SOCIAL CASEWORK

Principles and Practice

SOCIAL CASEWORK

Principles and Practice

by

NOEL TIMMS

LONDON

ROUTLEDGE & KEGAN PAUL

First published 1964
by Routledge & Kegan Paul Ltd
Broadway House, 68-74 Carter Lane
London, EC4V 5EL
Reprinted and first published as a Routledge Paperback 1966
Reprinted 1971

Printed in Great Britain
By Unwin Brothers Limited
The Gresham Press, Old Woking, Surrey, England
A member of the Staples Printing Group

ISBN 0 7100 4663 4

CONTENTS

Contents

ACKNOWLEDGEMENTS

I WOULD like to thank those social workers in probation, child care and almoning, those psychiatric social workers and family caseworkers who have allowed me to use extracts from their case material. It has been decided, in consultation with these workers, that no specific acknowledgements should be made so that the secrecy of the records would be safeguarded as fully as possible. The content of the book will, however, signify the extent of my indebtedness.

These workers come from the main branches of social work and from both sexes! Some professional groups of social workers are still predominantly female, but an increasing number of men are entering the profession. Consequently, I have decided in the text to abandon the usual convention whereby the caseworker always plays 'she' to the client's 'he'.

Part of chapter seven has already appeared in *Blackfriars* December 1962. I am grateful to the Editor for allowing me to use this material in the present work.

Note: Since the first edition almoners have formally changed their title to medical social workers.

Chapter One

THE CASEWORKER AND THE AGENCY

INTRODUCTION

THE need for a general textbook of British social casework practice is widely acknowledged in this country and the present work aims at satisfying certain aspects of this need. This is a time of fruitful and even exciting change in social casework and there is room for several different kinds of book on the subject, though the temptation perhaps is to try to encompass the range of possibility in one volume. In this book an attempt will be made to describe some of the main problems facing caseworkers as they try both to help their clients and to theorize about their methods and objectives; to discern the knowledge they use and apply; and to appraise the significance of the social agencies in which they work. The intention is not to present and justify an overall categorization of the casework process, for example, as treatment[1] or problem-solving,[2] but to explore casework operations on an eclectic basis, using as pivots in the discussion ideas of human relationships and of agency function.

British social workers have in the past relied heavily on American writings on social casework. In recent years the balance has been somewhat redressed by the production of original work in this country, but it remains true that our range is neither as extensive nor as comprehensive as the American. This is to be regretted. Obviously some aspects of social casework will be applicable in many countries and there is no necessity for each society to devise a completely fresh idea of casework for its own use. There is a great deal of fruitful thought in American work that can be assimilated by British social workers towards the solution of their theoretical and practical problems. No country needs to look constantly within its own boundaries for a unique inspiration on every topic. Such an insular approach is patently absurd. Equally mistaken, however, is the view that particular traditions, particular ways of making arrangements in a society are readily exportable and that they can be adopted by any other nation without translation or modification in the light of their own experiences.

This view is sometimes inflated into a general objection to American work on the grounds that its theorizing and practice are the product of a culture very different from our own. Exponents of this viewpoint seldom describe what they hold to be the essential differences. A sounder basis on which to judge the usefulness of American (or any other) ideas on social casework is provided by comparing their theorizing with our own social work experience. Social casework began in Great Britain, but despite the creative writing of individuals in the late nineteenth century and in more recent times, we have seldom paused to consider and appraise our own total experience in this field. Such a task is important at the present time, not simply because we can then assess the differences between American experience and our own, but also because we can be confident in our own contribution to a general view of the theory and practice of social casework.

Present American writing on casework is characterized by a considerable (and exaggerated) emphasis on certain aspects of ego-psychology and by a marked (and unfortunate) insularity.[3] British social work experience would seem to offer some remedy for the latter by offering a corrective for the former. This corrective, as will become apparent in the following pages, is mainly to be found in a deeper view of the significance of the function of the social agency, and of social relationships, and an appreciation of unconscious fantasy. (The distinction usually made between conscious 'fantasy' and unconscious 'phantasy' is not of fundamental importance in the present work, and I shall use the term 'fantasy' (except when quoting or discussing other people's views of 'phantasy') because I do not wish to draw a rigid line between conscious and unconscious mental activity.)

The term 'casework' was first used about a hundred years ago, but until quite recently its circulation has been on the whole confined to social workers. It is to be found now in contemporary novels and in discussions of power and the professions in present-day society. Indeed the recent criticisms of casework by Wootton and others have publicly recognized the existence of casework in a way that has no parallel since the Fabian attack on the Charity Organization Society at the turn of the century. Yet within social work and in more public allusion, criticism or defence, casework has rarely been defined to anyone's satisfaction. It remains elusive and even its sympathizers are forced to admit that attempts to describe it often reveal—to borrow a phrase of Oscar Wilde's—'all the utility of error and all the tediousness of an old friend'.[4]

Social workers will probably always have to accept a measure of uncertainty about the nature of their occupation, both generally and in regard to particular cases. This is partly because of the difficulty of making precise and detailed statements about interventions in the life of one human being by another—this will be discussed later. It is also because the identity of social work has to be thought anew as society and our conceptions of society change, and as the administrative structure, through which social work help is given, responds to the challenge of previously unseen or undefined need. In each individual case the social worker is concerned with establishing her identity for a particular client and with creating a function specific to the case, albeit within a framework of general identity and established function. Her 'acts are nothing if not original, done afresh and thought afresh for the particular occasion, however they may depend . . . on training and good slowly-built method'.[5]

Undue concentration on uniqueness and individuality, however, has often prevented the social worker from formulating generalizations. A fear of intellectualization has sometimes hindered the critical appraisal of concepts in daily use. Thus, the present state of social work literature reveals mainly an accumulation of unassorted ideas. This seems particularly so for casework. In writing and in professional discussion casework can be 'case work' or 'case-work', it can be 'scientific', preventive, therapeutic, deep, or intensive. Yet beneath these variations it is possible to discover variations on a number of key themes. It is by concentrating on these that we can perhaps alter the characterization of much casework teaching in the past as 'a benevolent casuistry and an interminable story-telling'.[6]

Some of the definitions of casework in this country and in America have been considered elsewhere,[7] but Swithun Bowers's fairly recent attempt has been widely accepted. After reviewing

American definitions since 1915, Fr. Bowers offered the following: social casework is 'an art in which knowledge of the science of human relations and skill in relationship are used to mobilize capacities in the individual and resources in the community appropriate for better adjustment between the client and all or any part of his total environment'.[8] This definition represents a considerable advance on its predecessors, but is still open to a number of criticisms. It is deeply entangled with the art/science controversy in casework; it contains some heavily persuasive terms (*science* of human relations) and it does not avoid the misuse of the holistic approach found in much social work writing. What is an individual's total environment except everything that is? It also fails to give sufficient emphasis to the different kinds of component in casework.

Caseworkers are coming to appreciate more clearly the complex structure of their discipline. One of the most succinct and lucid recent statements about it is to be found in Perlman's recent description: casework 'is complex by virtue of the varied knowledges which feed it, the ethical commitments which infuse it, the special auspices and conditions of its practice, the objectives and ends which guide it, the skills which empower it'.[9] Clear distinctions are thus made between knowledge, general values, settings and goals. Until we distinguish in this kind of way the different assertions that can be made in casework, we cannot begin to be sure what we are saying.

An example of casework writing which does not observe clear distinctions between kinds of assertion may illustrate the advantages of consistent differentiation.

Social work rests ultimately on certain *assumptions* which cannot be proved, but without which its methods and goals have no meaning. These *axioms* are, for example; human betterment is the goal of any society; so far as economic and cultural resources can be developed, the general standard of living should be progressively improved; ... the social bond between man and men should lead to the realization of the age-old dream of universal brotherhood. The *ethic* derived from these and similar axioms leads to *two nuclear ideas* which distinguish social work as one of the humanistic professions. The first is that the human event consists of person and situation, or subjective and objective reality, which constantly interact and the second that the characteristic *method* of social work incorporates within its processes both scientific knowledge and social values in order to achieve its ends.*[10]

In this passage Hamilton presents an obscure progression—values (called indiscriminately 'assumptions' or 'axioms') lead somehow to an 'ethic' which in turn produces 'ideas', one of which purports to be about 'method' but is in fact a very generalized description of any practice that can be called professional. With this confused notion of the structure of casework it becomes exceedingly difficult to identify the different kinds of assertion and to describe their relationship to each other.

It is not my intention simply to advocate a rigid vocabulary in which 'assumptions' are never called 'axioms' and 'propositions' are never called 'ideas', but I do argue that we need to be clear about the kind of assertion we make. It is only then that we can look for appropriate ways of justifying the assertion. For example, some of the statements made by caseworkers refer to generalized values (e.g. respect for the individual personality). These value assumptions cannot be tested, but they can be criticized and attempts can be made to establish good reasons for their adoption. Other assertions refer to descriptions and explanations of human behaviour—for example, people coming to an agency are under stress (descriptive) because of cultural and psychological factors (explanatory). Such assertions can be tested, either within or outside the casework discipline.

The themes of casework can perhaps be more clearly seen if for a moment we abandon a discussion that must be, to some extent, abstract and examine a recorded interview. Many of the terms used in casework can be adequately appreciated only when the operations they are used to describe are made apparent.

Miss M., a single woman, aged 48, was in hospital with thyrotoxicosis. She asked to see the almoner in connection with her payments from the National Assistance Board. The almoner consulted the doctor: the thyroid condition was not severe and not of long-standing and it was hoped that, with rest and drugs in hospital, an operation could be avoided. The doctor considered that there could well be psychological factors contributing to its onset, but that the patient was probably too 'neurotic' to be helped by anyone. She had attended hospitals for different conditions for many years. He agreed

* My italics.

5

that she seemed to need acceptance and support and that the almoner should see her as long as she wished it.

1st Interview

Miss M. spent the first interview telling the almoner how badly the National Assistance Board had treated her and how they had humiliated her on a number of occasions. The upsets were described in great detail. She felt it was because she was unlike their usual run of clients in that she always appeared well dressed. She explained that she was able to dress well because a sister, married to a doctor, gave her a lot of clothes.

In telling the almoner about the attitude of the Assistance Board, she brought out details of her circumstances. She explained that she was not married, but had had a child 12 years ago 'the wrong side of the blanket'. This was said in a rather defiant fashion and she watched the almoner very closely for her reactions. The almoner tried to convey acceptance, but actually had very little chance to say anything at this interview at all as the patient spoke practically non-stop. For the past 7 years her health had not been good so she had been unable to work and for this time, she had been living in an old, very inconvenient bungalow where she had had to carry all her water. Interspersed with these other details, she spoke about all the people she knew in X and in the hospital through her brother-in-law who is a doctor. Several times, she tried to draw the almoner into personal discussion of people, mainly doctors, in the hospital. The almoner tried to stress that she understood how humiliating Miss M. would find her present position and that she also understood how important it was to her to have the good opinion of these people she had mentioned.

Miss M. did not appear unduly concerned about her health. She had obviously discussed it a great deal with different doctors and had a reasonably good understanding of it. She said rather casually that she thought worry had had a good deal to do with her present hospitalization. This was at the end of the interview so the almoner suggested that she might like to see her again to talk about these worries. She gave a brief description of the function of an almoner and said she would talk to the doctor about her. This did not appear to arouse any anxiety.

An examination of this brief record reveals a number of important elements. We see the caseworker (an almoner) working in a particular agency (the social work department) situated in a larger institution (the hospital), in collaboration with other staff (doctors etc.). A person has asked for help over National Assistance, but seems to be more concerned with other matters. The caseworker tries to understand what is troubling Miss M., explains the kind of service she can offer and, in fact, begins to be of service by communicating acceptance and understanding, by commencing some form of appraisal of Miss M. and her difficulties, and by avoiding the role of 'friend'. These elements: the agency, with its organization, personnel and objectives; the client in some difficulty; the worker, with his or her knowledge and skill, have been the themes of casework throughout its history. I have elsewhere suggested that they could be combined into a definition of casework as 'work on cases guided by certain principles and the use of knowledge and human relation skills with the object of fulfilling the function of a particular agency'.[11] It should perhaps be stated in addition that casework is one of the methods of social work; the others usually being described as group work and community organization. Ideally, the social worker should be able to use whichever method seems appropriate to the situation and there is evidence that those trained to practice primarily with individuals or with single families are attempting to develop their skills in working with groups.[12] However, the emphasis of most courses of training has been on either casework or group work; and the first of these was established so long before the second that social casework and social work have often seemed synonymous. Social work can now be exhaustively described in terms of its three main methods. To ask what social work is besides its methods (and their objectives), is like asking to meet the family after one has been introduced to each of its members.

The elements of casework and their interaction will now be discussed in some detail.

The Agency

The term 'agency' has a misleadingly American sound, but it was used in British casework literature in the late nineteenth century. Present-day usage refers to the institution within which the caseworker practises; sometimes it is the larger institution that is intended (e.g. the local authority) and at other times it is the smaller social work microcosm (e.g. the psychiatric social work department in a mental hospital). The institutions in which caseworkers practice (child guidance clinics, children's departments of the local authority, hospitals, courts and so on) have all been established to achieve certain broad social purposes and caseworkers have a part to play in achieving them. This is so whether the institutions are manned and directed largely by social workers (e.g. the voluntary family casework agency) or by personnel trained for practice in other disciplines (e.g. doctors, policemen etc.). And it remains true whether caseworkers are concerned with helping people to make use of the services provided by others (e.g. the hospital) or with using the methods of casework directly to achieve social work objectives (e.g. a social work agency helping problem families). A distinction is commonly drawn between the 'primary' and the 'secondary' settings of casework practice. Perlman, for example, characterizes the former as those which 'use the methods of social casework as the major means of administering their services', whilst 'in the secondary setting casework is used to help the individual make use of a service rendered by another professional group'.[13] This distinction has a certain descriptive value, but casework is always a means of achieving the objectives of the agency, whether this is a primary or secondary setting. Moreover, casework in any agency so often involves collaboration with other personnel (social workers in other agencies, doctors, teachers etc.) that this kind of distinction has only a limited use. It is because of this collaborative element that I believe casework should be seen generally as 'work on cases'.

The purposes for which institutions have been created are often called in the vocabulary of social work the 'function' of the agency. This notion is of central importance for social casework. The idea of agency function provides one of the simplest means of distinguishing casework and psychotherapy: the psychotherapist might describe his aims in a number of different ways, but not in terms of achieving agency objectives or fulfilling the function of the agency. It also links the social worker and the agency with the community. The agencies are established to carry out such broad social functions as healing and rehabilitation in the case of hospitals, ensuring good parental care in the case of children's departments of the local authority, and so on. The worker is expected to contribute to these objectives and to clarify and develop his own function within these broad social purposes. Yet, the most important aspect of agency function is that it constitutes the meeting-

point of social worker and client; it is what brings them together
and gives meaning and sustenance to their continued contact. This
viewpoint has been insufficiently emphasized in recent British publications. It is either simply ignored[14] or swamped by the overwhelming emphasis given to 'the relationship'. The Morrison
Committee, for instance, saw casework as 'the creation and utili-
zation, for the benefit of an individual who needs help with personal problems, of a relationship between himself and a trained
social worker'.[15] Yet it is the function of the particular social
agency that gives the relationship its purpose and which helps it
to evolve. Casework does not begin with a relationship, but
with a worker and a client meeting in a particular kind of social
agency.

An alternative approach to the problem of agency function to
be found in recent British writing on casework is that which
maintains a rigid distinction between a worker's official functions
and his or her casework. Thus, Kastell talks on the one hand, of
the official duties of the child care officer and, on the other hand,
of something described as 'casework drive'.

> One of the first things the child care officer is called upon to do is
> not to give casework help, but to make an accurate assessment of a
> situation. For she is in part official, a social worker within the setting
> of an agency that has both duties and powers bestowed upon it, and
> in part caseworker; and she must learn to find a balance between these
> two functions according to the demands of each case.[16]

It is the argument of this book that these are not two functions,
but one. The worker in a children's department or in any other
setting helps by means of the method of casework to achieve the
objectives of the agency. Social casework has objectives of its own
only in the sense that the caseworker's approach to problems of
social functioning is governed, as we shall see, by certain general
values in connection with the individual and society. As long as
these values are not violated by the institutions in which caseworkers practice, there would not appear to be many objectives
which casework could not help in achieving. It is quite usual for
reference to be made in contemporary social work writing to the
'limitations' of the agencies in which social workers practice. It is
assumed, apparently, that casework is carried out in spite of them.
It is my argument that no agency can accomplish everything and

that the specialization implicit in the idea of agency function is helpful for both client and worker.

Yet, important as the idea of function is, it is not free from ambiguities, some of which may have become apparent in the discussion so far developed. Many writers refer to 'function' in the singular, but it would seem more useful to think of the functions of an agency. It is hardly possible, for example, to summarize under one heading the different kinds of work appropriately undertaken by an almoner in a complex institution like a modern hospital. Other writers wish to make a clear distinction between the function of an agency and agency policy or methods.[17] This view recognizes the importance of establishing some vantage point from which policy or methods might be reviewed and criticized, but it is by means of policy and method that the concerns of society to meet particular needs are mediated. It is policy and method with which the person in difficulty engages himself. For him they are the function of the agency. It is policy and method which the caseworker utilizes in helping herself and the applicant to test out if he wants help in the particular forms in which agency is authorized to offer it.

In using, then, the idea of the functions of an agency I would not wish to draw too sharp a distinction between 'the basic function of the agencies to meet social needs'[18] and their particular definition of the ways and means best calculated to meet such needs. I would wish to make a distinction between the general functions of an agency and the ways in which caseworker and applicant decide the functions can be interpreted in any particular case. 'Function' in any particular case refers in the first place to society's concern (or, as in the case of the Pacifist Service Units in the War, a group's concern) that certain needs should be met; secondly, to the application of methods and policies designed to meet these needs; and thirdly, to the work of caseworker and applicant as they decide how these methods and policies can be used to meet need in the specific case.

So far the argument would suggest that the caseworker is deeply involved with the agency she serves. It could be summarized in the opinion that the caseworker cannot be seen as someone who *happens* to work in some agency or other. The implications of this view for the caseworker now require some elucidation.

The agencies in which caseworkers practice might all be very generally classed as welfare agencies, but this does not say any-thing about their specific nature or about their specialized tasks. It is fashionable in social work at the present time to decry special-ization and to emphasize a 'generic' approach to the institutions which caseworkers serve. The position now seems similar to the earlier American view that 'the various separate designations (children's case worker, family case worker, probation officer, visiting teacher, psychiatric social worker, medical social worker, etc.) by which its (social work's) practitioners are known tend to have no more than a descriptive significance in terms of the type of problem with which they respectively deal. The outstanding fact is that the problems of social casework and the equipment of the social case worker are fundamentally the same for all fields'.[19] In this country we have, in our plans for new social work training, perhaps moved too quickly on the basis of this kind of generic idea without working towards a clear idea of the significance to client and worker alike of each specialized agency.

An example of the approach to which I refer can, perhaps, be seen in the treatment of the problem of 'authority'. It is frequently stated today that this is not the special problem of any one group of agencies (e.g. the probation service); it is rather a 'generic' problem, common to the practice of social casework in any agency. This is a rather abstract approach: in fact, arguments about 'generic' training are customarily in the form of rather abstract statements about 'man in society'. A more fruitful ap-proach would be through a specific understanding of the particular manifestations of authority in each special setting. It is, however, essential to attempt some analysis of the term before it can be used.

Authority is a subject that has a significance for social workers; they seem at once attracted and repelled by it. It may be defined as legitimized power to control or influence the behaviour of another. The source of legitimization or authorization may lie 'outside' any given relationship between two people; the authority of the probation officer, for example, comes from the court, whether the probationer perceives this fact or not. Authorization may, on the other hand, lie within the relationship itself, when one participant begins to accept the other as 'an' authority for him. Finally, authorization may be partly a question of what develops in a relationship and partly something given from the 'outset'. When we speak—as social workers increasingly do—of the expert authority of professional knowledge, or the right to give a professional opinion, we refer partly to a client's acceptance of this and partly to the right of the professional to claim such acceptance (i.e. to his authorization through training and, perhaps, experience). We can also make some useful distinctions between different kinds of power.[20] For example, the caseworker in a family casework agency may be perceived by the client as a person who has access to certain resources (a money grant, clothing etc.) and the power to reward behaviour by granting access to them. This perception might well be correct, though the caseworker might think it more important to encourage the client to accept her as some kind of expert in human relationships. The clients of any agency will correctly perceive that workers have power because of their knowledge of the complexities of the organization within which they work and their ease of access to personnel with greater authority and prestige. This kind of power is, of course, authorized by the worker's place in the organization.

So far we have treated authority on a rational level, but one of the reasons for the reluctance of social workers to discuss the concept is to be found in its irrational undertones. A discussion of the subject must include a reference to the irrational power of authority figures. The authority the court gives the probation officer is, as we shall see, extremely limited and clearly defined and even the authority of the expert has essential limitations, since no one can claim to be an expert in everything. The power of authority figures, however, is neither authorized nor circumscribed; it operates mainly through fantasy. The concept of fantasy will be examined later, but at this point in my argument I wish only to explore the possibility that specific fantasies of power may be associated with each of the main settings of social work.

It seems possible to associate certain authority figures with the work respectively of the almoner, the psychiatric social worker, the child care officer, the family caseworker, and the probation officer. The authority figure most commonly projected on to the almoner will be that of the fantasy doctor who will see the patient's innermost possessions because he is able to 'cut him open'. This fantasy figure deals in death and dismemberment as well as healing by magic. There will be some resemblance between him and the figure associated with psychiatric social work, though perhaps the main feature here will be the connection with madness. The psychiatrist will be able to read the patient's innermost thoughts and can shut people away from their familiar world because he finds they are mad. The child care officer, on the other hand, will more directly embody a fantasy figure because she exercises authority in her own right. She will often be seen as the perfect mother, or as the rival with a natural or foster mother for the child: she can be seen by both as 'the witch' who steals children belonging to others. The worker in the voluntary family agency may be seen as the representative of the unnamed 'them' or as the good parent who gives inexhaustibly, but who can become a harshly depriving person lavishing attention and affection on other children (i.e. other clients). Finally, the probation officer may be seen as the harsh, punishing father, who keeps others in minority status through fear of their rivalry.

This brief characterization of the authority figures associated with the specific settings of social work should not be rigidly interpreted. Fantasies about madness and about the figures of power who control it may well be found amongst clients in several of the social work settings. Yet they will perhaps be more common in psychiatric social work and where they do appear in that setting they will require attention since they are so closely connected with the functions of the agencies in which psychiatric social workers practice.

The possibility that certain kinds of fantasy figure may commonly be associated with the authority of each setting emphasizes the significance of any worker's choice of a particular field of work. The choice of a career in child care, for example, is no doubt the result of a number of factors, but we should reckon among these, attraction to a particular kind of work because of the wish to be involved, and to come to terms, with the fantasies associated with it in our own minds. These fantasies are connected both with the source of power in any particular setting and also with its actual operations. The general functions of the child care service may be considered in terms of caring for children in need of 'good' parents, judging the adequacy of natural or substitute parents, acting to improve or terminate already established parental roles, providing the kind of substitute home that will meet the needs of the individual child. Thus, the important processes for the child care service are caring, judging, acting and providing, and these are carried on in an area of special difficulty, the parent–

child relationship. We may assume perhaps that the person who becomes a child care officer wishes to work through some of his or her feelings, fantasies and problems in relation to children and their parents. In general, this may be true of all social workers, but it has a special significance for the child care officer because of what she comes to embody in reality and fantasy for her clients in the course of her work, and because part of her function is to recognize the separateness of children from natural parents and foster parents at the same time as she tries to hold the child's world together.

So far we have been considering the significance of the agency, and the argument has been in favour of an examination of the specific nature and meaning of each kind of service provided. It may well be that we can then make some generalizations about social work in any kind of setting, but these will be more firmly based than present *a priori* assumptions. In order to appreciate the full impact of the setting on social casework we should adopt a three-fold approach to the study of each kind of organization: (i) What work has the community set the agency to accomplish and what are the specific functions of the social worker within this broad social purpose? (ii) What is the specialized clientele of the agency? Just as the social worker is not someone who simply happens to be an almoner, probation officer etc., so the client is often not a person who happens to have come, or been referred, to a particular agency. How do clients reach a particular service and what happens to them in the course of their approach or referral? Becoming the client of a specialized agency may have a particular significance for the individual. Does referral of a patient, discharged from a mental hospital, to the local authority service assume for the patient the hopeful sign of a 'cure' or the recognition that his case is hopeless from the point of view of medical treatment? Finally, in this sub-section, we should inquire what is happening in other spheres of a person's life whilst he is a client of the caseworker and what happens to him before, during and immediately after termination of casework help. For instance, the hospital patient who becomes an almoner's client is also the object of the professional attentions of a wide range of other personnel; he and the almoner may often have to work within a time limit subject to alteration by the doctors and by changing hospital policy and continuing contact of an intensive kind after discharge from hospital will usually be possible only by referral to another agency. (iii) We need also to study the fantasies associated with the sources of the caseworker's authority and with the processes entailed in the exercise of the agency's general function and the caseworker's own functions. If we approach the casework specializations along these lines, we may discover that the caseworker is not an expert in generalized problems of human relationships, but a person trained to be 'open' to these problems when they arise in the fulfilment of the functions of the agency. Such an approach could be described as rigid—and this is one of the words of strongest criticism in the contemporary social work vocabulary. Yet openness to the 'wholeness' of a person is not incompatible with adherence to the functional basis of social work.

This discussion of the significance of the agency may seem to be far removed from the case of Miss M. (on p. 6), but we saw that in her first interview the almoner gave a brief description of her function and watched for any reactions as she told Miss M. that she would talk to the doctor about her. The almoner was helping Miss M. to see her part in the work of the hospital, her co-operation with the doctors and the main focus of her work on health and social problems connected with it. Special features of the setting, moreover, appear to have meaning for this patient: she stressed that her status derived largely from relationships to doctors and she tried to engage in a 'friendship' with the almoner largely on the basis of gossip about them. Miss M. seemed, in other words, to be emphasizing how much at home she felt in this medical world and the almoner would doubtless have asked herself why the patient needed to make such an emphasis, what fear and what resentment might be receiving indirect expression in this way? The almoner encouraged Miss M. to talk about her worries (more by her attitude, since verbal encouragement seemed unnecessary) and tried to convey some understanding of the feelings she was expressing. She began also to try to 'make sense' of what the patient was saying, to formulate some appraisal of her situation. Before we consider the knowledge and the processes involved in this, we must discuss the caseworker at the beginning of his or her contact with a possible client.

The Caseworker
The caseworker is someone who has equipped himself through

formal training or experience or both to work in a social work agency and to give help to its clients through a professional relationship and co-operative endeavour with other agencies and members of other disciplines. Part of the professional relationship is, as we have already seen, deeply embedded in the agency and its functions. 'In case-work, as contrasted with psycho-therapy, one does not work primarily through the medium of one's own personality. In addition to the personality of the client and the personality of the worker there is a third factor of great importance in the case-work situation. This is the specific function of the agency in which one operates.'[21] Yet this is explained, conveyed and exercised through a professional relationship in which the personality of the caseworker is deeply involved.

The notion of involvement has at times appeared incompatible with that of professional objectivity. Surely, one goes for help to a professional person both because he has specialized knowledge which one lacks and also because he is able to take an objective view of the situation, since he is not deeply connected with his client in an emotional relationship? However, an objective view does not imply necessarily a 'cold' or distant approach and if the caseworker is to offer an effective service he must be personally involved, though not totally lost, in relationships with clients. The caseworker wishes to express concern for his clients and he cannot do so if he feels none. It is also considered important that the caseworker develops insight into a client's personality and problems and this is a process that involves the caseworker's own feelings and memories. Halmos,[22] and Clare Winnicott[23] have recently drawn attention to the importance of the development of insight, defining it as a recalling of those sentiments in the observer's life which appear to characterize the observed behaviour of the other. Finally, if the caseworker is expected to use as part of the casework process, the feelings invoked in him by the client (this will be discussed later), then clearly his own feelings will become quite deeply implicated. Emotional involvement is thus a necessary part of casework; it is not something to be avoided nor a mere by-product. The danger to be avoided is not that of involvement, but that of loss. Caseworkers must participate with feeling in relationships with clients, but they must also be able to bring themselves out of such relationships from time to time and ensure that the differences between themselves and their clients as individuals are maintained. Some features of the psychoanalytic situation which have some useful parallels have been well described by Moore: 'The analyst must, to understand me, come to the brink of loving me. But in the end he must draw back, he must resist the "counter-transference", he must remain an other. He must do so for my sake, for I did not come to him for love, but for analysis. He must do it also for his own sake. For analysis is a personal encounter.'[24]

The basis of the kind of social work help that 'comes to the brink of love' is undoubtedly previous personal experience and training. The latter is a matter of knowledge and skill and will be discussed in later chapters; here consideration will be given to personal experience. The experiences of prime importance are those responsible to a considerable degree for the development of the personality: the events and relationships of infancy and early childhood. The importance of family relationships was recognized by the more perceptive pioneers of casework in the nineteenth century. Helen Bosanquet, for instance, urged workers to treasure as the basis of their task all opportunities of helpfulness in their own families. Most of the experiences of infancy and childhood, whether positive or negative, cannot ordinarily be recalled to memory, but we can all remember occasions in the past when we have been helped. Our ability to maintain connectedness with them constitutes a necessary basis for casework, just as reflection on them helps us to discern some of the principles of effective practice.

Reflection on situations in which we have received significant help will probably reveal that they have been based on the exercise of a particular kind of authority, on the establishment and maintenance of a system of effective communication, and on a feeling of acceptance which has not only helped in the solution of the particular problem in hand, but also increased our feeling of self-value. In other words, we have been helped at a particular point in time in a way that could be generalized to other occasions when we face a problem. Now, authority has already been discussed in this chapter and it will be sufficient to say that the authority referred to here is that of competence and of personality: we were helped because the person had a combination of skill and knowledge and because they were the kind of person we could accept as 'an' authority. The remainder of this chapter will be concerned with communication and acceptance. The ability to communicate and to receive and understand communications from others, be they clients, social work colleagues or those trained in other fields, and to convey acceptance are two of the most important skills in casework.

The subject of communication is attracting a considerable amount of general attention and social workers are beginning to appreciate that it has some relevance for their activities.[25] Here, as in other aspects of the work, the fruitful beginnings made by the late nineteenth-century social worker have been neglected. Helen Bosanquet, for example, wrote a short but penetrating essay entitled 'An Apology for False Statements', which is basically concerned with the idea of failure in communication in casework.[26] 'Every individual', she stated:

> collects his meanings from his own private experiences: and when we think how the experiences of individuals differ, the wonder is that we come to any mutual understanding at all. We do not take our meanings ready made from the dictionary; we put them together bit by bit as we grow and see and ask questions; and, in as much as no two people ever have just the same experiences, or receive just the same answers to their questions, it is probable that no two people ever really understand one another, or are at all times able to communicate intelligently.

Later in the essay she gives an example of a break-down in communication:

> Take such a question as this, which I imagine must be a fairly common one: 'Have you ever been so badly off before?' We want to get at the cause; is it periodical or accidental? He (the client) has not even a glimpse of our drift, and sees only another opportunity of emphasising *his* fact, the uniqueness and intensity of his situation; while very likely the only difference between his present position and that of twelve months ago is the difference between present suffering and the mere recollection of past suffering, and everyone knows what a difference that is.

She concludes by asking, 'is it not safe to assume that in a considerable number of cases opinions from which we differ require interpretation rather than refutation'.

On the whole, Helen Bosanquet took a rather pessimistic attitude to the problem of communication, but as our knowledge of the communication process increases it becomes clear that this is not justified. If we examine the several models of communication so far developed, we can arrive at a general notion of the elements of communication which does present a helpful way of viewing at least some important aspects of casework. Communication is, of course, a purposeful activity: we communicate with the intention of affecting people and events. Sometimes the purpose is achieved as soon as the message we send is received and at other times the message is instrumental towards a purpose in the future. The messages that are sent have often a manifold content, the parts of which may be congruent or incongruent with each other. Thus, the mother who opens out her arms to her child, and with a voice that is harsh and cruel orders him 'to come to mummy at once', is by physical movements sending the child the message, 'come to these loving arms', and by her voice sending the incongruent, accompanying message, 'come to these unloving arms'. So, in any communication there seem to be four main elements: the sender, the receiver, the message and the means by which it is delivered. A complete model would also require means of putting the message in a suitable code before its despatch and of decoding on arrival, but for present purposes the elements listed will suffice.

How can this broad notion of communication be applied to casework? If we return briefly to the interview with Miss M. we can perhaps begin to see some of the applications. Taking the apparently simple fact that she is known as, and calls herself, 'Miss', even though respectable status has evident importance for her, we can ask what is she trying to communicate? She talks to the almoner of the humiliation she felt at the N.A.B. office, but she may also be trying to convey some of her present feelings as she asks for help again, though in a different setting. She seems by her talk of doctors to be asserting some kind of eligibility for help from the hospital's social worker. Her purpose in telling the almoner about her illegitimate son is clearly not informational, as she communicates by means of her expression and, perhaps, bodily movements.

The importance of communication in casework is again apparent if we consider the conditions of effective communication. These may be summarized as knowledge, attitude and skill. The caseworker must have sufficient knowledge of the content he wishes to communicate. A person may, for instance, require some information about the social services. The caseworker must also have a knowledge of the communication process. The discussion of communication in terms of elements has perhaps created the impression that this is a largely mechanical affair, but it is essentially a dynamic and a reverberating process. The caseworker should have studied this process and absorbed what knowledge we have of the factors that make people 'deaf' to some communications, that create 'noise' in a system, and of those other factors that tend to increase fidelity of communication. The attitudes that affect communication could broadly be described in terms of their objects—the self of the sender, the other to whom the message is sent, and the content of the message. Thus, a caseworker who has a high sense of his own value and a low sense of the value of certain others (e.g. clergymen) and a difficulty with homosexuality could not be expected to establish very effective communication on sexual matters with a clergyman placed on probation for offences against boys. Skill is partly a question of applying knowledge appropriately and partly a matter of drills and habits. Perhaps the two most important skills in communication that the caseworker can acquire are the ability to receive and analyse multi-level messages and to choose channels of communication appropriate to the situation.

In the case of Miss M. the predominant channel was that of verbal communication. Caseworkers have perhaps emphasized this at the expense of other means of communication. Pacifist Service Units (and later Family Service Units), however, have demonstrated some of the advantages of communicating with certain kinds of clients by means of direct concrete service in the home. This frequently proved a way of communicating the worker's interest and concern as well as demonstrating perhaps more effective ways of performing household tasks. Sometimes, however, workers did not always appreciate that their demonstrations might also be communicating the worker's lack of confidence in the client's ability. Workers on a recent research project have reported examples of their own way of using non-verbal communication[27] and Lambrick[28] has recently published some examples of sensitive communication with patients by means of written communication, touch and symbolism.

Finally, attention must be given to the caseworker's attitude of 'acceptance'. This is not an easy concept to grasp, but it has a central importance in casework and as such requires early consideration in any discussion of casework. A recent review of the main British references to 'acceptance' indicated the elusive nature of this concept[29] and Biestek in an essay based on American literature has stated that 'it remains one of the vaguest terms in our professional language'.[30] We can make some progress by observing a distinction between the nature, the purposes and the process of acceptance. Acceptance is primarily an attitude of active sympathy and an awareness of the client's suffering, even though he makes other people suffer. It is sometimes equated with passivity, but it is in fact a readiness to work hard at identifying, and 'receiving' without rejection and condemnation as much of the client's personality as can be seen. Acceptance is usually discussed in terms of the 'bad' aspects of the client's personality, but it should refer to an attitude to the 'whole' client, good and bad. Searles has described this reaction as a 'loving relatedness', which 'entails a responding to the wholeness of the other person'.[31] Difficulties arise, however, when one asks what the caseworker does with what he has accepted. Does he 'accept' and, therefore, condone, encourage or collude in, behaviour which the caseworker believes to be immoral, illegal or both? Is casework not undertaken to change rather than accept at least certain kinds of behaviour? If the caseworker receives and accepts the client's 'badness', *ought* he not to take some measures to protect himself from its effects?

These are important questions which have received insufficient attention in social work. It is possible to maintain a non-condemnatory attitude towards the fact that a person has sinned or done something he feels to be 'bad', and this is largely because the caseworker is often able to say—and with justification—'I can (or am trying to) understand that such and such is the case and also why it is. This is, of course, much easier where the behaviour in question is 'bad' only in the client's eyes. What happens when it is in the caseworker's view objectively bad? It is again possible to accept the person even though the caseworker may also have to make clear both for his own sake and for the good of the client that certain behaviour is, in his view, bad. In other words a distinction is made between the client and his behaviour. This is, however, difficult to maintain when we consider not particular episodes of behaviour, but persistent behaviour, since the ways in which a man persistently behaves *are* his character. It is possible to say that his character is understandable in the light of his previous experience, but this has perhaps undertones of determinism.

Social workers need to establish the nature of acceptance more clearly, even though some of its aspects can be seen fairly precisely. We can increase our grasp of this concept if we consider also its purposes and its process?

If the caseworker is to enter the world of his client it is clear that he must accept this world. The caseworker wishes to understand the client and acceptance seems both the product and the basis of such understanding. Yet the caseworker's understanding is for the client's benefit and the caseworker's acceptance of his client will, it is hoped, help the client to accept himself, to take a more realistic view of himself. More immediately acceptance should bring the client some measure of relief.

The process of acceptance can be usefully seen in terms of communication. The client sends the caseworker a message containing implicitly or explicitly information about some feeling, action etc. which he regards as 'good' or 'bad'. The worker receives the message, decodes it and then sends back through verbal or non-verbal channels a number of messages, along the following lines: 'I have received and understood your message; I can hold what I have accepted and I do not need to forget it, overemphasize it etc. and it will not damage me or make me envious; what you have conveyed does not make me condemn you, it is part of you because . . .; I am still concerned to continue our relationship.' Before we can say a feeling, thought or action has been accepted it is important to ensure that the client has received from the caseworker the message that his previous communication about the feeling etc. has been received and understood. 'Acceptance' in ordinary language is used in two different ways—'I accept that as a fact' and 'I accept your invitation'. Thinking in terms of communication helps us to ensure that 'acceptance' in both senses is conveyed to the client.

NOTES

[1] This seems to be the basic view contained in Hamilton, G., *Theory and Practice of Social Case Work*, Columbia University Press, 1951, though it is also influenced by the idea of 'good rules' based on a sense of moderation.

[2] This view has, of course, been succinctly presented and cogently argued in

Notes

Perlman, H., *Social Casework—A Problem-Solving Process*, University of Chicago Press, 1957.

[3] The edition of Hamilton cited above contains no references to English work, while Perlman has only one.

[4] Wilde, Oscar, *The Critic as Artist*, London, 1880.

[5] Notes of the Month, *Charity Organisation Society Review*, August 1893.

[6] Halmos, P., 'The Training of Social Workers and the Teaching of Psychology', *Social Work*, Vol. 6, No. 1, January 1949.

[7] For the survey of American definitions see Bowers, S., 'The Nature and Definition of Social Casework', *Social Casework*, Oct., Nov., Dec. 1949. Some British definitions have been briefly considered in the present writer's *Casework in the Child Care Service*, Butterworths, 1962.

[8] Bowers, S., op. cit.

[9] Perlman, H., op. cit., p. 3.

[10] Hamilton, G., op. cit., p. 3.

[11] Timms, N., op. cit., p. 3.

[12] See e.g. Sheppard, M. L., 'Psychotherapy with a Small Group of Chronic, Schizophrenic Patients', *British Journal of Psychiatric Social Work*, Vol. V, No. 4, 1960; Bissell, D., 'Group Work in the Probation Setting', *British Journal of Criminology*, Vol. 2, No. 3, Jan. 1962; Roberts, V. K., 'An Experiment in Group Work with Foster Parents', *Case Conference*, Vol. 9, No. 6, Nov. 1962. For a useful review of the literature on group behaviour see Crichton, A., *Personnel Management and Working Groups*, Institute of Personnel Management, 1962.

[13] Perlman, H., 'Generic Aspects of Specific Case-Work Settings', *Social Service Review*, Vol. XXIII, No. 3, Sept., 1949.

[14] For example, in Ferard, M., and Hunnybun, N., *The Caseworker's Use of Relationships*, Tavistock Publications, 1962.

[15] *Report of the Departmental Committee on the Probation Service*, Cmmd. 1650, 1962, p. 24.

[16] Kastell, J., *Casework in Child Care*, Routledge & Kegan Paul, 1962, p. 19.

[17] This seems to be the position in a recent stimulating discussion on the subject by Clare Winnicott, 'Casework and Agency Function', *Case Conference*, Vol. 8, No. 7, Jan. 1962.

[18] Winnicott, Clare, op. cit.

[19] Social Case Work: Generic and Specific: *A Report of the Milford Conference*, American Association of Social Workers, 1929.

[20] For a useful discussion of different kinds of power—coercive, reward, legitimate, referent and expert—see French, J. R., and Raven, B., 'The Bases of Social Power', in Cartwright, D. (ed.), *Studies in Social Power*, University of Michigan, 1959.

[21] Aptekar, H., Basic Concepts in Social Case-Work, Houghton, 1941, p. 8.

[22] Halmos, P., 'Personality Involvement in Learning about Personality', in *The Teaching of Personality Development*, Sociological Review Monograph I, 1958.

[23] Winnicott, Clare, 'The Development of Insight', Sociological Review Monograph II, 1959.

[24] Moore, A., 'Psychoanalysis, Man, and Value', *Inquiry*, Vol. 3, 1960.

[25] See e.g. the present writer's 'Communication and Collaboration', *The Almoner*, Vol. 16, No. 3, June 1963.

[26] Bosanquet, H., *The Standard of Life*, London, 1898.

[27] *The Canford Families*, Sociological Review Monograph No. 6, 1962, pp. 170–1.

[28] Lambrick, H., 'Communication with the Patient', *The Almoner*, Vol. 15, No. 7, Oct. 1962.

[29] See the author's *Psychiatric Social Work in Great Britain (1939–1962)*, Routledge & Kegan Paul, 1964, pp. 147-146.

[30] Biestek, F., *The Casework Relationship*, Allen & Unwin, 1961, p. 67.

[31] Searles, H., 'The Effort to Drive the Other Person Crazy', *British Journal of Medical Psychology*, Vol. XXXII, Pt. 1, 1959. The phrase of Searles quoted in the text might seem to merit the criticism I made earlier in the chapter of Bowers's definition of casework: it might appear a misuse of the holistic approach. Two uses of holistic terminology can be found in social work discussion: (1) 'wholeness', in the sense of 'totality'; (2) 'wholeness' in the sense of a reference to unacknowledged or 'absent' aspects of a situation or person which explain the acknowledged and present aspects. The second sense seems more helpful and it is this that informs Searles's approach. See also, Philp, A. F. and Timms, Noel, *The Problem of the 'Problem Family'*, Family Service Units, 1957, pp. 39–40.

Chapter Two

PSYCHOLOGICAL AND SOCIAL KNOWLEDGE

SO far we have been concerned with a preliminary discussion of
the concept of agency function and of certain aspects of the caseworker's attitude (acceptance) and of her skill (communication).
One of the caseworker's most important aims is to understand the
client and by conveying her understanding to help him to move
towards the identification and solution of his problems in social
functioning. There is, of course, no easy road to this kind of
comprehension and the caseworker has to undertake the work of
understanding before she has the right to say to her client, 'Yes,
I think I can see what you feel', and, later, 'I can see why you feel
it'. In such work she can rely on the orderly process of appraisal
and help, on her perception of the changing situation between
herself and the client, and on the differential application of several
kinds of knowledge. Sometimes, the caseworker has given emphasis to other factors in her service to clients, to the detriment of
technical principles and of knowledge. Rall, for example, has suggested that, 'Effective case-work service is not a matter of following rules, nor can it be secured through the possession of theoretical knowledge.'[1] Such a viewpoint fails to appreciate the distinction between the necessary and the sufficient conditions for
effective casework. Clearly, effective service is not *only* a matter of
following rules or of possessing theoretical knowledge, but these
are none the less among its most vital ingredients. The knowledge
caseworkers use and the principles they observe will be the subject
of this, and the following, chapter.

The knowledge used in casework derives mainly from the disciplines of psychology and sociology and there is no body of casework knowledge as such. This statement contradicts many contemporary claims about casework knowledge in general or in

particular fields which range from quietly confident forecasts of assumed future progress to panegyric statements of supposed present fact. Bartlett, for example, in her recent detailed and clear study of Social Work Practice in the Health Field states: 'Unquestionably, medical social work is building up its own body of knowledge out of its experience in practice and teaching, but this knowledge has not yet been formulated'.[2] It is precisely this last fact that makes it difficult to be sure (and knowledge gives the right to be sure) whether medical social work is *building* anything. A similar enthusiasm is to be found in commentaries on the disciplines on which social workers rely. It has become customary to refer to 'very rapid advances made in the social and behavioural sciences'[3] and to the application and testing in social work of 'a growing body of psychological and sociological theory'.[4] Undoubtedly, recent developments in psychiatry, psychology and sociology represent a number of fruitful beginnings from the viewpoint of the social worker—existential psychiatry,[5] ego-psychology,[6] learning[7] and role theories.[8] Yet some caution is required before these starting-points, exciting as they are and useful as they promise to be, can be considered as advances that have been consolidated or insights that have been integrated into a *body* of theory. The present should perhaps be seen as a time of careful (though not timid) experiment as well as of enthusiastic proclamation. The history of social work does not reveal an even development of ideas and one influential notion has been succeeded by another with little or no appraisal or consolidation of theory. Thus, social work has relied in turn on models of Economic Man, Man the Debtor to Society, and Oedipal Man. We are now perhaps at the stages of Sub-cultural (or East London[9]) Man, on the one hand, and of Generic (or Abstract) Man, on the other.

Of the disciplines that have contributed to casework the most widely used has been that of psychology, particularly psychoanalysis. Even this cannot, however, be seen as a homogeneous source of ideas. The term 'psychoanalysis' refers loosely to a number of different schools (Freudian, Adlerian, Jungian etc.) and to distinguishable theories within the same school. Thus, a distinction is usually drawn in discussions of the Freudian approach between the content of different theories (e.g. ego theory, theory of the unconscious etc.) and between different kinds of theory (e.g. his metapsychological views on religion and his theory of the

Oedipus complex). Within such a range of theory and speculation social workers have naturally found some ideas more helpful than others. The emphasis has been successively on ego-libido analysis, relationship without the transference elements,[10] transference and the avoidance of other aspects of the relationship, ego-psychology with the appraisal of ego strengths and weaknesses and, finally, the ego as the major integrative force in the personality. Of the other groups of psychological theory the psychology of individual differences was one of the first to attract social workers and it is still of importance, particularly in relation to intelligence. Learning theory promises to be of considerable relevance in the near future, though perhaps largely in terms of a categorization of the helping process. As such it will be considered together with possible psychoanalytic formulations in the next chapter. In the field of social psychology it is already evident that social workers will draw heavily on theories about the behaviour of small groups, whether they are working primarily with groups (e.g. youth leaders) or as caseworkers (e.g. interviewing several members of a family at the same time). It is possible that field-theory[11] will also be more extensively used, though the central importance of the 'situation' was grasped comparatively early in the development of casework. Mary Richmond stated that 'The social worker's "Case" is the particular social situation or problem—not the person or persons concerned'.[12]

Psychological theories, then, have been the main influence on casework and their usefulness has clearly not been exhausted. Social workers are also beginning to pay increasing attention to 'social' knowledge. This again needs to be analysed into its component parts—knowledge of social conditions, of the social services and the working of social policy; knowledge derived from research into social class and industry and into social institutions generally; and finally, the use of sociological concepts and theories. In the last category emphasis has most recently been placed on role and role-theories. Knowledge of these different kinds helps to deepen and widen the intuition of caseworkers from their earliest days concerning the essential relationship between personality and society.

PSYCHOLOGICAL THEORIES

Limitations of space preclude a detailed discussion of each of the psychological theories mentioned above, and a certain arbitrariness in selection is inevitable. Emphasis will be placed on those psycho-analytic theories which have in the past most influenced British casework and those developments which seem to offer most help for the future.

Freudian theory, as we have already indicated, is a large and complex collection of concepts, hypotheses and speculations, covering a wide range of subjects. It is possible, however, to summarize Freud's theories concerning the structure and development of the personality. Human life is seen as the successive mastery of stimuli which are of two kinds, internal and constant (inherited instinctual forces) and external and continuous (the pressure of the environment 'outside' man). The structureless collection of internal stimuli is called the 'id'. This represents the unconscious part of the personality which works not according to reason and logic, but to the primary processes which recognize no law of contradiction and no principle of reality. An important and persisting activity of the unconscious is described as fantasy, a kind of primitive thought using sets of feelings rather than concepts. Mediating between the 'unconscious' stimuli, on the one hand, and the fierce forbidding super-ego, on the other, is the ego, that aspect of the personality directly responsible for maintaining the equilibrium of the whole personality. Its operations are conducted largely in terms of a series of defensive tactics (the mechanisms of defence). The equilibrium of the personality is subject to a series of threats as the libido (or sexual instinct) develops through a number of clearly marked stages changing its aim and its object. These stages are usually described as the oral, anal and phallic. The last clearly places the personality in the field of relationships with persons other than his mother and it is the resolution of the ensuing crisis (the Oedipal situation) which, according to Freud, originates the super-ego or internalized forbidding parent. The ways in which the person 'navigates' these stages has an important bearing on his future character. Intimately connected with this view of the structure and development of the personality are Freud's ideas on psychoanalytic therapy and in particular the importance given to the persistence throughout adult life of childhood wishes and fears, whether acknowledged or not.

This is an extremely condensed presentation of some of Freud's most important ideas about personality development which shows his theories as a static collection of rather flat statements rather than changing and developing approximations to the complex and dynamic truth about human beings. Yet it may serve as a backcloth against which later important developments in psychoanalytic thought and changes in the selective use of his theories by caseworkers may both be discussed.

The idea of the 'unconscious' exercised an early fascination for caseworkers which has continued undiminished to the present. The notion of the unacknowledged aspects of the personality must have a central place in casework, though there are certainly differences of opinion about the content of 'the unconscious'. Caseworkers who follow a Jungian psychology will see it as containing a positive wisdom far beyond that conveyed by the idea of a mass of instinctual wishes. Others may be led to question the view of the unconscious as a *disorganized* mass of impulses. However, the basic point is that some functions and purposes of the personality remain unconscious because the person has 'good reasons' for refusing to acknowledge them. The 'unconscious' can most profitably be used as a reference to 'experiences that the person cannot permit himself to actualize. The questions in understanding unconscious phenomena are, "How does the individual reject or accept his possibilities for being conscious of himself and his world?" How is it possible that he should shut out something which on another level he knows, and even also on this *level knows that he knows*'.[13] Viewing the unconscious in this way helps to overcome two major difficulties in the use of the concept by caseworkers. The first of these consists in the habit of referring to the unconscious as something like a chaotic basement, far beneath the superstructure of the conscious mind. The emphasis here is, of course, on 'depth' and the distinction is sometimes made between the work of the psychotherapist and the caseworker on the basis of the depth of their respective explorations of the psyche. This is not a very helpful approach. It is preferable for the caseworker to think in terms of unconscious processes or manifestations rather than locating their source somehow or other *in* the unconscious. As Dilman has observed, 'The statement about unconscious envy is a statement about what can be seen in the same way that the snake hidden in, but not behind, the bush is seen'.[14] In other words, it is the 'unconscious' that is in the feelings, attitudes etc. that we unknowingly express rather than the feelings, attitudes etc. that reside somehow *in* the unconscious.

The second difficulty concerns the view of the 'unconscious' as the source of psychic determinism. According to this, man's objectives in life are seen as disguised forms of instinctual satisfaction which man must pursue. In fact, using the notion of unconscious behaviour helps us to see that man is a more purposive creature than might have been supposed.[15] He is not an organism driven to inevitable Hedonism by an ineluctable force. Actions and processes of thought cannot be seen merely as ways of passage from stimulation to its abatement. Instead, we need to use a model of man pursuing a wide range of objectives and of therapy as a way not of altering behaviour but of enlarging his vision of his purposes and the means he adopts to accomplish them. As MacIntyre has observed: '. . . in psychoanalysis there is a large element of the treatment which consists in the patient coming to see that certain of his beliefs are misconceptions and that certain of his actions only make sense on assumptions which when they are made explicit he is prepared to reject. The patient's rationality is brought into play . . .'.[16]

Freud's approximation of the structure of the personality as id-ego–super-ego has also been used by caseworkers in this country, and early psychiatric social work in child guidance clinics sometimes took the form of helping mothers to relax the exacting standards of their super-ego. More recently, the focus of attention has moved away from releasing some of the repressed sexual and aggressive feelings towards examining and supporting the ways in which the personality maintains its own integrity and fosters its own growth. In other words, the approach to the personality now emphasizes the ego. Within this context two developments are of crucial importance for the caseworker: the study of the mechanisms of defence and the significance now given to the functions of the ego, in particular its work of integrating the personality.

The ego has the task of coping with anxiety so that equilibrium is maintained within the personality and in relationships with the environment. In pursuing this work the ego can use a number of defensive tactics. These have been studied by Anna Freud,[17] and the work of Melanie Klein[18] has also contributed to our understanding of the ways the personality seeks to defend itself against both the id impulses and pressure from the super-ego. Thus, the ego under stress employs mechanisms of regression to an earlier period when life was more tolerable and demands from others and from oneself were less exacting. The ego can satisfy certain instinctive demands by hiding them from the super-ego under the cloak of rationalization, borrowing a 'good' reason for a prohibited action. The ego can also—and most frequently does—use the mechanism of repression, whereby disallowed thoughts and feelings are expelled from consciousness and continuously kept from consciousness by the use of psychic energy. Melanie Klein has suggested that the most important defences employed very early in life are those of splitting, of projective identification and of introjection. Splitting comes into operation as a means of dealing with feelings of love and of hate directed to the same object (originally the mother's breast), which is seen both as good and bad. As a precondition for establishing the good object within the 'personality' it is essential that the 'good' breast is split off from 'the bad'. Projective identification refers not to identification of the ego with an object (introjection), but replacement of the ego ideal by an external object. Thus, National Socialists in Germany who took their leader for their ego ideal were projectively identifying with him.

The study of the defensive manœuvres of the ego is important because it helps the caseworker to describe certain aspects of personality. It is a way of directing attention to the means employed by the personality in solving certain kinds of conflict. Thus, the important aspect of this subject is not the learning of a list of defence mechanisms, but the appreciation that practically any process within the personality can be used defensively[19] and that the problem against which defence is sought is that of anxiety. Knowledge of the different kinds of anxiety and the ways in which the personality may react to them constitutes a crucial area of study for the caseworker. Freudian theory regards anxiety predominantly as a danger signal and three main kinds of danger have been described: real danger from an outside source, danger that the standards of the super-ego might be violated and danger that the ego might be 'flooded' by uncontrollable instincts. This approach, thus, identifies real anxiety, super-ego and instinctual anxiety. An important extension of these ideas is to be found in the work of Melanie Klein, who has distinguished two kinds of anxiety in early infancy—persecutory and depressive. These anxieties are connected with two stages in the development of the young personality, called the paranoid and the depressive positions.

> The paranoid position is the stage when destructive impulses and persecutory anxieties predominate and extends from birth until about three, four, or even five months of life. . . . The depressive position, which follows on this stage and is bound up with important steps in ego development, is established about the middle of the first year of life. . . . The infant introjects the object as a whole, and simultaneously he becomes in some measure able to synthesise the various aspects of the object as well as his emotions towards it. . . . Depressive feeling and guilt give rise to the urge to preserve or revive the loved object and thus to make reparation for destructive impulses and phantasies. . . .[20]

This is a controversial theory even in psychoanalytic circles, but it emphasizes an important feature of interpersonal relationships which can be formulated in terms of the question, What am I *doing* to others in my real and fantasy relationships with them and what are they doing to me?

The ego, then, is seen as that part of the personality which deals with anxiety. Recent theorizing, however, particularly in America has stressed its wider, integrative functions. French, for instance, has stated that

> The Ego is an integrative mechanism whose usual function is not to defend itself against the instincts but rather to learn how it can satisfy the needs of the organism. Even when the Ego is confronted with a conflict, the normal Ego's primary task is to try to find a solution rather than defend itself against recognising the conflict and against having to struggle to solve it.[21]

Within this context the functions of the ego are usually seen as the perception of inner and outer reality, differentiation of the self from others, learning by trial and error and identification, and action as an integrated whole. It has often been suggested that one of the 'diagnostic' objectives of casework is the assessment of ego strengths and weakness—the ability to perceive correctly, to judge realistically, to act or to postpone action, and to bear frustration. The new emphasis on ego-psychology has served a number of useful purposes. It has, for instance, re-emphasized the importance of studying the client's own problem-solving apparatus and ability and it has re-directed attention to the unified person who is characteristically in action rather than acted upon. Two qualifications, however, should be made. Firstly, despite statements to the contrary, ego-psychology is often applied in casework in a way that minimizes the less positive, more unconscious aspects of the personality. Rieff has called attention to this danger in the theory itself: 'it may be charged that the ego-psychology wing of psychoanalysis overestimates the parliamentary capacities of the mind and discounts the negative, conflictual elements which Freud saw in it'.[22] Secondly, ego-psychology often underestimates the significance of relationships both in the constitution and the operations of the ego. Freud's deep pessimism in regard to social relationships which he saw as predominantly restrictive and coercive still seemed to overhang the extension of his ego theory by others.

A remedy for both difficulties is to be found in the theories which allow both for the unity of the personality and for the presence 'within' it of conflictual and 'dark' elements and also place the developing ego in a social rather than an individual matrix. The outstanding speculations in this direction are contained in Fairbairn's object relations theory.[23] This theory assumes the existence from birth of a unitary ego which becomes structurally differentiated through the process of interaction with 'outside' objects which are internalized. In this theory, as Guntrip has rightly observed, 'the ego not merely *reacts to* and *adapts to* its objects, but is also *constituted* by its object—relations. . . . Our deeper emotions and impulses are then, not fixed instincts, but ego-reactions to personal objects in an inner world, surging up to complicate our reactions to our external objects—the outer world'.[24] In the course of interaction the ego is differentiated into three structures—the central ego, which is in touch with the outside world, the libidinal ego (that aspect of the total psyche in a state of deprivation, frustration and impotent rage) and the anti-libidinal ego representing object relationships to parents. These sophisticated formulations are not crucial for social work as long as Fairbairn's general views of the unitary but differentially structured ego and of the importance of relationships are appreciated. Perhaps the impact of his theory can be conveyed by this quotation from Fairbairn:

The ultimate principle from which the whole of my special views are derived may be formulated in the general proposition that libido is not primarily pleasure-seeking, but object-seeking. The clinical material on which this proposition is based may be summarised in the protesting cry of a patient to this effect—'You're always talking about my wanting this and that desire satisfied, but what I really want is a father.' It was reflection upon the implications of such phenomena as this that formed the real starting-point of my present line of thought.[25]

So far we have attempted to describe some of the aspects of psychoanalysis that caseworkers have used and others that they might profitably study for future use. We have considered the concept of the unconscious and the structure of the personality with particular reference to the ego. Caseworkers have also used some of the crucial assumptions made in Freudian theory. Of these perhaps the most influential has been that of the persistent influence of childhood wishes and feelings throughout later life. The idea that unfavourable development at any of the main stages of libidinal development (oral-anal-phallic) has a determining influence on one's future character (so that one can talk of the oral, anal and 'mature' character) has not exercised much influence on casework. Recent work, however, on character disorders has given fresh significance to this idea, as we shall see.

The experiences of childhood have assumed importance for caseworkers for a number of reasons. They are important in moulding personality and because the behaviour of many clients can be understood as a 'carry-over' of childhood wishes, fears and relationships. Many clients seem in general to be feeling and acting at an immature level of development and many caseworkers are closely concerned directly and indirectly with children (the child care officer, the family caseworker, the psychiatric social worker in child guidance, the probation officer and so on). Theories that seek to explain the importance of childhood can be found in abundance, but a useful preliminary approach is to consider them as theories of crises and theories of learning. This distinction cannot be rigidly applied, and an attempt will be made to draw them together in terms of object-relations theory. None the less it serves a purpose.

Two of the most important crises theories can be found in the work of Melanie Klein and of Erik Erikson. Some aspects of

Klein's work are open to serious criticism: the central place given to the death instinct is perhaps the clearest example. Yet, even if the existence of this instinct is doubtful, caseworkers can benefit from the emphasis given in Kleinian theory to aggression against the self and others and its function, according to the theory, at crucial turning points of the developing personality—the paranoid-schizoid and the depressive positions. The first revolves around the infant's reaction to a world into which he has projected a great deal of his innate aggression, so that, in consequence, he feels persecuted by his own bad feelings which he has split off and projected away from himself on to what, thus, becomes a 'bad' or partly 'bad' object. In the depressive position the infant is able to bring together the 'good' and 'bad' parts of an object (the breast, the mother) and begins to relate to a 'whole' object. '. . . With the introjection of the object as a whole the infant's object-relation alters fundamentally. The synthesis between the loved and hated aspects of the complete object gives rise to feelings of mourning and guilt which imply vital advances in the infant's emotional and intellectual life.'[26]

It might perhaps be considered that Kleinian theories of development have little relevance for the caseworker. Such an impression would be apparently confirmed once her over-emphasis on intra-psychic life has been appreciated. Melanie Klein pays insufficient attention to such environmental factors as the differing effects of actual variations in motherly care. In spite of this, however, much of her work can be interpreted as an object-relations theory and her views of personality development are helpful to caseworkers in a number of ways. In a later chapter we shall be concerned with problem families whose behaviour, feelings and ways of relating are often described as 'immature'. Much of their behaviour seems to indicate that they have not yet reached the stage of relationships to 'whole' people and that they are avoiding their depressive position, the acknowledgement of the harm they feel they have done. The caseworker who helps mothers with their babies, will perhaps be better able to see the importance of allowing babies some sadness, while all caseworkers will be able to derive from Kleinian views an appreciation of the place of guilt and mourning as positive factors in personality development. Thus, a caseworker faced with the recently widowed client will be able to appreciate that the recent death may well reactivate some of the much earlier responses to real or fantasied loss, that the client needs time and support in working through a revived depressive position, and that the work of mourning is a necessary step to adequate recovery.

Erikson has suggested that a human life can, from the point of view of personality development, be divided into eight stages, each of which constitutes a crisis. Whether the crisis is resolved at each stage and the manner of the resolution influence decisively the outcome of later stages. The stages have been described in terms of their objectives and the conditions which would signify failure at that particular point in development:

I. *Trust v. Mistrust*, in this period emphasis is placed on what the infant receives and his perception of the world as a reasonably safe place;

II. *Autonomy v. Shame, Doubt*, this is also described as the muscular-anal period, and the two forms of behaviour of most significance are holding on and letting go;

III. *Initiative v. Guilt*, here Erikson emphasizes what he describes as the social modality of 'making', and it first appears in the sense of 'being on the make';

IV. *Industry v. Inferiority*, when the child learns to win approval and recognition by producing things;

V. *Identity v. Role Diffusion*, this is the phase of adolescence in which the establishment of a sense of inner sameness and continuity is important;

VI. *Intimacy v. Isolation*, this is the age of young adulthood when the personality is testing out whether it can retain a sense of identity at the same time as it is involved in intense and demanding emotional relationships;

VII. *Generativity v. Stagnation*, here the focus of interest should turn away from the self and towards establishing and caring for the next generation;

VIII. *Ego Integrity v. Despair*, this stage marks the culmination of the others, 'it is post-narcissistic love of the human ego—not of the self—as an experience which conveys some world order and spiritual sense . . .'.[27]

This scheme must inevitably distort the picture of human development, but it does focus attention on some important aspects. Some stages are less clearly characterized than others; particularly perhaps No. 8, a kind of beatific vision which, being secular, loses its point. Yet there is no doubt that many of the problems facing children and adults can be summarized in Erikson's terms. Particularly useful, for example, is his view of the adolescent stage of development.

The idea of stages of development has been criticized on the ground that growth occurs in constant sequences. It is perhaps within this context that the views of some of the learning theorists should be discussed. Take, for instance, the different views on the origin of neuroses to be found in the work of Dollard and Miller[28] and of Mowrer.[29] Dollard and Miller use the concepts of psychoanalysis within a framework of learning theory derived from Hull. The neurotic, in their view, is basically a 'stupid' person whose confusion has arisen in the following way: a person seeks to achieve certain goals, driven by what are considered to be the basic drives of sex and aggression; he meets responses within the environment which occasion fear and which lead him to avoid the goal he sought. This situation interrupts learning because the individual is preoccupied with thoughts motivated by the unreduced drives. The neurotic person is someone 'who is in need of a stock of sentences that will match the events going on within and without him'. The new sentences make possible an immense facilitation of higher mental processes. With their aid he can discriminate and generalize more accurately; he can mature himself for remote tasks; he can produce hope and caution within himself. . . .[30] Mowrer's view of neurosis is the reverse of the general Freudian view which emphasizes excessive socialization (or the severe super-ego). Mowrer's solution to the problem of the neurotic's persistence in self-defeating behaviour is to outline two kinds of learning—problem-solving and conditioning (or emotional learning). The child has an ambivalent attitude towards his parents and when faced with demands from them learns to avoid conditioning by using his problem-solving learning. Thus, neurosis results from a super-ego deficiency; it is the social drives (conscience) that are repressed rather than the primary drives (sex and aggression).

The idea of childhood as a time of basic learning is clearly important and some of the formulations of the learning theorists are of use in casework. For example, Dollard and Miller's emphasis on 'labelling' explains why some clients find it helpful when the caseworker puts into words the feelings they are trying to express. An important part of the child's learning needs, however, to be expressed in more personal terms than those of stimulus, response and cue. The child's most important lessons are those of perception, perception of the self and of others, as well as of the world of material objects. Thus, the Freudian stages of development are perhaps best seen as a series of interlocking phases in which the personality learns how to see and to use himself and others in a number of different situations. A person successively faces in the years of infancy and early childhood situations in which he tries to relate to people who give (food, love, comfort) and who also, of necessity withhold (food, love, themselves etc.), to people who make demands on him and who encourage him, people who control him and urge him to begin self-control, and who love him, but who also love others and who are not always present. This way of regarding childhood development had been succinctly described by the Winnicotts in the following terms:

> Without someone specifically orientated to his needs the infant cannot find a working relation to external reality. Without someone to give satisfactory instinctual gratifications the infant cannot find his body, nor can he develop an integrated personality. Without one person to love and to hate he cannot come to know that it is the same person that he loves and hates, and so cannot find his sense of guilt, and his desire to repair and restore. Without a limited human and physical environment that he can know he cannot find out the extent to which his aggressive ideas actually fail to destroy, and so cannot sort out the difference between fantasy and fact. Without a father and mother who are together, and who take joint responsibility for him, he cannot find and express his urge to separate them, nor experience relief at failing to do so.[31]

In this section the considerable importance given to a psychology of object-relations will by now have become apparent, and my final comments on the Freudian concept of unconscious phantasy will be made within the same orientation. This is the most recent concept to have been reassessed in terms of its significance for inter-personal relationships. The work of Laing is of fundamental importance in this respect.[32] 'Human actions', he has stated, 'are barely comprehensible without an understanding of the phantasies in terms of which persons experience and relate to each other.' He sees phantasy as a mode of experience involving

38

'issues of full/empty, good/bad, destruction/reparation, anxiety/ security, and so on'. Thus, in phantasy we experience a relation- ship between ourselves and another as that between something full and something empty, something good and something bad and so on. This way of experiencing other people is an important part of our total experience of relationships with others. 'The relatedness of self and other that can occur on a phantasy level is as basic to all human relatedness as the interactions that most people most of the time are aware of.'

The caseworker is concerned with the individual *in* his relation- ships and within this context he asks a number of questions. By what psychological means do people continue to exist as persons with an identity which is apparent both to themselves and to others? How do they maintain a sense of relative well-being as they pursue their purposes in a world of others? How do they meet their fears of themselves and others and how do they try to accomplish their desires? These are obviously very general ques- tions and any attempt to answer them risks being platitudinous, poetistic, or incomprehensible. Yet a profession that is essentially concerned with helping people must assume a view of human nature and also use it explicitly in its actual operations. An object- relations psychology seems most useful from the viewpoint of casework. Such a psychology rests on an accurate recognition of the basic difference between man and animals. This difference lies in man's capacity for dialogue and his ability to form a system with other men, a system which 'contains' and affects both himself and others. Man in creating and maintaining these systems of relationship creates the necessary means of a *human* life and the possibility of his own change.

KNOWLEDGE OF SOCIETY

In considering some psychological theories in casework I have suggested that importance should not be attached to the idea of instinct (or push and pull forces within the personality). As Peters has observed, 'Social life is never, like the jungle popularized by evolutionary theorists, a matter of mere survival; it is a matter of surviving in a certain sort of way'.[33] This 'sort of way' can be interpreted as referring to two different though connected 'limits'. As we have seen in the previous section, man is concerned with survival, but not at the cost of the means by which he survives as man (object-relations), of his own self-love or esteem. In addition to these 'psychological' limitations to a mere wish for survival at all costs, there are 'social' limitations. Man also wishes to survive within a particular social tradition, within a known and knowable social environment. It is with this second element that we are concerned in this section.

The term environment covers an unspecifiably large range of phenomena; it refers to everything that is judged to be 'outside' the person. It includes large- and small-scale organizations, social institutions, and the culture of the whole society and its sub-groups. Sociological knowledge can, however, increase our understanding of the environment, whether we are concerned with the family or the wider society in which it carries on its work of socialization. It can also increase our knowledge of the relationship between the person and his society. This is perhaps the most important aspect for the social worker, as reformers and social workers in the late nineteenth and early twentieth centuries appreciated. Henry Jones, for example, writing on 'The Working Faith of the Social Reformer', stated that the relationship between man and the environment should be seen as '*a process*: a process by which the outer world is formed anew within the individual's mind and will, or by which the individual forms himself through taking the world into himself as his own content'.[34] The continuity between this notion and some of the contemporary views of role-taking will become apparent later in this chapter. Social history was once considered to consist of history with the politics omitted and similarly the object of the study of society might be conceived as society with personality left out. This is not the argument of this chapter.

'Knowledge of society' is admittedly a vague phrase and, if it is to be extended beyond the stage of rather superficial description, it should clearly be analysed into its different components. As far as social workers are concerned, there would appear to be three kinds of knowledge within the wider term: knowledge of social conditions, social policy and the social services; of social institutions; and of sociological concepts and theories. Knowledge of these groups of phenomena helps social workers to describe and understand their clients' problems and guides their helping efforts.

Early caseworkers and reformers—certainly in their writings—

heavily emphasized the social orientation of their efforts. Social work with individuals was part of a wider movement for the amelioration of society. 'I see', wrote Bernard Bosanquet in 1915, 'some new lights inform us from time to time that "case work" alone is to be left to the Charity Organisation Society. The idea would make our founders turn in their graves. Case work which is not handled as an engine of social improvement is not, I should have said, Charity Organisation Society work at all.'[35] Just before this date Loch had been urging caseworkers to turn their attention to 'bad areas': 'our plea is for the association of good, patient, and skilful treatment in the individual cases, with a direct, constant and unflinching effort to remove the evils that produce immoral stagnation, to purge bad areas, to remove bad conditions'.[36] This plea did not produce very significant results, but it is as valid today as fifty years ago. Social workers need to know about social conditions, local and national, and to apply such knowledge in the appraisal of individual cases. To take some obvious examples, the significance of a man's unemployment for a period of time depends, to some extent, on the level of employment in his area. Unemployment at a time of local and national 'full' employment 'feels' different to the client, and possibly has a different meaning to the caseworker in terms of appraising the man's role performance than the same occurrence at a time of low employment. Similarly, judgments about a client's maturity depend, partly at any rate, on a knowledge of the material resources on which he can rely to solve his problems and this emphasizes the importance, for instance, of knowledge about the extent of poverty in our society. Again, though the appraisal of adolescent behaviour depends on a knowledge both of psychology and of the pressures that our changing society exerts on the growing child, it may also require special knowledge of the locality. For example, a group of teenage boys living on a new but isolated council estate were charged with a series of offences with a succession of girls, some of whom formed a regular group. Understanding these offences would certainly call for the application of knowledge about the homosexual and heterosexual phase of adolescence, but it would also require some appreciation of the pressures specific to the locality.

Knowledge of the social services is clearly part of the social worker's equipment, as Rodgers and Dixon have stressed in their recent study of the social services in a northern town.[37] People come to the social worker for information about other services or require referral to them as a part of casework. The world of welfare, like the rest of our society, has now become so complex and specialized that a knowledge of its provisions and operations has become an expertise in itself. To refer, however, to the operations of welfare is to emphasize the place of a knowledge of social policy in the social worker's equipment. It is not sufficient to know the provision, one must also know how the services actually work. Take, for example, Townsend's recent work on the residential care of the old.[38] It may be that the quality of residential care in the caseworker's own locality differs from that described in the book. None the less, a knowledge of the general ways in which services are provided for this particular group in the community can and should deepen the worker's imaginative grasp of the impact of services on the recipients. This is important since the caseworker will need to appreciate what his or her clients may expect from a service and how they might be treated. As we shall see, the kind of image we have of ourselves is deeply influenced by the ways in which we are actually treated.

The worker needs a firm and continually refurbished knowledge of her own service. The importance of communication has already been stressed; the social caseworker never communicates with a client *in vacuo*, but always from a functional base. Caseworkers need to know the complexities and significance of the organization in which they work, both to render effective service and also to assess the agency's impact on the client. Thus, as we shall see, the almoner should know both the significance of the hospital as a 'container' for people who have been defined as sick enough to need separation from the community and special care, and also the ramifications of hospital hierarchies, the formal and informal channels of communication, the locus of actual power.

The caseworker should also appreciate the specific content of knowledge necessary for effective work within her agency. It is difficult to categorize this, since it is partly social and partly psychological. It is included in this section since it is exercised and sometimes acquired from the caseworker's functional base in society.

A detailed consideration of the knowledge specially required for practice in each field is not possible in a work of this size, though it is clearly a priority in the further study of social work. As a first approximation, however, it may be useful to analyse the fields of casework in terms of the following categories: the nature of the organization's specialized clientele and the special roles they play in relation to the agency; the specialized personnel other than the caseworker who deal with his or her client—what they do and the knowledge they require in order to work effectively; the response of the organization and of society at large to the client in his main organizational roles *vis-à-vis* the agency. Knowledge of these kinds would appear to be necessary for practice in each field.

The specialized clientele of the almoner, for example, are people playing the sick role, which, as long as it is fairly strictly adhered to, is accepted by the hospital and those in the patient's environment. The sick person is obviously primarily the concern of doctors, nurses etc. who are trying to treat and care for him. The doctors, in order to cure the patient, must seek accurate information, diagnose scientifically and treat swiftly and effectively. What implications have these factors for the almoner's knowledge? She must appreciate the ways in which the sick role is defined and the fact that a person's definition of himself as ill is as likely to be influenced by cultural factors as by aspects of his personality. The almoner should know about sickness as a medical as well as a social entity, not in order to diagnose or treat the illness, but so that she can be reasonably sure of the course of an illness, its treatment, prognosis and likely residual effects. There will also be special aspects of the illness that will directly concern her function; for example, its social aspects and the likelihood of psychogenesis or emotional factors in causation, cure or rehabilitation. A knowledge of the ways the doctor will work and the knowledge he seeks will bear directly upon the almoner's method of collecting and interpreting data. Bartlett has observed that 'In working in a scientifically oriented field such as health, social workers must have sufficient command of concepts and theory to convey the essential content to their associates'.[39] These examples from the field of medical social work illustrate the use of the categories outlined above and indicate the way they might be applied to other fields. In the child care service,[40] for instance, the problems of central concern are separation, substitution and rehabilitation and the worker will be especially concerned with 'the natural history' of separation. She will perhaps find Bowlby's view of the three stages of reaction—protest, despair, detachment[41]—useful in understanding a particular situation herself and in helping others who play more directly parent-substitute roles to share her understanding.

Studies in Britain and America[42] have given attention to the importance of social class in the operation of the social services. Social classes would not perhaps usually be called social institutions; they would seem to have the nature rather of potential groups, which might or might not become social movements. The influence of class factors, however, appears to be worthy of serious consideration by social workers. One of the difficulties, of course, in the way of such consideration is the elusiveness of the concept itself. Sociologists appear to have seen class as a question of subjective feeling and definition (one is the class one feels one is) or as an objective relationship to the means of production in a particular society. For some, social class can be defined by occupation, by the length of full-time education, or the pursuit of a way of life. It is social class defined in terms of the last criteria that has attracted most attention from past and present commentators on social work, who have stressed the importance of a knowledge of the norms of the client's social class in the assessment of his behaviour, and the folly of exerting pressure on one social class to conform to the standards of another. In other words, the importance of knowledge about social class has been seen in terms both of 'diagnosis' and 'treatment'. What requires more study, of course, are the particular factors in a class way of life which may hinder communication between worker and client. Bernstein, for example, in some interesting recent research[43] has drawn attention to differences in perception between the working and the middle classes. He has distinguished between the public language of the former and the formal language of the latter. The public language allows little individual choice whilst the formal language is much less structured and permits greater individualization. He also sees the working class as much less concerned with long-terms aims than the middle class. It is, however, important to place such observations in an historical context and to ask, for example, what opportunities has the working class had in its historical development to learn that long-term goals are worth planning for? This should perhaps encourage social workers to extend their view of social class beyond a consideration of distinctive norms. If, as seems possible, the differential use of the social services is partly associated with class factors, is this due to their identification with a middle class way of life, to a failure in communication based on differences in perception, or in educational experience, or the definition of the helping situation in terms of social power? People may feel that in coming to a social service they are in the power of others considered to be their superiors and the applicant's power can be exercised only in explicit or implicit refusal of the service.

Of the many social institutions which help to mould our social life perhaps the most important is the family. It is important for the social worker because it is the prime means of helping children to become human persons and members of a particular society and also because it is the main guarantee of the maintenance of adult adjustment. Studies of the family have increased in Britain in the last few years and the material they provide can be used by the social worker in several ways. A study of general changes in the family can help the social worker to appreciate changing ideas of 'normality' and the importance of any resulting contrasts. Thus, the significant change in the pattern of women's work, particularly in relation to wives and mothers, influences both those who wish to work and those who actually do not. Studies of family organization and role distribution within the family have helped social workers to discard some of their myths in regard to the 'normal' family[44] and to appreciate the many different kinds of family pattern that are still conducive to apparent happiness. In some studies the work and attitudes of the husband and father have been graphically portrayed[45] and the social worker has, thus, once again been encouraged to see their important influence on family life and organization. Mothers (and daughters) have perhaps received an undue amount of attention from social workers and, in spite of periodic protestations from social workers themselves, the tendency appears to continue. The reasons for this are beyond the scope of this book, but it is to be hoped that any alteration will take the form not of a reparative over-attention to fathers, but of a focus on the role relationships of husband–wife, father–mother–child and so on.

So far we have considered the importance for casework of knowledge of different aspects of society—social conditions, social policy, class and such institutions as the family. Reference has of necessity already been made to sociological terms (e.g. class, institution etc.), but special attention will now be given to them in order to illustrate their relevance to social casework. Of the terms that could be considered 'role' has been selected as of primary importance.

This term has been prominent in recent discussions of casework in Britain and America. Perlman, for example, has suggested that the large number of people who do not continue beyond their initial contact with the social agency may be explained in terms of differences in role ascription between the applicant and the caseworker.

> If the caseworker conceives of intake as a 'study' or 'exploratory process' and the applicant conceives of it as a help-getting experience, the two participants will have a hard time understanding one another. If the caseworker conceives of the applicant as his 'client', that is, a person who is ready to use his services, and the applicant conceives of himself and the caseworker in who-knows-what ways, they will have a hard time communicating with one another.[46]

Another writer has suggested that the problem is not lack of information about the norms governing the role of client, but a conflict between the generally established and recognized norm of autonomy and self-sufficiency in the adult role and the new norm of dependency in the client role.[47] In England, Waldron,[48] Woodward[49] and other caseworkers have reported their use of the concept of role in the clarification of ways of helping people.

In judging the usefulness of the concept of role it is important to attempt some clarification of its meaning. It is possible to find amongst the many and varied uses of the term two basic elements, reciprocity and patterning. Clearly, reciprocity is involved in the very notion of role, since the role of father makes no sense without that of the child. The behaviour which makes a consistent whole and which we describe as the role of father gains its meaning and consistency by reference to the role of another, the child. An individual is called upon to play a large number and range of roles from the position of father, husband, worker, worshipper, to name only a few. Role refers to the behaviour, responsibilities and rewards appropriate to each of these positions. Roles may be classified in several different ways: according to the manner of recruitment (some roles are ascribed by reason of a person's sex and age, while others are chosen); whether they are occasional (a customer) or pervasive (a mother); concrete or abstract (an abstract role would be that of courteous behaviour in social relationship). We speak frequently of role-playing and this perhaps conveys the idea that roles are somehow superficial, easily discarded aspects of behaviour. As the discussion has already indicated we are deeply involved in the roles we take or are called upon to play.

These basic ideas have been elaborated in two main directions. Some theorists have stressed the normative aspects of role, whilst others have seen role-making and role-taking as a continuing process whereby an individual's attitude to himself and to others is determined by his judgment of their role towards him. Each notion of 'role' can contribute to the caseworker's understanding.

The caseworker, as we shall see, in order to understand the problems presented to her attempts to appraise the behaviour of the client in the interview situation. Such appraisal must obviously pay some regard to the client's ideas about the kind of behaviour that is expected in a social agency and about the sort of person the caseworker is and what she may do. Caseworkers themselves have at different times assigned different roles to their clients or are at present undecided about which roles to assign. Thus, in the child care service the role of the child care officer in relation to the foster-parent is obscure and 'at various times the foster-parent has been thought of as a caretaker for the agency's children, as a resource for these children, and, more recently, as an extension of the staff and a member of the child care team'.[50] In appraising the client's situation the idea of role helps the caseworker to recognize the many different roles each individual plays, and that one role may become predominant to the detriment of the performance of the others. The problems which people bring to the caseworker can very often be classified in terms of a break-down in one or more significant roles and the caseworker will endeavour to find the reasons for such a failure, whether it is due to a role conflict that has been recently accentuated, to a failure in role definition between the participants, to a lack of resources necessary for playing the role, or to the fact that the person has had no opportunity to learn the role. Thus, the use of the concept of role in its normative sense can lend a clarity of focus in both 'diagnosis'[51] and 'treatment' in social casework.

Of deeper significance, however, is the idea of role-taking and role-making as a continuous process of testing and incorporation contributing to the creation of a person's 'self' role. A notion of this kind seems necessary if we are to think of the 'self' as something more than an assortment of various roles. The child from an early age can be observed rehearsing the feelings and copying the actions of the significant adults in his life. He is in this way giving meaning to such feelings and actions by taking the role of the other within himself and thus acquiring one of the basic skills in communication. He is also acquiring meanings for his developing sense of self. As a result of interaction between this developing self and the interpretation of the other's conception, valuation and expectation of the self, the child gradually acquires a predominant or cardinal role. This idea of the fusion of roles has not been extensively studied, but Fallding,[52] after a recent critical examination of some of the approaches already made, has concluded that the unity attained through the cardinal role is basically one of accountability to an enduring family group. He has suggested a broad threefold classification of the family—the adaptation type, in which each parent has given the other a charter of independence; the identification type, in which the parents have identified their interests with those of the family and the false-identification type, expressing conflict between the other two patterns. It is perhaps possible to interpret other work in this field as suggesting that each individual develops a fundamental attitude towards himself which pervades all his actual role behaviour. Thus, Philipps and Rabinowitcz have identified the three categories of (1) avoidance of others, (2) self-indulgence and a turning against others and (3) self-deprivation and a turning against the self.[53]

Role-making and role-taking refers to a basic tendency to interpret the behaviour of others as a series of social acts. Their interpretation is modified in the course of inter-action between the self and others.

> Interaction is always a *tentative* process, a process of continuously testing the conception one has of the role of the other. The response of the other serves to reinforce or to challenge this conception. The product of the testing process is the stabilization or the modification of one's own role. (This) idea of role-taking shifts emphasis away from the simple process of enacting a prescribed role to devising a performance on the basis of an imputed other-role. The actor is not the occupant of a position for which there is a neat set of rules . . .

but a person who must act in the perspective supplied in part by his relationship to others whose actions reflect roles that he must identify.[54]

An example may clarify this viewpoint. If a man has an appointment with a priest he will expect him to behave according to the norms attached to the position of clergyman. But as he talks and transacts his affairs with the priest he identifies units or patterns of behaviour (roles) towards him. This identification is at first tentative and it becomes more firm as he tests the reality of these roles in interaction with the priest. He interacts by responding to the suggested role through complementing and, thus, confirming it, or by denial of the reciprocity, or by maintaining the uncertainty and ambiguity. This idea of tentative interaction based on an interpretation of the other's behaviour as a series of consistent wholes (expectations, evaluations, etc.) is clearly of importance to a consideration of the casework process.

Take, for instance, the following brief extract from an interview between a psychiatric social worker in a child guidance clinic and Mr. Brown, the father of a boy of 12 who is receiving treatment. Mr. Brown places great value upon intellectual pursuits and shows a considerable fear of the consequences of allowing freedom of expression to his emotions. This extract is taken from the fourth interview:

> Mr. Brown said that he had tried, he really had: he had kept control of his own feelings and allowed his son to answer him back. His son had abused him and had run out of the house. The trouble with this thing was that you did not know where it would end. He looked at the caseworker in a challenging way. The caseworker said that Mr. B. was telling him that his suggestions about the expression of feeling were not useful and that in fact they might be dangerous. Mr. Brown said that it sounded different when the worker said it. The worker wondered what the difference seemed to be and Mr. Brown suggested that the worker made his words seem childlike.

In this extract, the client seems to be concerned with himself in the role of a child towards the caseworker and as the interview proceeds he relates to the caseworker in accordance with different aspects of this role. At first he shows himself as the good child who has tried to carry out an imposed task, but he has interpreted the task incorrectly; he has still controlled his feelings, though he has allowed his son to give rein to his critical views of his father. Perhaps Mr. Brown now sees himself as the impertinent child, but this raises unthinkable prospects. His look towards the caseworker can be seen as a silent appeal or rebuke, an invitation to confirm or deny aspects of his assumed child-role. The caseworker's reply seems to maintain the role ambiguity, and Mr. B. interprets this as a child-making gambit on the worker's part.

In this section we have considered social knowledge of various kinds which could be of use to the caseworker. The temptation is, of course, to add to the list until it constitutes an impressive series of research projects for the future. The acquisition of the kinds of knowledge already suggested may seem onerous, but it will also be apparent that no cases will require the application of the full range of concepts, theories and data. Some kinds of knowledge may in many cases only indicate the general areas in which the caseworker must acquire her own information of particular cases; while others will be of more use in the clarification of 'treatment'. Yet each kind of social knowledge brings some assistance to the caseworker's general and particular understanding of the social world which permeates the individual lives of her clients.

NOTES

[1] Rall, M., 'The Effective Use of Case-Work Principles in the Family Agency', *Social Service Review*, Sept. 1950.

[2] Bartlett, H. M., *Social Work Practice in the Health Field*, National Association of Social Workers, New York, 1962, p. 130.

[3] *Report of the Working Party on Social Workers in the Local Authority Health and Welfare Services*, H.M.S.O., 1959, p. 244.

[4] *Report of the Departmental Committee on the Probation Service*, Cmd. 1650, H.M.S.O., 1962, p. 23.

[5] See e.g. Binswanger, L., 'Existential Analysis and Psychotherapy' in Fromm-Reichmann, F. and Moreno, J. L. (eds.), *Progress in Psychotherapy*, Grane and Stratton, 1956. May, R., 'The Context of Psychotherapy' in Stein, M. (ed.), *Contemporary Psychotherapies*, Free Press of Glencoe, 1961.

[6] See e.g. French, T. M., *The Reintegrative Process and Psychoanalytic Treatment*, Vol. III of the *Integration of Behaviour*, University of Chicago Press, 1958. Parad, H. J. (ed.), *Ego Psychology and Dynamic Casework*, F.S.A.A., 1958.

[7] For an interesting discussion of learning theories see Hilgard, E. R., *Theories of Learning*, Appleton-Century-Crofts, 1948.

[8] See e.g. Neiman, L. J. and Hughes, J. W., 'The Problem of the Concept of Role', *Social Forces*, Vol. 30, Dec. 1951; Sarbin, T. R., 'Role Theory', in Gardner Lindzey (ed.), *Handbook of Social Psychology*, Vol. II, New York: Addison-Wesley, 1954; Rose, A. M. (ed.), *Human Behaviour and Social Processes*, Routledge & Kegan Paul, 1962.

Notes

[9] The reference here is to the work of the Institute of Community Studies which has carried out a number of important investigations into various aspects of social life in East London.

[10] In the early 1940's students on the Mental Health Course were taught to encourage 'relationships', but to avoid 'transference'.

[11] For an attempt to use field theory in a formulation of social work theory see Grinker, R. *et al.*, *Psychiatric Social Work: A Transactional Case Book*, Basic Books Inc., New York, 1961.

[12] Richmond, M., *What is Social Case Work?* New York, 1922, p. 27.

[13] May, R., op. cit.

[14] Dilman, I., 'The Unconscious', *Mind*, Vol. LXVIII, No. 272, Oct. 1959.

[15] For a critical discussion of this view, however, see Alexander, P., 'Rational Behaviour and Psychoanalytic Explanation', *Mind*, Vol. LXXI, No. 283, July 1962.

[16] MacIntyre, A., *The Unconscious*, Routledge & Kegan Paul, 1958, p. 5.

[17] Freud, A., *The Ego and the Mechanisms of Defence*, Hogarth Press, 1937.

[18] Klein, M., *et al.*, *Developments in Psycho-Analysis*, Hogarth Press, 1952; Klein, M., *et al.*, *New Directions in Psycho-Analysis*, Hogarth Press, 1955.

[19] See e.g. Klein, M., *Envy and Gratitude*, Tavistock, 1957, pp. 61-6 for a useful discussion of defences against experiencing envy. She considers idealization, flight from the mother to other people, devaluation of the object or of the self, stirring up envy in others etc.

[20] Klein, M., *Preface to The Psycho-Analysis of Children*, Hogarth Press, 1948 (Third Edition).

[21] French, op. cit., p. 32.

[22] Rieff, P., *Freud, The Mind of the Moralist*, Gollancz, 1959, p. 62

[23] Fairbairn, W. R. D., *Psychoanalytic Studies of the Personality*, Tavistock, 1952.

[24] Guntrip, H., *Personality Structure and Human Interaction*, Hogarth Press, 1961, p. 30. This work discusses in an extremely useful way the theories of Freud, Klein and others in comparison with the completely object-relations theory of Fairbairn. See also *British Journal of Medical Psychology*, Vol. XXXVI, Part 2, 1963.

[25] Fairbairn, W. R. D., op. cit., p. 137.

[26] Klein, M., *Developments in Psychoanalysis*, Hogarth Press, 1952, p. 294.

[27] The material for this paragraph is based on Erikson, E., *Childhood and Society*, Imago, 1951, Chapter Seven.

[28] Dollard, J. and Miller, N., *Personality and Psychotherapy*, McGraw-Hill, 1950.

[29] Mowrer, O. H., *Psychotherapy: Theory and Research*, Ronald, 1953.

[30] Dollard and Miller, op. cit., p. 281.

[31] Winnicott, D. W. and Britton, C., 'Residential Management as Treatment for Difficult Children', *Human Relations*, Vol. I, No. 1, June 1947.

[32] Laing, R. D., *The Self and Others*, Tavistock, 1961, particularly Chapters One and Two. The quotations in this paragraph are taken from Laing's first chapter.

[33] Peters, R., *The Concept of Motivation*, Routledge & Kegan Paul, 1960, (2nd Ed.), p. 127.

[34] Jones, H., 'The Working Faith of the Social Reformer', II: 'The Misuse of Metaphors in The Human Sciences', *Hibbert Journal*, Vol. IV, 1905-6, p. 309.

[35] Bosanquet, B., 'Politics and Charity', *Charity Organisation Review*, Nov. 1915.

[36] Loch, C. S., 'A Further Development', *Charity Organisation Occasional Papers*, 4th Series, No. 28.

[37] Rodgers, B. N. and Dixon, J., *Portrait of Social Work*, O.U.P., 1960.

[38] Townsend, P., *The Last Refuge*, Routledge & Kegan Paul, 1962.

[39] Bartlett, H. M., op. cit., p. 51.

[40] For a full description of the knowledge required for work in the child care service see the author's *Casework in the Child Care Service*, Butterworths, 1962.

[41] Bowlby, J., 'Grief and Mourning in Infancy', *Psychoanalytic Study of The Child*, Vol. XV, 1960.

[42] See e.g. Hollingshead, A. B. and Redlich, M. D., *Social Class and Mental Illness*, Chapman and Hall, 1958; Gursllin, O., Hunt, R. G. and Roach, J. L., 'Social Class, Mental Hygiene and Psychiatric Practice', *Social Service Review*, Vol. XXXIII, No. 3, Sept. 1959; Douglas, J. W. B. and Blomfield, J. M., *Children Under Five*, Allen and Unwin, 1958.

[43] Bernstein, B., 'Some Sociological Determinants of Perception', *British Journal of Sociology*, June 1958.

[44] Goldberg, E. M., 'The Normal Family—Myth and Reality', *Social Work*, Jan and April 1959.

[45] Dennis, N., *et al.*, *Coal is our Life*, Eyre and Spottiswood, 1956.

[46] Perlman, H., 'Intake and Some Role Considerations', *Social Casework*, Vol. XLI, No. 4, April 1960.

[47] Rosenblatt, A., 'The Application of the Role Concept', *Social Casework*, Vol. XLIII, No. 1, Jan. 1962.

[48] Waldron, F. E., 'The Choice of Goals in Casework Treatment', *British Journal of Psychiatric Social Work*, Vol. VI, No. 2, 1961.

[49] Woodward, J., 'Notes on the Role Concept in Casework with Mothers of Burned Children', *The Almoner*, May 1961.

[50] McCoy, J., 'The Application of the Role Concept to Foster Parenthood', *Social Casework*, Vol. XLIII, No. 5, May 1962.

[51] On the application of the role concept to the problems of diagnosis in casework see the useful discussion in Perlman, H., 'The Role Concept and Social Casework: Some Explorations, II: What is Social Diagnosis?', *Social Service Review*, Vol. XXXVI, No. 1, March 1962.

[52] Fallding, H., 'The Family and the Idea of a Cardinal Role', *Human Relations*, Vol. 14, No. 4, Nov. 1961.

[53] Philipps, L. and Rabinowitcz, U. S., 'Social Role and Symptomatic Behaviour', *Journal of Abnormal and Social Psychology*, Vol. 57, No. 2, Sept. 1958.

[54] Turner, R. H., 'Role-Taking: Process versus Conformity', in Rose, A. M. (ed.), op. cit.

Chapter Three

THE PRINCIPLES OF CASEWORK

SO far casework has been discussed in terms of the kinds of knowledge used in the fulfilment of the objectives of a social agency. The specific nature of casework is to be found partly in its connection with agency function, partly in the kinds of knowledge used and partly in the observance and application of 'casework' principles. This term is one of the most widely and loosely used of what I have elsewhere described as the 'structural' words of the profession.[1] In this chapter a broad distinction is made between the general values and the technical principles of casework, though it will become apparent that this distinction has no absolute significance. Since much of the 'technique' of casework is a matter of the informed response of one human being to another, it is clear that technical principles will be embedded in values in regard to both their sources and their mode of operation. However, the distinction serves a useful if transitory purpose.

VALUES IN CASEWORK

What has often been termed the 'philosophy' of casework has not received adequate treatment in professional writing or thinking. It is a subject that has sometimes fascinated the social work educator,[2] occasionally interested the philosopher[3] and theologian,[4] and nearly always left workers in the field unmoved and uninterested. Reasons for the unsatisfactory nature of the studies so far attempted are not hard to find. Practitioners, it is claimed, must always give first allegiance to their professional activity, and social work education has not so far given much attention to helping the student to philosophize in a helpful manner: it has not always been appreciated that 'intellectualizing' is parasitic on genuine intellectual activity. References to the philosophy of casework are often unnecessarily ambitious, aiming to cover the widest possible range of subjects—propositions about the possibility of human betterment and of knowledge of man,[5] and about man and his society seen as an organic whole and the individual caseworker's responsibility to improve his agency's service.[6] A distinction is required between such 'formal' assumptions[7] as 'man is knowable' and other kinds of value observed in casework. In attempting to study the values and assumptions of casework it is fruitless to attempt to cover all possible classes and combinations. It is impossible, for example, to attend to assumptions that underly the whole activity of casework (equivalent in some studies apparently to those that underpin *human* activity) as one also considers the values upheld within the boundaries of the activity in question.

Furthermore, existing studies of casework (or social work) philosophy, whether comprehensive or occasional, seem to confuse analysis with persuasion. Bisno's monograph,[8] for instance, seeks to establish the underlying concepts and values of social work, but it is in fact concerned with advocating a programme contrasted with what in the author's views (from rather inadequate sources) seem to be the dogmatic and puritanical beliefs of Roman Catholicism as applied to social work. His programme consists of a number of statements about the nature of the individual, of society, and of the functions and methods of social work. Some of these seem to be statements of sociological and psychological fact (e.g. 'experiencing' is an essential part of the learning process; family relationships are of primary importance in the early development of the individual); others are more far-reaching and controversial (human suffering is undesirable and should be prevented; man does not 'naturally' act in a rational manner). A second example of confusion can be found in a much earlier discussion by Van Waters[9] who suggested that 'the technical problems of philosophy, the nature of knowledge, and the ultimate essence of things' did not concern the social worker: 'he could do his work as readily in the mental world of Plato as in that of Dewey'. This is, in fact, a masked philosophical judgment, since in maintaining that our ideas make no difference to the world in which we live the author is adopting a particular philosophical position.

So far the argument has suggested that the subject of 'the philosophy of casework' has attracted little interest amongst field-workers and that studies so far attempted have been ambitious in range, but uncertain in aim. Such an approach may, of course, have complicated the author's task of presenting the general values of casework and may also have succeeded in somewhat depressing the reader. It is a sound maxim of casework practice to begin by outlining what is or may be possible rather than by stressing what services the caseworker cannot render. Adopting this more positive approach, what can be said about the general values of casework; how can we begin to consider this subject?

We refer frequently to the values of casework (or of social work) as if they had a stable and continuous history, but a comparison of values upheld by nineteenth-century social workers and those acknowledged today both shows the extent to which this view needs correction and serves as a useful introduction to the general subject of values in social work. A comparison of these values in earlier and later periods shows both continuity and contrast.

An Historical Contrast

The contemporary social worker and her nineteenth-century counterpart both seem to emphasize the value of the individual. 'The fundamental basis of all casework', stated a recent British work:

> is the belief that the individual matters. He matters in himself, and not merely as a unit of cannon-fodder, labour-power or population, not as a vote, not as a useful citizen, not as a potential criminal, an invalid, an anti-social nuisance; but because every man has the right and the duty to work out his own salvation, and because, within the necessary limits of his society, he must also be allowed the chance to do so . . . in the last resort the case-worker believes that the individual is an end in himself.[10]

A nineteenth-century social worker in America seemed to be expressing the same view when he said, 'Charitable work in the best sense must be done by the individual . . . for the individual. . . . If the individual is lost, all is lost.'[11] Yet earlier caseworkers also had considerable difficulty in abstracting the individual from the complex of his social obligations. Chalmers, who is often regarded as one of the founding fathers of casework, in fact stated that 'The principle that each man, simply because he exists, holds a right on other men or on society for existence is a thing not to be regulated but destroyed.'[12] Similarly, C. S. Loch based much of his social work theorizing on the view of man as a debtor to society, as a potential or actual contributor.

Social workers in earlier and later times have assumed the possibility of change and improvement in human affairs, though this has sometimes been based on a plastic view of human nature, giving very little credence to the possibility of genuinely traumatic experience. Take, for instance, the following quotation from an issue of *Moral Welfare* (1922), which exactly captures the rather optimistic reactive view of the nineteenth century:

> One little boy, who was cruelly molested by a man one dark winter's night, and had his nerves utterly shattered, came back a different creature after five months by the sea. . . . Sometimes a trial of our methods proves successful, and a naughty girl goes to Girl Guides, or to a Net Ball Club, and finds an outlet for her energies in healthy recreation.[13]

Growth is also a concept emphasized by social workers in both periods, though again they made different uses of it. In the nineteenth century, it tended to support a limiting 'wait and see' principle. 'Should we not', said C. S. Loch, 'learn simply how they (the poor) live and think first, and then, with a kind of reverence for what is growing around us, interfere with the circumspection that comes of knowledge, or perhaps in a surer wisdom not presume to interfere at all?'[14] In contemporary social work the idea of growth is used in an attempt to describe the aim of social work and to delineate the kinds of 'treatment' appropriate at each stage of emotional and social development. Social workers have always seen the importance of the family—it was in the nineteenth century that the family was first described as the 'unit of casework'—but comparatively recent developments in psychology have changed the social work emphasis on the family, regarding it not as the source of obligation, but as the predominant influence on future personality development.

Perhaps the contrast between the two periods of social work can most vividly be seen in the different ways in which the casework situation was defined. Sympathy and concern have perhaps always been highly valued in social work, but the situations in which these values were expressed have changed considerably. In the nineteenth century the caseworker saw himself as a business-like judiciary who gave clients a fair hearing and who applied the laws of social progress to each individual case. The client was expected to account for his behaviour and to regard all circumstances as opportunities; what mattered was what man could become. The contemporary caseworker sees himself as the member of a profession, the agent of society and of the client, who is engaged in a therapeutic activity based on affective neutrality and specific authority and which is available on a universal basis. The client is not held to an accounting relationship, but 'accepted' and 'understood', partly through the application of social and psychological knowledge.

This brief historical contrast shows the kinds of value that have found expression in social work and a more detailed discussion of some of these aspects will now be attempted.

The Value of the Individual

Contemporary social workers, as we have seen, emphasize the value of the individual as such. 'Each human being should be regarded by all others as an object of infinite worth';[15] 'personality is precious';[16] the social worker should respect 'the pre-eminent worth and dignity of the individual human being'.[17] This list of examples, which could be extended indefinitely, raises a number of important questions which have received insufficient consideration in the professional literature. What is the basis of this value? To what are social workers committed if they claim to uphold it? What is the relationship between this value and the other cornerstone of social work, the value of society. As Pollard has stated, 'There is a multitude of definitions of social casework. All imply a dual concern; to help not only the individual in relation to society but also society in its relations with individuals.'[18]

There seem to be several possible bases for the value given by caseworkers to the individual as such. It could represent an existentialist recognition of the uniqueness of every person and each situation or a valuation of an individual's potential accomplishments. It could be linked with opinions about democracy or it could represent a simple declaration of a value held as such and requiring no further grounding. Alternatively, it could be seen as a recognition of the Christian belief in the infinite and unique value of every soul through divine creation and redemption. Stated in these terms the value appears highly abstract and, though we need to reflect systematically at this level, it is preferable within the limitations of the present work, to consider the more practical implications of this value.

Firstly, it implies respect for persons and an acceptance of the 'whole' person. The latter implication has already been discussed in chapter one and only a comment on its holistic aspects appears necessary at this stage. Social workers refer frequently to the importance of responding to the client's 'total' personality, but, of course, one would never be in a position to know everything about a person. 'Response to the total personality' should be seen rather as an attitude and an endeavour. The attitude is that of openness to as much of the personality as we can absorb, giving 'equal' attention to the 'good' and to 'bad' aspects. The endeavour is the attempt to build a coherent picture of the person rather than record numerous discrete items. As Polanyi has observed, 'particulars can be noticed in two different ways. We can be aware of them uncomprehendingly, i.e. in themselves; or understandingly, in their participation in a comprehensive entity'.[19]

Respect for persons may also appear an abstract value, but it appears easier to grasp and to handle than statements about unique or pre-eminent value, where there is either by definition no scale against which the value can be measured or the choice of scale seems open to random and arbitrary choice. The meaning of 'respect for persons' can be discerned by emphasizing each of the main words in turn, respect and person. An examination of the ways in which 'respect' is used in ordinary language (Children should respect their elders; I respected him as an opponent; we respect the clergyman's 'cloth' etc.) suggests that the word refers to behaviour appropriate to a recognized status. 'Respect' does not imply certain acts or a range of acts, but refers to the manner of our behaviour in the relationships in question. How, then, should we behave towards 'persons' and in what manner should we transact business with them? The 'person' figures largely in such different philosophies as existentialism and Thomism (to name only two) and some of their implications for casework have begun to be studied.[20] The subject can, thus, be seen to be wideranging and complex, but it is possible to delineate certain characteristics of a 'person' of importance for casework.

If, once again, we examine the ways in which the word 'person' is used, we find a wide range of meanings—next person, please; he made me feel like a person; she's a *real* person; person to person and so on. Omitting instances in which 'person' is a synonym for 'anybody–somebody' (as in 'next person, please'), it would appear that a person is something more than the roles he may be playing at any one time and more than a bundle of roles; he is a unique and autonomous constellation of qualities and ends. To treat someone as a person, therefore, is to behave towards someone with dignity and consideration, and not to base our valuation of him on any actual roles he may be playing towards us. An example of a failure to observe a broad basis of valuation can be found in the following observation (1908) on the caseworker's right to ask the client questions:

> What right have I to ask these questions, and to enquire into the private affairs of this man, who is almost a stranger to me, and who has the same right as I might have myself to resent this interference? The answer is that we are supposing this family has asked for your help. The man is not, therefore, a normal member of the community . . . it is unnatural, abnormal, that he should depend upon others. I am not saying that he is necessarily to blame. Your child is not to blame for his sickness, yet being sick he needs treatment such as would be quite unsuitable to him in health.[21]

Here the role of 'socially' sick deprives a man of some of his rights as a 'normal' person; it is the occupancy of that role that is made the (narrow) basis of the worker's valuation of him.

A person is also a rational creature who can pursue reasonable ends in a reasonable way, even though he may often be driven by internal and external forces. In treating someone as a person we acknowledge his ends and help him to achieve them in so far as it is in our power and legitimate to do so. Help should be given in a way that robs clients neither of their purposes nor of the efforts they are making to achieve them. As Maclagan has said, 'We must have regard not simply to their *ends* but also to their *efforts*'.[22] This implies that the caseworker respects the autonomy of the individual and avoids playing Providence to the client's Creature. The client is seen as a person who is usually able to reach decisions about matters that concern him: he is ordinarily considered as capable of exercising what is described in casework literature as the right of self-determination.

The concept of client self-determination or the freedom to choose has been given a special place in nearly every consideration of the values upheld in social work, though its pre-eminence has recently been questioned.[23] The concept refers to a client's right to accept or refuse casework help, to participate actively in processes intended to help him, to give or withhold specific consents within casework, and, in brief, his right not to surrender living the life he wants to lead. The principle is violated when an unmarried mother is hurried into a decision about her child's future, and when a client is simply informed that she should not have any more children, or when clients are manipulated into choices which are 'best' according to the caseworker's estimation. Principles, however, need to be applied and we, therefore, require criteria which show us when the application has been appropriate.

Clearly, the client's freedom is limited by the rights of others in his own family and in the wider society and, as we shall suggest later, it is no part of 'respect for persons' to help people to evade their commitments. These rights are defined partly by law and partly by a wide range of social custom. The clients of a social agency, for example, may be said to have a right to good professional service, a reasonable amount of time etc. and the freedom of a demanding client to choose the amount of help she wants and will accept must be limited by the rights of other clients. Much less clear is the limitation on client self-determination contained in the notion that 'Since the capacity to make decisions varies from client to client, the worker is aware of the client's mental and physical capacity to act for himself and does not force him to self-determination beyond his capacity.'[24] This kind of formulation has a tendency to move from statements about the capacity to make a decision to those about making 'positive and constructive decisions'.[25] In the most obvious instances of this kind of limitation (e.g. the severely subnormal) we are sure that client self-determination cannot be applied simply because the persons in question could not make what was generally regarded as a decision, irrespective of its quality. To suggest that other groups of people lack a capacity for 'sound' decisions is, of course, to formulate an entirely different proposition which requires much closer examination. For example, we are informed that 'Caseworkers have differed in their evaluation of the capacity of unmarried mothers, as a group, to make sound decisions.'[26] It seems that in this kind of statement we encounter a new principle, that of best-self determination.

What is happening, of course, is that social workers move rapidly between different definitions of freedom. Sometimes freedom is seen as self-determination, with the emphasis on ability to make decisions without human interference; at other times, it is self-realization, the circumstantial freedom to act as one pleases (it is in this sense, for instance, that Perlman is using the term when she states that in fact 'full self-determination is an illusion');[27] while a third view of freedom stresses 'self-perfection' or freedom from 'slavery' to certain habits. This idea of self-perfection can also be illustrated from Perlman, who has written that 'where emotional stress or involvement is so great that our perception of what is realistic is dimmed . . . our capacity to be self-determining with judgment and objectivity is obviously impaired. The choices we make under such circumstances are not free choices'.[28] The difficulties that caseworkers have encountered, though not always recognized, in a consistent formulation of the principle stem perhaps from alternating conceptions of human possibility. On the one hand, caseworkers have asserted a faith in the potentiality of the human being to change himself and his society, whilst on the other hand, espousing a group of psychological theories which would appear to place severe limitations on the capacity of individuals to change.

To appreciate the possible confusions in the principle is important, but it is clearly not enough. How can we begin to use the principle in casework? The notion of helping clients to do as they please, when they please is of no assistance in this connection. It is no part of casework with an adolescent to respond to every change of wish; a caseworker introducing himself to a problem family mother does not regard as a decisive refusal her obvious reluctance to admit him into the house; a caseworker will often initiate discussion of matters not raised by the client. So, client self-determination is concerned with decisions, not whims, and in judging what a client 'really' (or consistently) wants the caseworker does not rely exclusively on what the client says, but also on what is communicated by other means. Decisions, however, are never made by perfectly rational people in a social vacuum. They are made in complex situations by people whose perception is always 'somewhat dimmed', and whose objectivity and judgment is always impaired—to an extent. This does not mean that decisions made under these circumstances are less 'free', only that they are human. Self-determination safeguards the client against any general surrender of rights by becoming a client, but it does not free him from his normal obligations and these must often form part of the social worker's judgment. Thus, the problem in regard to unmarried mothers is not their capacity to make decisions, but the fact that the rights of the infant have also to be considered and respected.

Decisions, then, and the making of decisions are the content of self-determination. Anyone who can *make* what is recognizably a decision (and this is more than saying 'I decide', since this only describes part of the process) should be protected in exercising the right of self-determination. Yet this principle is almost a characterization of the process of casework, which may be said to involve very often the client's exploration and discovery of his self. In this context self-determination is not something that is, as it were, found in any human situation; it is something that is created.

Finally, to treat someone as a person implies that one takes the facts of his situation seriously and this involves the social worker inevitably with the other's values. As Emmet has observed, 'facts are seldom "mere" when they are facts of social situations because they are seen within the context of ways in which people live together, and the common values these involve. And anyone who responsibly accepts such a way of living accepts its commitments'.[29] These ways of living together are shared, to a greater or lesser degree, by the social caseworker and her client, and respecting someone as a person implies recognition of his consequent obligations and of one's own.

It is perhaps in religious belief and practice that a person's values are most clearly apparent and yet the relationship between religion and casework has received little attention in social work in this country or America.[30] There are probably several reasons for this, including the influence of Freudian views on religion and a reaction against the religiosity of some nineteenth-century social workers. A new appraisal of the subject seems opportune, and the questions now requiring answer could perhaps be based on an assumption of the importance and significance of religious belief and feeling in human beings; this is not something to be hidden away or dissolved by analysis. Once again only a brief discussion of this topic is possible in the present work. The question considered here concerns the ways in which religious or moral subjects may helpfully be discussed within the boundaries of casework.

Consider these two brief extracts from casework, the first from a letter to a client and the second from an account of a home visit:

(i) The psychiatric social worker had received a letter from an outpatient of a mental hospital who had been her client for several months.[31] The letter referred to the client's worries about God's will: 'God has become someone terrible who must be answered and the only answer I have is failure.' The worker replied that she knew how hard the client has been trying and that she feels sure that in the long run this will not have been in vain. 'We all have times when we hate people, but this does not mean we are bad or are failures, and surely God knows about this and understands. Sometimes it does look as if He asks the impossible of us, but perhaps it is because we are often more severe on ourselves than He is—and that we underrate His capacity for love and forgiveness.'

(ii) Second home visit to Mrs. Gregers, referred to a voluntary family casework agency by the Health Visitor. After greeting the worker, Mrs. G. handed him a Jehovah Witness pamphlet and asked him to read it. The worker said he would and said it looked as if this religion was important to her. She replied that it should be to all, and she asked rather aggressively what was the worker's religion. He said that this particular religion meant a great deal to Mrs. G., but he had come to help her with her social problems, like those discussed last time (her debts, her feelings towards Mr. G., her worry concerning her son's delinquency). Mrs. G. said she found a great comfort in her religion; perhaps the worker could also find comfort. All other religions were false, did the worker not realise this? The worker said he thought a religious discussion would probably not be helpful at this stage and asked Mrs. G. how her son had been in the last week.

In each instance the client raises a religious issue and also communicates in religious terms some questioning of the relationship with the caseworker. In the first case the client feels that God, and perhaps the caseworker, see her as nothing but a failure, while in the second, Mrs. G. says she finds comfort in her religion, possibly contrasting this with what she feels she receives from the caseworker. The first case is handled more successfully, partly, of course, because the worker shares some, at least, of the client's religious beliefs; if she did not she would not have the right to use the words she did. She could also stress to her client God's compassion and in this she was more fortunate than the second caseworker. She has taken the client's formulation of the problem in religious terms seriously, though she has also indicated that she does not see the client as a failure. She could perhaps also have helped her client to examine the implications of her statement that 'God has *become* someone terrible'. In the second case, the worker does not apparently share the client's religious belief. A franker statement of his own position combined with a suggestion that Mrs. G. perhaps found it difficult to see how someone of a different religion could be helpful, might have produced better results. It may well be that Mrs. G. will use her belief to block any offers of help, but an exploration of what more precisely she finds helpful about her religion seems indicated as a first step. This would 'allow' Mrs. G. her religion as a pervasive influence in her life which cannot be segmented into a number of self-contained needs, some of which are labelled for the caseworker's guidance 'spiritual, keep out!'.

Sometimes, of course, the caseworker is directly involved with a client concerned with making a moral choice or facing a moral problem. Two examples of this can be found in the cases of Mrs. M. and of Mr. P.

(i) Mr. and Mrs. M. are Roman Catholics in their middle thirties. They have nine children and Mrs. M. is fearful of her own mental stability if she has another. Mr. M. sees no necessity for control and says he intends to have intercourse whenever he requires it. Mrs. M. does not go to church very regularly and a social worker helped her to go to a Family Planning Clinic, on the assumption that she was not a practising Catholic. The M.'s are now being visited by a caseworker from a voluntary family casework agency and Mrs. M. says she is in considerable conflict. She wants to go to confession, but feels she cannot discontinue taking artificial means to prevent conception. At the same time she feels that some dreadful calamity will befall her children because of her practice of birth control. She asks the caseworker, 'What ought I to do?'

(ii) Mr. P. is a Roman Catholic also. He is living with Mrs. L., but not having sexual relations with her. He hopes that she will soon be free to marry him in the eyes of the Church. Naturally, he finds the situation stressful and he tells the caseworker that he feels extremely guilty about his masturbation. He feels this is a very terrible sin which will bring unlimited punishment upon him. The caseworker expresses some understanding of his feelings and says that he does not think masturbation is 'a terrible sin'.

In each of these cases the worker has an obligation to respect the religious views of her clients, whatever her own views on the moral teaching in question. Whilst Mrs. M. *may* be indicating by her irregular church attendance that she has some doubts or confusion about her religion, the social worker has no right to decide that a client is not a practising member of a particular religion and to act as if she was not. The caseworker cannot tell Mrs. M. what she ought to do, but she can do more than simply say 'this is your decision'. She can recognize the conflict that Mrs. M. faces, help her with her feelings about the 'dreadful calamity' and emphasize that she and her agency will try to help Mrs. M. whatever she decides to do. The caseworker will also attempt to involve Mr. M. in his wife's dilemma and she may well contact the parish priest, with Mr. and Mrs. M.'s consent, in an endeavour to facilitate any communication between the family and the clergy. There is much spiritual comfort that might be given to Mrs. M. in this situation, though it must be admitted that this is the kind of moral dilemma that frightens some priests. The caseworker will probably help Mrs. M. most effectively, not by looking for a problem to be solved, but by regarding it as a painful and distressing situation that must be endured and worked through.

In the case of Mr. P. the caseworker gave an opinion on a question of morality. It might perhaps have been fruitful to explore why Mr. P. expected the caseworker to play a confessor's role, but the caseworker instead attempted to relieve Mr. P.'s guilt. The useful distinction between moral guilt and pathological guilt can be applied in both these cases. It would be no part of the caseworker's task to attempt to relieve guilt consequent on moral fault; pathological guilt, on the other hand, which sees both the moral offence and the punishment as almost unlimited in extent belongs not to religion but to superstition. The caseworker would be entitled to attempt to understand and relieve this second kind of guilt.

So far we have examined some of the implications of the high valuation by social workers of the human personality, paying particular attention to notions of respect and of client self-determination. Before considering professional and technical principles, I wish to discuss two further aspects of the general values upheld in casework, the principle of human kinship and the goals of casework.

Caseworkers have sometimes exaggerated their valuation of the individual into a general personality cult, stressing the 'release' of the personality at the expense of social rights and values. The caseworker is not a psychotherapist; he or she works in a social agency which, as we have seen, has been established out of a protective concern for society as well as a 'redemptional' concern for the individual. This raises both theoretical and practical problems. Theoretically, the question concerns the fundamental basis of social work; is social work built on the two valuations of the individual and of society or is one value derived from the other? Pollard has recently answered this question in the following terms: '. . . Society's significance for social workers . . . is obviously very great, but it is in principle derivative—derived from the absolute significance of the individual, since society is but the network of individual's relationships with each other and with groups of individuals.'[32] Without going into complex issues concerning the status of propositions about society,[33] it is clear that it is precisely through the different networks of relationship that conflict ensues between individual and social rights. Such conflicts cannot be resolved by tracing them back to the same value basis and they suggest that in fact social work is based on two values, that of the individual and that of human kinship. On a practical level choice sometimes has to be made on the basis of one rather than the other. Systems of priority, for example, are based on notions of fairness which derive from the principle of human kinship rather than the unique value of the individual. Clients might sometimes prefer to do without social work help, but they are obliged to maintain communication with the social caseworker over at least a minimum range of topics. In such cases (child neglect, for example,) the caseworker is basing his intervention on the principle of human kinship.

The general objectives of casework have so far been seen as fulfilling agency function, but this involves considering the spirit as well as the letter of these functions. For example, notions of what constitutes 'good' child care are built-into the child care service and perhaps change in emphasis as they are interpreted by succeeding generations of workers. Similarly, the voluntary casework agency's function to help 'the family as a whole' has characterized some important developments in this and the previous century, but obviously notions of a 'happy' or a 'good' family have changed with developing ideas of the work society has given the family to do. These ideas of 'good' child care and 'good' family life are clearly values upheld by social workers. To recognize them as such, however, is the beginning rather than the end of exploration. Wootton's recent study of social pathology stopped at the revelation of a series of value judgments partially masked by terms like 'mental health', 'adjustment' and so on.[34] It did not proceed to investigate whether such values could be more accurately expressed or whether they could be considered well or ill-based. The values expressed in the objectives of social work (which includes casework) should be studied in each of these directions.

How have social workers formulated their general aims? They have sometimes talked of creating a new kind of society. Loch, for example, hoped to see a society without dependents, one in which each person carried the burden of his own responsibility. Other social workers have thought in terms of helping people to carry their significant role-relationships with greater effectiveness from society's point of view and increased comfort from their own. Ideas of adjustment have also been canvassed, though it has never been made clear to which sets of norms the adjustment should be made. The movement for mental hygiene, which first influenced British social work in the 1930's, encouraged social workers to view their activities in terms of mental health, but the range of norms implicit in this concept varied, of course, with the differing definitions of mental health. Was it absence of mental-illness, a statistical average or an evaluative norm, or something much nearer the traditional concept of man as a rational and social being? More recently, the idea of equilibrium has been suggested as a guide for social work. 'Social work', stated the Younghusband Report, 'is directed towards helping individuals and families to cope with their problems and so to achieve at any given time a better personal and social equilibrium.'[35] This is a good example of a possibly fruitful idea requiring much more elaboration. As it stands the idea that the worker's function is to assess disturbances of equilibrium in the individual, in his family and in his social relationships suffers from a rather optimistic vagueness. Between which elements in the individual and in his relationships is the balance to be held? Is it to be held between interests, or between love and hate? How can we recognize different states of inbalance and their different causation? If every social problem is fundamentally one of inbalance, does this mean that the systems held in equilibrium can never break down? These and many other questions require investigation before we can be sure quite what we are saying when we talk of achieving equilibrium through social work.

PROFESSIONAL AND TECHNICAL PRINCIPLES

Caseworkers define their service as professional. This implies a general objective pursued by the profession, such as we have discussed briefly in the last paragraph, and also a number of criteria for 'good' practice. Some of these are of a general kind and some more specific. General principles of professional practice suggest the worker's main focus of responsibility. The professional is obliged to give the best service he can to help his client achieve his own ends without violating important social, legal and moral norms. He should not attempt to achieve direct gratification of his needs through the client and this involves the responsibility of self-knowledge. It also emphasizes that the professional worker should not attempt to practice beyond the general limitations imposed by his own competence and by agency function. He should accept the responsibility of referring cases when appropriate to other agencies and to other disciplines.

More specific responsibilities undertaken by the professional concern respect for the information the client gives and the importance of punctuality, privacy and attention when the client is being interviewed. In respect of these responsibilities we see how both general and instrumental values are implicit in the same aspects of the worker's behaviour. We respect the client's information both because people would be unwilling to tell caseworkers about themselves if they thought such information might be irresponsibly treated, and also because we think that people have a right to privacy. Similarly, we emphasize punctuality, keeping of appointments, consistency of the worker's attention not simply because this kind of predictable experience is helpful to the client, but also because we think people ought to be treated in this courteous respectful manner.

Confidentiality of information is a professional principle that has been given considerable emphasis in social work. An analysis of this principle suggests that there are two basic questions. What is the nature of the original compact between client and worker? Under what circumstances would a violation of this compact be justified? We know very little about the general expectations of applicants at the beginning of casework and it is possible only to conjecture about what they think they have authorized the caseworker to do on their behalf. On this basis, however, what can usefully be said? Firstly, the applicant expects reasonably competent service and will not find it helpful to be asked to make numerous decisions about the kind of service he is to receive. We do not, for example, ask the applicant's permission to keep records of the interview, though we would not conceal the fact if he wished to ask about or even question the procedure. Secondly, the applicant appreciates that what he tells the worker he tells to the agency; casework is not a personal and private matter between two individuals. Sometimes, the client in the course of receiving casework help will request the worker to treat a particular piece of information 'in confidence'. This raises a number of issues. The client may in fact be requesting the worker to pay special attention to the message he is about to send. Or he may wish to emphasize the *personal* relationship—he may be saying 'this is a gift for you only'—or to show how well the caseworker is regarded compared to other workers. These possibilities should be explored, but the client should also be helped to accept that the worker is in a position to receive confidences only because he operates from the functional base of a particular agency. Thirdly, the client expects to be consulted if it seems necessary for the caseworker to send information to other agencies. For example, a family caseworker who wishes to refer a child in a problem family to a child guidance clinic would be expected to obtain the consent of the parents both to the referral and to the giving of information to the clinic.

Thus, the applicants may be said to have entered some kind of compact once they have agreed, implicitly or explicitly, to become clients. This compact does not imply that the worker will not discuss information with others in the agency or with those who might be acting in a consultative capacity, but it does entail that the client's information will always be used responsibly for his good. Yet it must be remembered that the compact is with a particular agency and not with the world of welfare at large. The client will expect to give specific consents when confidential material is passed to other agencies. The requirement of such consents acts also as a guide to the caseworker, since in foreseeing some of the client's questions about the necessity for his action he is enabled to clarify the reasons for his intended action. The caseworker cannot always accept the client's refusal of permission to pass on information, though there would not appear to be any reason why the client should not be informed of the worker's intention. Thus, where a social worker learns that incestuous acts are currently being committed by a father and daughter the worker should inform the appropriate authorities, if his or her attempts to encourage the parents themselves to take action to bring the affair to an end are unsuccessful. The caseworker should inform the parents both of the action she will take and of her reasoning.

One aspect of confidentiality that has not perhaps received sufficient attention is that entailed in inter-agency relationships. For example, in the case of Mrs. D. (to be discussed more fully in chapter eight) the National Assistance Board informed the caseworker that proceedings might be instituted against her for fraud, but that the worker was not to tell Mrs. D. She accepted the N.A.B.'s request for confidentiality, thinking that Mrs. D. would not know about the possibility of prosecution. In fact, Mrs. D. was told that her books had been recalled for this reason and she expressed some puzzlement that the worker did not know this from the N.A.B., since they had informed the previous worker when she had been drawing allowances in excess of her entitlement. This incident illustrates how carefully social workers should consider any requests from other agencies to regard information as confidential.

The technical principles of casework, or general maxims about the most effective ways of reaching casework goals, develop as our ideas of human nature change and expand. Of the numerous principles that might be listed only the most important can be mentioned in the present book. These include personalizing the help and partializing the problem whenever possible, client involvement in defining and solving the problem and the recognition of the importance of feeling. It is one of the assumptions of casework that the same kind of help is not required by every client of a social agency. Nineteenth-century social workers in fact drew a distinction between wholesale and retail social service, emphasizing the latter's superiority. At the present time the Younghusband Report has attempted a three-fold classification of the kinds of problem people bring to social workers in terms of difficulty. Caseworkers should carry out their work in the light of this assumption attempting to focus all the time on precisely what the client is communicating, now at this time, what is the problem as exactly as it can be seen? The caseworker is, thus, open to the individual emphasis, the personal nuance of the case. Yet he cannot and should not try to do all things for every man, especially simultaneously. The caseworker can absorb and make sense of only a limited amount of material and the client can work most effectively if he does not feel that everything must be done to solve all his problems at once. The worker's openness to the client does not imply randomness of effort or unsureness of aim, even if every attempt to understand is only an approximation. To talk of partializing a client's problem can sometimes, of course, represent the worker's tidying away of what cannot be faced or a premature closure of his appraisal. Yet we need both to remain as open as we can to the client's continuing communications at the same time as we try to help him structure and make sense of his situation. If we do not, client and worker may float together happily or disastrously down the stream of consciousness.

The notion of the client's involvement in working towards a solution of his problems can be viewed in many ways. It can be seen as a reflection of his rights, but in this context it will be approached as a technical principle, since if the client remains uninvolved he cannot be convinced that the objective of the exercise is to solve a *problem* and that the problem is *his*. The principle indicates that the caseworker's responsibility is to facilitate the activity of another. This is not simply a matter of obtaining the client's consent: the client's permission for his own manipulation could not be accepted by the caseworker. It is a matter of continuous striving together.

In this work of striving the caseworker will often be trying to call on hidden sources of strength in the situations, unused powers of foresight and control. Or he may be seeking to develop them. Yet such powers will be effectively exercised only if the nature of the material on which they are to work is clear. This entails that the caseworker values the expression of the client's feelings. He values them because they are aspects of the personality, but also because their expression helps the client to begin to understand their force and mode of operation. The personality consists of reason and of rational and irrational emotions, and the problems faced by the person will also have these essential aspects. It may be that caseworkers talk too easily of their client's feelings. As Arnold wrote:

> Below the surface stream, shallow and light,
> Of what we say we feel, below the stream,
> As light, of what we think we feel—there flows
> With noiseless current strong, obscure and deep,
> The central stream of what we feel indeed.

Yet in pursuing feeling to its source there is no doubt that casework is engaged on an excursion as helpful as it is necessary.

NOTES

[1] Timms, N., 'Theorising about Social Casework I', *British Journal of Psychiatric Social Work*, Vol. V, No. 2, 1959.

[2] E.g. Bisno, H., *The Philosophy of Social Work*, Public Affairs Press, 1952. Pumphrey, M., *The Teaching of Values and Ethics in Social Work Education*, Vol. XIII of the Curriculum Study, Council of Social Work Education, New York, 1959.

[3] E.g. Bosanquet, B., *The Philosophy of Casework*, C.O.S. Occasional Papers, Fifth Series, No. 11.

[4] E.g. Tillich, P., 'The Philosophy of Social Work', *Social Service Review*, Vol. XXXVI, No. 1, March 1962.

[5] Pumphrey, M., op. cit., p. 44.

[6] Cockerill, E., *et al.*, *A Conceptual Framework for Social Casework*, University of Pittsburgh Press, 1952.

[7] For a summary of the main kinds of assumption in casework see Timms, op. cit.

[8] Bisno, H., op. cit.

[9] Van Waters, M., 'Philosophical Trends in Modern Social Work' in Lowry (ed.), *Readings in Social Casework 1920–1938*, New York, 1940.

[10] Cormack, U. and McDougall, K., 'Case-Work in Social Service', in Morris, C. (ed.), *Social Casework in Great Britain*, Faber and Faber, 1954, pp. 31–2.

[11] Buzzelle, G., 'Individuality in the Work of Charity' (1886) quoted in Woodroofe, K., *From Charity to Social Work*, Routledge & Kegan Paul, 1962, p. 120.

[12] Chalmers, T., *Political Economy*, Preface, p. ix, Glasgow, 1832.

[13] *Moral Welfare*, Oct. 1922.

[14] Loch, C. S., 'An A.B.C. for Almoners', *Charity Organisation Review*, Oct. 1897.

[15] Pumphrey, M., op. cit., pp. 43–4.

[16] Dressler, D., *Practice and Theory of Probation and Parole*, Columbia University Press, 1959, p. 136.

[17] Lutz, W. A., *Concepts and Principles Underlying Social Casework Practice*, National Association of Social Workers, 1956.

[18] Pollard, B., *Social Casework for the State*, Pall Mall, 1962, p. 1.

[19] Polanyi, M., 'Knowing and Being', *Mind*, N.S. Vol. 70, p. 458–70.

[20] McCormick, M. J., *Diagnostic Casework in the Thomistic Pattern*, Columbia University Press, 1954. Laing, R., 'An Examination of Tillich's Theory of Anxiety and Neurosis', *British Journal of Medical Psychology*, Vol. XXX, Part 2, 1957–8.

[21] Lyons, Miss, *The Art of Helping*, C.O.S. Occasional Papers, 4th Series, No. 17, 1908.

[22] Maclagan, W. G., 'Respect for Persons as a Moral Principle', *Philosophy*, Vol. XXXV, Nos. 134 and 135, July and Oct. 1960.

[23] Bernstein, S., 'Self-Determination: King or Citizen in the Realm of Values', *Social Work* (U.S.A.), Vol. 5, No. 1, Jan. 1960.

[24] Biestek, F., *The Casework Relationship*, Allen and Unwin, 1961, p. 110.

[25] Ibid.

[26] Ibid.

[27] Perlman, H., 'The Caseworker's Use of Collateral Information', *Social Casework*, Vol. 32, No. 8, Oct. 1951.

[28] Ibid.

[29] Emmet, D., *Facts and Obligations*, Friends of Dr. Williams's Library, 12th Lecture, 1958.

[30] Useful comments on the subject can be found in: Tilley, M., 'The Religious Factor in Case-Work', *British Journal of Psychiatric Social Work*, No. 4, 1950; Spencer, S., 'What Place has Religion in Social Work Education?', *Social Service Review*, Vol. XXXV, No. 2, June 1961.

[31] This case (Vera, L.) is treated at greater length in chapter nine.

[32] Pollard, op. cit., p. 11.

[33] See e.g. Mandelbaum, M., 'Societal Facts', *British Journal of Sociology*, Vol. VI, No. 4, Dec. 1955. For a contrasting view see e.g. Watkins, J. W. M., 'Historical Explanation in the Social Sciences', *British Journal for the Philosophy of Science*, Aug 1957.

[34] Wootton, B., *Social Science and Social Pathology*, Allen and Unwin, 1959.

[35] *Report of the Working Party on Social Workers in the Local Authority Health and Welfare Services* (Younghusband Report), H.M.S.O., 1959, p. 175.

Chapter Four

SKILL IN HUMAN RELATIONSHIP

TO claim that a caseworker has skill in human relationship may appear foolhardy or sinister: to suggest that her skills should be consciously developed through professional training may evoke ideas of detailed manipulation or omnipotence. Yet in spite of the dangers of misinterpretation, it must be asserted that caseworkers work through the relationships they establish as a result of inter-action with their clients. They work *in* relationships and through their ability to build and maintain systems of communication with different groups and kinds of people. It is by means of relationship that agency functions are conveyed and mediated. The central importance of the caseworker's personality in establishing and fostering relationships was certainly appreciated by the early case-workers. Octavia Hill, for example, writing on the necessity for social work training, argued that:

> We are educating not a mechanic to practise manual work, not a lawyer whose intellect must be developed and mind stored with facts, not a physician who must gather knowledge and dispense advice, but a worker who, though she may need a certain manual skill, and clear intellect and knowledge, is primarily a human being who may use manual and mental power for the help and blessing of numbers of families. That being so, all will depend on what she is. . . .[1]

Sometimes the early caseworkers participated sensitively and appropriately in relationships with their clients to considerable if quiet effect, but at other times they attempted to create and use relationships in ways unredeemed by thoughtful introspection, sensitivity or even tact.

The present period of casework is sometimes represented as one of impressive technical change compared to the past. References are frequently made to the modern 'tools' of casework—the interview, the professional relationship, the worker's own personality have all been cited as examples. This kind of language may, however, be misleading. A tool is an instrument that can be picked up and used to achieve a particular objective in a definite series of work operations. It is difficult to see how the professional relationship, for instance, can be seen as a 'tool'. It is more rewarding to see casework as participation in a developing relationship and response to a range of different and changing role expectations.

'Technique' is another term in frequent use in casework. Students sometimes say they wish to learn the techniques of casework. Some writers regard treatment as the application of techniques[2] and others have attempted to create elaborate typologies in order to link distinctive treatment techniques with specific groups of problems.[3] Other writers have been content with more modest designations. Perlman, for instance, has quoted a description of treatment largely in terms of the different kinds of comment the caseworker might make: sympathetic, reflective, focusing, facilitating, confronting and connecting.[4] This is virtually to think in terms of the worker's response in a number of different roles. British caseworkers have shown very little interest in delineating their professional techniques, though some important technical developments have occurred, as we shall see. Something of our self-consciousness in discussing 'techniques' can be seen in one of the very few controversies recorded in a British social work journal. In 1954, the journal *Case Conference* carried articles and correspondence[5] on the technique of 'grunting' or listening in silence to whatever the client says without expressing sympathy, surprise (or even, perhaps, interest). This technique was advocated for a whole class of people (those with marital problems), and it was contrasted with a technique of 'fuddle-duddle' with an emphasis on receptivity and sympathy. The terms used to describe responses which would be perfectly appropriate in certain situations did not, of course, encourage readers to consider such responses seriously and both supporters and opponents of 'grunting' seemed to believe that the automatic application of a technique would result in successful casework. As Philp suggested in a final letter in the controversy, 'contributors are in danger of putting the clock back to the food ticket era. The ticket satisfied an immediate need for food; the grunt for a sympathetic encouraging response. Neither does more than give some temporary satisfaction of an immediate

75

need though both may be useful in creating the possibility of further assistance'.

'Technique' can refer to a body of numerous and complicated operations or to a more or less standardized procedure to attain a particular and limited objective. References to the technique of psychoanalysis illustrate the first meaning and to the technique of transference interpretation, the second. There would not appear to be many aspects of casework that could be called techniques in the latter sense. There is something inappropriate in talk about the technique of advice or of material aid, for instance. Such activities play an important part in casework, but they cannot be used in isolation to achieve objectives other than those of the whole process. They should be considered as activities that are or are not appropriate to the roles the caseworker plays in the process of casework. This does not mean, of course, that they cannot be separately considered, only that in operation they form part of a larger complex which gives them effective meaning. It is possible that casework may develop towards more standardized procedures of treatment; in this as in other disciplines technical aspects have shown considerable instability. At present, however, the search for techniques and the notion of treatment as the application of a series of techniques do not seem particularly fruitful.

In this chapter we shall examine the ways in which relationship skills are used to accomplish the broad purposes of 'diagnosis' and 'treatment'. These will be separately considered, though in actual practice they proceed simultaneously and in interaction with each other. This viewpoint contrasts vividly with that of earlier case-workers who attempted to collect all the information necessary for 'diagnosis' before actual 'treatment' began. As a caseworker wrote in 1914 '. . . when inquiry is complete and the facts have become clear, when we have come to perceive the kind of man with whom we are dealing, and can trace the steps which have brought him to his present strait, then it will be time enough to decide what our attitude towards him ought to be'.[6] Caseworkers now consider that they increase their understanding of a client through 'treating' him and 'treat' him largely through attempting to understand him. For purposes of study, however, a distinction between these two essential processes is both possible and necessary.

DIAGNOSIS

This process is at the heart of casework because of the assumption that everyone does not need the same kind of help in the same way. It remains relatively unexplored in British social work writing, but in America it has been subject to considerable shifts of opinion. Mary Richmond, who first used the expression 'social diagnosis' in the early years of the present century, emphasized the concept of 'evidence' and its judicial appraisal as she expanded and systematized the range of sources from which social workers could collect their facts. The influence of psychoanalysis in the 1930's turned caseworkers towards the intra-psychic life of their clients and to personality dysfunction in general. The Functional School of casework, however, began to question the caseworker's right to make a diagnosis, which was seen as a kind of violation of his will to self-determination and a doomed attempt to predict the essentially unpredictable outcome of a relationship. More recently, American social workers have considered the desirability of creating typologies for their discipline. Greenwood, for example, has suggested that:

> A well-developed practice has at its disposal a highly refined diagnostic typology that embraces the entire gamut of problems confronted by that discipline. There has been formulated for each diagnostic type a series of generalizing propositions, both descriptive and prescriptive. The former propositions describe the properties, behaviour, etiology, and life-cycle of the type; the latter prescribe the steps to be pursued in ascertaining whether a given problem is classifiable within a type. Together, these propositions make up the diagnostic principles of a practice.[7]

The feasibility of this kind of project in social work will become apparent as we review the difficulties of diagnosis.

The term has, of course, a medical origin and direct analogies between medicine and social work have been drawn since the late nineteenth century. The Principles of Decision published by the Charity Organization Society in 1881, for example, stated that 'Each case of distress is to be considered as that of a sufferer from some malady, of one afflicted in mind, body, or estate. . . .' The attractiveness of diagnostic typologies derives partly from the desire to emulate the discipline of medicine. Yet, to 'diagnose' in medical terms means to classify a group of behaviours as a case of something, an instance of a particular disease. In social work, however, there are no 'illnesses'; there is no 'sociophrenia', for instance. The object of social casework inquiry is not simply the things that happen to people, the organisms that invade their social being, but also the things people make happen. And people make things happen for all the varied reasons they act at all. There is also in the social work idea of diagnosis an important and illuminating ambiguity, since the term is frequently used to refer to both process and product, the path of discovery as well as a description of the arrival-point. The process element in diagnosis has received insufficient attention.

It used to be assumed that the process of casework diagnosis was one of fact-finding, though certain kinds of fact (e.g. that the applicant 'drank') received a disproportionate emphasis. In the process the applicant was one of several sources of information and his role was that of passive informant who was expected to answer questions frankly. The caseworker's role was that of a moralizing detective (if the applicant failed to answer the questions he must have something to hide) or a corkscrew, ('the joy of wrestling with the stiff-necked applicant,' wrote a worker in 1919, 'and of returning triumphantly to the office with vital information previously withheld and now revealed in fullest detail as the result of our persuasion—what moments equal these?').[8] The contemporary caseworker is less likely to emphasize the discovery of discrete facts and more likely to see his role as that of facilitating discoveries by the clients themselves. The process of diagnosis is not one of the inexhaustable accumulation of facts, though facts must be collected and ordered; nor is it one of the labelling of certain behaviour by an expert, though the significance of behaviour must be recognized. It is rather a process whereby the client and worker help each other to 'see' and grasp relationships. Connectedness may or may not be the essence of all things, as Whitehead suggested, but it is near the heart of casework diagnosis as a process that helps the client to connect past with present, feeling with thought, seemingly disparate roles with each other. In this framework a central place is given to the worker's intelligent 'reading' of the client and his situations. Some writers have seen the diagnostic process as a kind of syllogistic argument. Lehrman, for instance,[9] has depicted the caseworker pursuing a series of logical steps in the form—Mr. Jones is irresponsible: psychopaths are irresponsible: therefore, there is a probability that Mr. J. is a psychopath? Undoubtedly, the caseworker may have to proceed step by step in his approach to a diagnostic statement, but these are not the kinds of step he takes. The caseworker takes what readings he can of the client and his situation until the pattern of the case becomes clear. This is not simply a question of observation; rather it is a question of continuous observation of the self and the other in interaction.

> At no stage do we cease to participate in the life of the individual under observation. For we comprehend a living being at all levels by our subsiduary awareness of its particulars. These particulars are never observed in themselves; we *read* them as manifestations of an individual. We rely on them as pointers, as we rely on a probe or a written text, by making them part of ourselves for reaching beyond them.[10]

This, however, is to advocate a viewpoint, not to delineate a programme. There must be limits to what a social caseworker needs to know about his or her clients in order to help. Some, of course, would draw these closely around the problem with which help is actually requested by the client. For them diagnosis of 'deeper' problems is an imposition amounting to a claim to know others better than they know themselves. Two comments can be made on this approach. Firstly, the idea of 'knowing others better than they know themselves' can be interpreted in a strong or a weak sense. In its strong sense it would refer to knowledge from a viewpoint the person 'known' could never occupy. Thus, God could be said to know us better than we know ourselves. In a weak sense, however, reference would be to knowledge from a viewpoint that the person 'known' does not occupy at a given moment, but which he could in principle occupy. Thus, someone in a position to observe the unacknowledged pattern of another's behaviour may be said to know the other better than he knows himself, and once the 'known' person sees things from the observer's viewpoint he may well agree that the observer knew him better than he knew himself.

Secondly, too constricted a view of the actual request of the client fails to recognize the rich ambiguity of social living. People, in fact, request help in ways that vary in accordance with their perception of themselves and of others. In this connection, some recent comments by Szasz[11] on hinting are of interest. Hinting is seen as a means of indirect communication used for three main reasons. It is a way of sending a message, the affect of which is feared, either because it expresses a forbidden wish or because it is an aggressive reproach against a person who is loved and needed; it allows the expression of feelings, wishes, fears etc., without fully committing the subject to the message; it may enable the subject to have his wish granted without having to make a full and explicit request. If the caseworker ignores the client's hinting he will clearly be imposing an artificial limitation on the range of possible communication.

The caseworker, then, should maintain an open approach to his client, but his concern will revolve around certain key themes, and the important limiting factor that he is required only to learn sufficient about his clients to help them make use of his agency's services. What are the key themes in social work diagnosis or appraisal?[12] The following seem to be among the most important questions the caseworker begins to answer: what is the problematic situation on referral, whether the client goes to the agency or vice versa, and what significance have the difficulties for the client and his family? The caseworker also requires to know what solutions are possible for the client in his situation and the nature of the personalities involved. In particular, he wishes to establish how they perceive their world and themselves and what they are doing to significant others in their lives, and why. The caseworker needs to know both what is wrong and why it persists, and much of his information will be gathered around the client's failure to carry one or more of his significant social roles and sometimes around his difficulties in a new role (e.g. the independent, over-conscientious father who has to assume a sick role as a hospital patient).

An example of a beginning diagnosis may clarify what has been suggested as the content of diagnosis.

Ronald D. (aged 16 years) was placed on probation in 1960 for committing wilful damage at his old school; previous offences of shop-breaking were recorded against him in 1958 and 1959. The officer's pre-trial enquiry revealed the following information: Ronald lived with his mother and father and sister (aged 14) in the 'respectable' part of a small industrial town. His father had been a noncommissioned officer in the army and was now doing highly skilled work in a light engineering firm, where he had obtained a job for his son. He worked long hours and described his job in great detail to the officer. He said that had Ronald been in the army he would have known how to deal with him, and he seemed to resent the possibility that 'his boy' might be placed under the supervision of another man. He compared Ronald unfavourably with his sister and was inclined to blame his delinquency on his mother's favouritism. Ronald's mother complained of father's bullying, and felt extremely ashamed of Ronald's 'persistent crime', expressing a fear that it might lead 'to all sorts of things'. Ronald could not explain the damage against his school; he had had a successful school career, though he had never taken much part in organised group activities, having left the cadets because his father would not pay for his uniform. His ambition was to join the police force. He seemed to be worried about the situation at home and particularly concerned with his father's bullying of his mother. He explained that he wanted to keep the peace. Recently his father had started to quarrel with him and they had almost come to blows. Mother spoke very well of Ronald and the officer was impressed by his frank and open manner and his good disposition towards him.

What kind of tentative diagnosis could be offered to account for this situation and to guide the caseworker's choice of 'treatment'? We know nothing about Ronald's early history, but at the time of the offences he seems to be reacting to changes within the family and within himself. His father has difficulty in taking and playing the role of father to a boy of his age, depriving him (e.g. the cadet uniform despite father's own links with the army) and also wanting to help and, perhaps, control him (he obtained a job for him at his place of work). He compares him unfavourably with his sister, and it seems as if the parental and sibling systems have broken down into a conflict between two 'couples' (father–daughter; mother–son). This interacts with Ronald's renewed oedipal conflict at adolescence. He feels identified with mother and a strong obligation to keep the peace. In this situation the direct expression of aggression is inhibited by 'real' anxiety in case of punishment from his father and by his assumed role of 'good' boy who keeps the peace. His offences seem at once a protest of his manliness and also an expression of resentment against authority. For father the offences signify his own failure (in *another* role he thinks he could have managed the situation) and the possible

81

intervention of a new 'father' (the probation officer). Ronald's mother sees the offences as the frightening beginnings of a criminal career. In many ways the problem in the case revolves around control and Ronald should be helped to see the feelings over which he might learn to establish more reasonable control as he is helped to assume the role of an adult male by a probation officer who is much less threatened by him. At the same time the family situation is clearly both cause and effect of his problem and it would certainly be necessary to help the parents to encourage Ronald's development and also perhaps to begin to examine some of their marriage problems which have become displaced on to the children.

TREATMENT

The automatic response to generalized situations has never been advocated by caseworkers, though their actual practice has sometimes suggested otherwise. Loch gave caseworkers a wide choice of 'treatment' when he stated that: 'To teach, to persuade, to relieve, to refuse to relieve, to upbraid, to leave alone—may all be true judgments of charity . . . according to the purpose it has in view.'[13] He offered, however, no means of deciding when any of these activities was appropriate. The development of criteria for different kinds of treatment and the refinement of ways of treating clients has been a feature of casework in the last three decades, during which classification of treatment measures has been attempted in America and Britain. Hollis,[14] for example, has suggested a fourfold division into environmental modification by direct action (e.g. referring a client to a source of assistance and helping him to use it); psychological support (encouragement, sympathy etc.); clarification or helping the client to understand his predicament; and the fostering of insight (the reliving in therapy of past events so that the associated affect may be discharged and awareness achieved by the client). Cockerill and her associates[15] also propound a fourfold classification, but they list separate techniques of treatment within each grouping. For example, in 'mild neuroses, character problems, neurotic traits, and transitory anxiety states' four main techniques are envisaged: (1) clarification, showing the client the themes of his behaviour; (2) interpretation, to help him understand emotional factors in the present situation, but not the historical roots of such feeling; (3) helping the client to use fragmentary self-knowledge to form a rounded conception of himself; (4) interpretation of transference situations if they are likely to block the client's material or encourage him to act out his problems. In Britain, Irvine[16] has outlined a more simple distinction between two main kinds of treatment. This is seen largely in terms of two main roles which the caseworker might play, the parent-figure or the interpreter. In the first, the worker's own emotional responses, the presentation of herself as a 'real' person, and her attempts to nurture her client are the essential ingredients. In the second, the caseworker will be more concerned to encourage the growth of the client's insight and to play a more passive part in treatment.

These examples illustrate the range of 'treatment' activities caseworkers have considered appropriate to their discipline. Some of them have been more highly valued than others. In America in the 1940's 'supportive' treatment was often left to the inexperienced worker,[17] whilst Irvine[16] has commented on the general tendency of British social workers to regard 'insight' therapy as superior to other forms of help. The classifications of 'treatment' so far proposed suggest a number of important conclusions. Firstly, the classifications have different bases. Irvine's twofold distinction is grounded on the idea of emotional maturity, whilst Cockerill clearly makes direct use of psychiatric categories (e.g. neurosis). This suggests that caseworkers need to give much more attention to the question, if a casework diagnosis seeks to classify a client, in what terms is the classification to be made? It would seem that a diagnosis in terms of psychiatric illness is of very limited value. A classification in terms of role-failure or conflict and its causes would be more helpful, but it is preferable to think of the diagnostic product as a profile rather than a classification.

Secondly, writers have differed in the emphasis they have given to tying certain treatment methods specifically to certain objectives. Cockerill, for example, avoids overlapping between some at any rate of her groups of technique. This does not, on the whole, seem to be a feasible procedure. In any one case it is likely that the worker will use the whole range of 'treatment techniques'. Thirdly, we can see that 'treatment' is used in both the senses to be found in ordinary speech. 'I treated him badly' means that I behaved badly towards him, I behaved inappropriately in a particular role relationship or a range of such relationships. On the other hand, 'I treated him for such and such an illness' refers to a specific series of therapeutic acts directed to removing a particular disease. Irvine's classification seems to approach the first meaning more nearly than the others and this way of referring to 'treatment' is the most useful for caseworkers.

Treatment, then, can best be seen as a matter of the worker's potential response to a range of roles. It is not an operation that can be planned in detail in advance, though certain guiding principles can be elucidated and certain phases of help are more open to prediction than others. Freud suggested that 'Anyone who hopes to learn the noble game of chess from books will soon discover that only the openings and end-games admit of an exhaustive systematic presentation and that the infinite variety of moves which develop after the opening defy any such description. . . . The rules which can be laid down for the practice of psychoanalytic treatment are subject to similar limitation.'[18] The principles of casework treatment could be regarded in the same light, though the caseworker is helped to focus her help through her objective of fulfilling the agency's functions. Treatment in casework consists largely in the attempt to understand the client and to help him to use the services of the agency. This understanding depends partly on attitude and partly on the use of knowledge. The attitude can best be described in terms of a readiness to perceive, make, refuse or question the changing roles suggested by interaction with the client. This emphasizes that the process of treatment is more tentative, more complex and more creative than the playing of a generalized role, whether it is that of 'good parent' or interpreter.

This does not, however, entail that treatment cannot be systematically considered. Two main approaches can be found in the literature of casework, as workers have identified certain phases of activity and emphasized certain acts. In considering the phases of activity the initial contact with the client has been given most emphasis.

The initial or intake interview has been studied generally and with particular reference to probation and psychiatric social work.[19] It is an important stage in treatment at which many clients are lost or won, and it has its own special emphases and problems. The client has to experience actual help, even if it is simply help

Treatment

to express his meaning more clearly; he has to feel the concern and
the competence of the worker, and he has to begin to define the
kinds of problems he may be facing. He is receiving, as it were,
a sample of the kind of help he would receive if he decided to
participate fully in the proffered service. In the broad sense of the
term outlined above, it can be said that 'treatment' begins as soon
as client and caseworker meet. The caseworker will be concerned
to gain certain impressions of his client, but an over-reliance on
the gathering of information at the expense of attention to the
concerns the client is expressing at the time will produce neither
meaningful information nor the experience of being, at least
partially, understood.

These general considerations are in basic agreement with some
experimental work on the expected behaviour of a potentially
helpful person. Three sorts of expectation were identified in the
realms of sensitivity, structuring and communication. The client
expected the potentially helpful person to be able to identify and
reduce his tension in an initial interview and to structure the
interview, overcoming the client's decision-making difficulties regarding the progress of the interview. In the sphere of communication the helpful person was expected to (a) Assign importance to the problem the client has, thus bringing it into the
area of communication; (b) Show willingness to maintain communication; (c) Show willingness to broaden the range of communications made accessible to both the client and the helper.'[20]

Turning to the acts of the caseworker, we find that particular
emphasis has been given to material aid, advice and reassurance,
and the interpretation of the client's feelings and behaviour. The
first will be discussed in chapter eight. Advice was freely given by
early caseworker[s], often in a forcefully persuasive way, while reassurance was perhaps reserved for the 'good' client. Sometimes
financial assistance was conditional on the client following a particular piece of advice, which thus took on some of the attributes
of an ultimatum. In the 1930's, psychiatric social workers often
saw themselves as concerned with the upbringing of children
along mental hygiene lines, and they would accordingly give
advice as experts in child-rearing rather than as moralists. Thus,
advice in casework has had a changing content and has been given
in a changing spirit. Similarly, 'reassurance' has no constant meaning in the history of casework and has been used to refer to a

85

specific act (the relief of fear or anxiety by comforting words) or to the effect of a whole series of actions, some of which may not have been directly aimed at relief of fear. Thus, the client is said to experience reassurance at the conclusion of an interview because the worker's attitude has been one of consistent and undismayed concern.

The giving of advice has not been extensively considered in British casework writing. Requests for advice are made by clients on different subjects and in different contexts. Thus, a client may request simple information about social provision and the caseworker, relying on his knowledge of current statutory benefits, might advise him to call and discuss certain matters with the National Assistance Board. Provision of this kind of advice must become an increasingly important part of the caseworker's task as social legislation and regulation become more complex. Caseworkers, however, do not act as a simple signpost or notice board, since they should be alert to any indications that the client has difficulty in perceiving the nature of the suggested service or in approaching its personnel. Advice is often sought on other kinds of topic, on personal issues of considerable importance to the client—how should they deal with their child's temper tantrums; should they seek a separation from their husband; should they continue coming to the social agency etc.? What considerations should the caseworker bear in mind in dealing with such requests?

There are perhaps three main questions that the caseworker should ask in connection with a request for advice—what is being requested, why is the request made, and by whom? In other words a request for advice is judged in just the same way as any other communication from the client. When he asks for advice about the upbringing of his children, is he asking for a list of 'techniques' or rather for the opportunity to talk over and think through some of his doubts and indecisions? In this connection it is worth remarking that we value not so much people's views about what we should do, but their good opinion of us. Is the person requesting advice really without the factual information necessary to reach a decision, or should not the request be seen as a piece of purposive behaviour within the context of the developing relationship? Requests for advice may assume a particular role relationship (mother–child; teacher–pupil; novice–expert) or be part of an attempt to create it. So far, it may be concluded, we have seen that advice-requesting is not an activity that would always lead to advice-giving. For some clients, however, particularly those described as immature, advice may be appropriate even if it is not requested. In the case, for instance, of those who persistently neglect their children's needs, their own health and so on, advice might well be appropriate, though the client's feelings about the caseworker's pressure would also have to be recognized and discussed. This kind of activity may easily seem to bear a strong resemblance to that of some early casework moralizers, but there are essential differences. The advice of the contemporary caseworker should, ideally, be given within the context of a relationship; it is part of a supportive role, not an act of intrusion. It should stem from the awareness of the worker and be given in a way that allows the client to express his own feelings about it. Moreover, the objective of advice-giving is not simply a change in behaviour, but a means of learning and of increasing the client's self-estimation. If a piece of advice is followed and the outcome is successful, it will then be possible to show the client the difference between past and present and to confirm that this has not been accomplished by any magical process, but as the result of patient day by day work by both client and caseworker.

Interpretation is a casework activity that has been highly valued in Britain and the term has been used in a number of different ways, as I have indicated elsewhere.[21] For present purposes a distinction can usefully be made between the manner, the matter and the objectives of interpretation. It has often been assumed that interpretations are 'given' by the caseworker to the client in the form of statements about the client's implicit feeling or behaviour. For instance, a client of mine in a child guidance clinic frequently ended his interviews by apologizing for the cigarette ends and 'mess' he always left on the floor, though an ashtray was provided. I suggested that he was wondering what I thought of the messy feelings that he left with me each week. He smiled and said, as he walked out of the room, 'Yes, something like that.' The interpretation was in the form of a tentative statement about the client's behaviour based on a number of separate observations. It was 'given' because I felt the client was drawing my attention to the behaviour in question; he was, perhaps, ready to receive an interpretation. Thus, an interpretation is not an unsolicited 'gift' that the caseworker 'gives', but part of the co-operative work between client and caseworker. It is also important to remember that interpretive comments can equally well take an interrogative form: 'Whenever we begin to talk about this subject, you talk about something else. I wonder why you feel you have to keep me at arm's-length?'

The matter of interpretation has usually been seen as some aspect of the relationship between client and caseworker or between the client and significant others. In interpreting the relationship caseworkers have often thought in terms of the psychoanalytic transference. Transference phenomena are feelings and behaviour appropriate to the person's past infantile life which come to dominate his or her reactions to the analyst in the present. Freud made an interesting distinction between negative and positive transference and divided the latter into the 'transference of friendly or affectionate feelings which are admissable to consciousness and transference of prolongations of these feelings into the unconscious'. The former, he observed 'is the vehicle of success in psychoanalysis as it is in other methods of treatment'.[22] It seems that Freud was distinguishing between the transference of feelings from the past to the present and also from one area of the present to another. Both kinds of phenomena are observable in casework and some of the ways in which they might be interpreted can be seen in the case of Vera L. in chapter nine.

There are a number of feasible objectives for such interpretations. Sometimes it is necessary to call the client's attention to the way in which he is distorting his relationship with the worker, because the distortions are hampering the client's use of the service or because the main part of the work consists in drawing a continuous contrast between the reality of the worker and the client's projections. On every occasion an appropriate interpretation will probably bring a measure of relief to the client; his hostility or love is seen as arising from fears of his own weakness and the real concern of the worker is experienced. The client may also benefit from increased sensitivity to himself and the relationships he forms. This is often termed 'insight'. The quality of insight has already been indicated in chapter one, but caseworkers have not perhaps given sufficient attention to the different kinds of insight. French has distinguished three kinds[23] and his formulation appears applicable to casework. Introspective insight occurs when a person becomes aware of a previously repressed wish or fear; problem-solving insight refers to what a person needs to know in order to solve a problem or reach a goal; and practical understanding is what a person actually knows, though he may not be consciously aware of doing so.

So far, we have examined various aspects of casework treatment, but it has proved difficult to discuss them without reference to the kind of relationship that informs these separate activities. On the subject of 'relationship' caseworkers are tempted towards rhapsody, mysticism and, at times, a triumphant vagueness. These are inevitable risks if the idea is to be discussed at all. At the same time there is no room for complacency. We have to approach the idea of relationship by increasing approximations to the truth, even though we may never entertain a completely satisfying and communicable notion.

An historical view of the idea of a helping relationship in casework reveals a number of key themes, the place of friendship, questions about reciprocity and passivity, and the concept of a professional relationship. Some early caseworkers clearly created and maintained sympathetic relationships with their clients. It is impossible to doubt, for example, the warmth and effectiveness of the relationships Octavia Hill established, even though they were based on an assumed leader-led role relationship which was not entirely consistent with the theorizing of the period. 'I could have formed', she wrote, 'no idea of the docility of the people, nor of their gratitude for small things. They are easily governed by firmness, which they respect very much.'[24] Yet the concept of friendship created difficulties for caseworkers who emphasized objectivity and judicial fairness. Some of the difficulties can be seen in the statement that 'I think we have hardly the right to help a man until we have got, in some degree at least, to like him and understand him . . . on the other hand, we must not make favourites.'[25]

One of the solutions to this dilemma was the development of 'friendly visiting' as an activity somewhat distinct from casework. The friendly visitor was allowed to participate in the family life of clients in ways that were not initially, at any rate, open to the 'official' caseworker. The gradual amalgamation of the two ideas led naturally to questions concerning the reciprocity of the 'friendly' relationships caseworkers established with their clients. 'Why should (clients)', asks a writer in June 1912:

tell us all their lives, past and present, while we sit and listen and give
no confidence in return? . . . If we are to create real friendships we
must force ourselves to make the friendship true and wholehearted,
and I believe that the power of expressing our feelings, telling our
lives, will develop once practised. . . . The poor love giving just as
much as the rich do—probably more; we accept extraordinarily badly
. . . they have a right, they should, they will give in abundance of
their affections and friendly love, if only they are given a footing in
the threshold of our lives.[26]

This point of view still has important implications for a profession
whose members are constantly tempted by what D. H. Lawrence
called the greed of giving.

The idea of passivity was partly a reaction against the enthusiastic over-involvement of earlier caseworkers and partly a direct
imitation of one of the major techniques of psychoanalysis. The
notion was not adopted in Britain in its extreme form and talk of
caseworkers acting as 'photographic plates'[27] probably failed to
convey accurately what caseworkers were doing. During his interaction with the caseworker a client may well begin to learn and
'see' something of his own personality, but this is the result of the
work of discovery rather than an automatic 'development'.

One of the concepts caseworkers took from psychoanalytic
therapy in order to deepen their idea of the professional relationship was that of counter-transference. The technical meaning of
this term is not precisely clear. In a recent symposium on the
subject,[28] for example, Fordham stated that it consisted of unconsciously motivated reactions in the analyst evoked by the
patient's transference, whilst Winnicott suggested it could 'only
be the neurotic features which spoil the professional attitude'.
Caseworkers, however, have used the term generally to refer to
the projection on to the client of the worker's feelings and ideas
as an irrational response to the client. There are obvious dangers
in such a situation, but there is also a positive use that can be made
of the feelings the client provokes in the worker. They can be a
very useful indication of the sort of person the client is. Heimann
has recently made an observation in connection with this phenomenon in the training of analysts which seems applicable to
casework.

Often when a candidate's interpretations appeared to be quite outside
any *rapport* with his patient, I asked him what he had really felt. It

frequently emerged that in his feelings he had appropriately registered the essential point. We could then see that had he *sustained* his feelings and treated them as the response to a process in his patient, he would have had a good chance of discovering what it was to which he had responded.[29]

This notion of sustaining the response evoked by the other is of considerable importance in casework.

Present concern for the relationship in casework largely centres around the idea of a *professional* relationship. A professional relationship in general is one in which the worker has a specific authority of competence and knowledge in a particular field. It is a relationship of 'affective neutrality', to use a term of Talcott Parsons.[30] The object of the relationship is not the direct gratification of the worker's emotional needs, however much indirect satisfaction the work yields. It is a relationship offered on a basis that discriminates between people in terms of their ability to use the service and not in terms of class, colour or religion. These general features of a professional relationship are applicable to casework, but caseworkers have a special interest in the relationship because it is necessary for the essential fulfilment of their task and not an 'extra'. They will, therefore, need to take the idea of a helping relationship further and explore its meaning more fully. This necessitates the attempt to clarify what we mean by a relationship in the first place. A relationship is a system of interacting feelings and ideas, changing but maintained within certain boundaries. It is a set of enduring attitudes towards the self and the other so that neither has, as it were, to start from the beginning when they next meet. It exists even when the members of a relationship are physically apart. Each relationship has its own natural history, its beginning and its crises. We can, then, begin to make statements about relationships along these lines and in this way begin to gain a more clear idea of the meaning and significance of the concept. This is one of the essential explorations for casework in the future.

Can we, however, gain any precise knowledge about the factors in relationships that make them helpful or curative? It has recently been suggested that 'the process of what we call cure is simply at this time not clear; . . . cure cannot presently be adequately described in any system; . . . the concept of human relatedness is probably basic in psychiatric healing, and . . . this concept, unclear as it may be, need not be feared'.[31] Can the same also be said of casework?

Certainly, some social workers have accepted with enthusiasm the possibility that one of the most important aspects of their work cannot be defined. Their position could be justified on a number of grounds. It could form part of a general argument that no set of words can ever adequately express an idea, or one could maintain that such a limitation applied only to certain kinds of experience (e.g. infantile experience). Alternatively, it could be argued that some kinds of experience can be adequately conveyed in a particular language which cannot be translated into any other. Thus, ideas about relationships, it could be maintained, are adequately expressed only in poetry or in religious language. If we wish to argue that statements about relationships are doomed to failure, it is important to be clear about the kind of inadequacy we assume. My own view is that we do not need to accept a pessimism in regard to the general adequacy of language nor should we search for a special 'relationship' language with which to describe 'relationships'. We can use every available language to deepen our perception of relationships and their dimensions.

Several attempts have, of course, been made to name *the* therapeutic factor in professional help with personal problems. Some of these have been specifically related to psychoanalysis but they have relevance for the explanation of all kinds of 'relationship therapy'. Strachey, for instance, emphasized the function of mutative interpretations,[32] whilst French has questioned a 'mystical faith' in their therapeutic efficacy.[33] Recently, Frank[34] has given weight to the influence of the therapist and the faith of the patient. Shoben has offered an interpretation of psychotherapy in terms of learning theory. He suggested that psychotherapy occurred through three interrelated processes: 'First, the lifting of repression and development of insight through the symbolic reinstating of the stimuli for anxiety; second, the diminution of anxiety by counter-conditioning through the attachment of the stimuli for anxiety to the comfort reaction made to the therapeutic relationship; and third, the process of re-education through the therapist's helping the patient to formulate rational goals and behavioural methods for attaining them.'[35] Guntrip sees the meaning of cure as the attainment of maturity, and this is accomplished through the analyst becoming a real and good object for his patient.[36] Irvine has suggested that casework supplies the client with a new kind of experience in which old conflicts can find to some extent a new solution.[37] Finally, Suttie[38] and others have claimed that it is the analyst's love that cures the patient. Which of these ideas can most fruitfully be adopted by caseworkers?

The professional relationship in casework can be viewed as involving two processes, those of learning and of loving or caring to the brink of love.[39] The relationship supplies the conditions under which clients can, to some extent, resume or correct an earlier stage of socialization. To undertake this kind of learning the client requires on the part of the caseworker an attitude of receptive endurance and also an attentive structuring of the situation so that it begins to make sense, to take on a coherence. Thus, casework could be described as possessing a love-function and a truth-function. A recent empirical study of initial interviews concluded by calling attention to two distinct processes in casework.

> It appears that to formulate the significance of the relationship with the helper as a person to the client solely in terms of its perceived instrumental value for problem solution would not be accurate for a large proportion of clients. Rather, satisfactions experienced in the relationship itself seem to have much to do with the commitment to maintain a relationship. On the other hand, the commitment to be influenced by the helping person entails another kind of scrutiny, having more to do with estimates of competency, technical skill and anticipated thoroughness. Evidently for these clients, as for supervisors of practitioners, interest is a *sine qua non*, but Love is Not Enough![40]

Caseworkers are faced with clients who have extremely complex problems, which worry and disturb them, their families and the society. To help them face and attempt to solve these problems the caseworker has a number of resources—her own personality, the functions of her agency and some knowledge and skill. She has also the realization that whilst the literature has sometimes described casework aims in rather global terms, such as adjustment or the release of personality, she must rest content with minor projects and smaller satisfactions. Freud once suggested to someone who asked how he proposed to help him: 'No doubt fate would find it easier than I do to relieve you of your illness. But you will be able to convince yourself that much will be gained if we succeed in transforming your hysterical misery into common unhappiness.' This is the kind of realism that should also inform the practice of casework.

NOTES

[1] Hill, O., 'Trained Workers for the Poor', *Charity Organisation Review*, Jan. 1893.

[2] See e.g. Dressler, D., *Practice and Theory of Probation and Parole*, Columbia University Press, 1959.

[3] See e.g. Selby, L., 'Typologies for Caseworkers: Some Considerations and Problems', *Social Service Review*, Dec. 1958.

[4] Perlman, H., *Social Casework—A Problem-Solving Process*, University of Chicago Press, 1957, p. 160.

[5] The controversy began with two articles in *Case Conference* (Aug. 1954): McCullough, M., 'The "Grunting Method" and Matrimonial Conciliation'; Foren, R., 'On Not Grunting'. Correspondence followed in the October and November issues.

[6] W.G.M., 'What We Mean By Inquiry', *Charity Organisation Review*, Jan. 1914.

[7] Greenwood, E., 'Social Science and Social Work: A Theory of Their Relationship', *Social Service Review*, March 1955.

[8] 'An Ex-Student's Point of View', *Charity Organisation Review*, May 1919.

[9] Lehrman, L., 'The Logic of Diagnosis', *Social Casework*, Vol. XXXV, No. 5, 1954.

[10] Polanyi, M., 'Knowing and Being', *Mind*, N.S. Vol. 70, pp. 458–70.

[11] Szasz, T., *The Myth of Mental Illness*, Secker and Warburg, 1961, p. 300.

[12] 'Appraisal' seems in many ways a preferable term to 'diagnosis', but the latter is so widely used that a change of terminology seems unlikely.

[13] Loch, C. S., 'Christian Charity and Political Economy', *Charity Organisation Review*, Nov. 1899.

[14] Hollis, F., 'The Techniques of Casework', *Social Casework*, Vol. XXX, No. 6, June 1949.

[15] Cockerill, E., *et al.*, *A Conceptual Framework for Social Casework*, University of Pittsburgh, 1952.

[16] Irvine, E. E., 'Transference and Reality in the Casework Relationship', *British Journal of Psychiatric Social Work*, Vol. III, No. 4, 1956.

[17] Selby, L., 'Supportive Treatment: The Development of a Concept and a Helping Method', *Social Service Review*, Dec. 1956.

[18] Freud, S. (1913), *On Beginning the Treatment*, Standard Edition of Complete Works, Strachey, J. (ed.), Hogarth Press, Vol. XII, p. 123.

[19] See Perlman, H., 'Intake and Some Role Considerations', *Social Casework*, April 1960; Anderson, D. and Kiesler, F., 'Helping Toward Help: The Intake Interview', *Social Casework*, Vol. XXXV, No. 2, Feb. 1954; Schmideberg, M. and Sokol, J., 'The Function of Contact in Psychotherapy with Offenders', *Social Casework*, Vol. XXXIV, No. 9, Nov. 1953.

[20] Thomas, E., Polansky, N. and Kounin, J., 'The Expected Behaviour of a Potentially Helpful Person', *Human Relations*, Vol. VIII, No. 2, May 1955.

[21] Timms, N., *Psychiatric Social Work in Britain*, Routledge & Kegan Paul, 1964.

[22] Freud, S. (1912), *The Dynamics of Transference*, Standard Edition of Complete Works, Hogarth Press, Vol. XII, p. 105.

[23] French, T., *The Reintegrative Process in Psychoanalytic Treatment*, Vol. III of *The Integration of Behaviour*, University of Chicago Press, 1958, p. 18.

Notes

[24] Hill, O., *Homes of the London Poor*, London, 1875.

[25] Walrond, 'Co-operation and the Need of Trained Workers', *Charity Organisation Review*, Feb. 1893.

[26] 'Co-operation between Hospitals and Relief Committees', *Charity Organisation Review*, June 1912.

[27] Cormack, U., 'Interviewing and the Bombed', *Social Work*, April 1942.

[28] 'Symposium on Counter-Transference': Papers by Fordham, M., Heimann, P. and Winnicott, D.; *British Journal of Medical Psychology*, Vol. XXXII, Part 3, 1959–60.

[29] Heimann, P., op. cit.

[30] Parsons, T., 'Social Structure and Dynamic Process: The Case of Modern Medical Practice', Chapter X of *The Social System*, Free Press of Glencoe, 1951.

[31] Will, O., Jr., 'Comments on the Psychotherapeutic Intervention', in Stein, M. (ed.), *Contemporary Psychotherapies*, Free Press of Glencoe, 1961, p. 188.

[32] Strachey, J., 'The Nature of the Therapeutic Action of Psychoanalysis', *International Journal of Psycho-Analysis*, Vol. XV, No. 127, 1934.

[33] French, T., op. cit., p. 14.

[34] Frank, J. D., *Persuasion and Healing*, O.U.P., 1961.

[35] Shoben, E. J., 'Psychotherapy as a Problem in Learning Theory', in Eysenck, H. (ed.), *Behaviour Therapy and the Neuroses*, Pergamon Press, 1960.

[36] Guntrip, H., 'The Therapeutic Factor in Psychotherapy', *British Journal of Medical Psychology*, Vol. XXVI, Pt. 2, 1953.

[37] Irvine, E. E., op. cit.

[38] Suttie, I., *The Origins of Love and Hate*, Pelican, 1960.

[39] May Irvine has characterized the two processes involved in casework in a similar way. She sees them as a process of rapport and of ordering experience: 'Communication and Relationship in Social Casework', *Social Casework*, Jan. 1955. It is interesting to note parallels between these two basic factors in casework and similar important features in groups. Small group research suggests that two of the crucial elements in a group's life can be seen in terms of cohesion (or relationship) and task activity (structuring experiences so that the client learns).

[40] Polansky, N. and Kounin, J., 'Clients' Reactions to Initial Interviews—A Field Study', *Human Relations*, Vol. IX. No. 3, Aug. 1956.

Chapter Five

MEDICO-SOCIAL WORK

INTRODUCTION

HISTORICALLY the almoner, like the doctor, first appeared in the hospital as a visitor from outside. The experiment began at the end of the nineteenth century largely on the initiative of leading social workers (like Sir Charles Loch), and it was envisaged as an attempt to help some of the voluntary hospitals to fulfil their functions more effectively. The almoner's original task was seen as the prevention of abuse of hospital treatment by those who could afford to pay, and the referral to the poor law authorities of those already in receipt of relief and of the destitute. Her only positive work seemed to have been recommending suitable people to join Provident Dispensaries. To achieve her purposes the almoner relied on investigation and encouragement, the two main tenets of social work current at the end of the nineteenth century. Her main concern was not the patient as a sick person, but the applicant as eligible or not for the treatment given at the hospital. The pauper would be referred to the service appropriate to his pauper status and, as a doctor wrote in an issue of the *Charity Organisation Review*, 1902, 'We provide infirmaries for pauper sick not because they are sick persons, but because they are sick paupers; theoretically at least, they are paupers first. . . .'[1]

The almoner was seen at first as 'a woman trained and experienced in relief work, a woman of insight, prompt decision and firmness'.[2] This rather narrow view of her role was shared by social workers and by the hospital staff. Gradually, however, her work expanded, since, like the psychiatric social worker in mental hospitals in the 1930's and 1940's, she attracted all kinds of work to herself, simply because of her presence in and around the hospital. She became closely identified with the hospital especially in the 1920's when she was once more concerned with assessing the patient's ability to pay for treatment. Present writers on medico-social work criticize this aspect of their profession's history on the grounds that almoners were not developing the methods and approach of social work within the hospital. Snelling, for example, comments that 'the hospital world was an unsympathetic place for the growth of social work and (almoners) stayed in it only with contriving and even at times in disguise'.[3] Yet at the time it would have been difficult to identify the true features of social work that were being disguised, in view of the break-up of the social work world around 1910 and the stunted growth of training and ideas in the following years. In 1941, a senior member of the profession after surveying the field concluded that 'The early pioneers would be disappointed to find that, except for the minor differences in outlook of a later generation, our approach to our patient and our treatment of the personal difficulties brought to light by the crisis of illness are almost exactly the same as those which they used twenty-five or thirty years ago. . . .'[4]

This pessimistic conclusion underestimates at least two aspects of the almoner's role that had become apparent by the 1930's and remain of importance today. Firstly, the almoner had begun to develop a role as a person who humanized the institution in which she worked. A description of the work published in 1935 by the Institute of Almoners suggests that the almoner was prepared to listen when the doctor was very busy, that she helped the patient to be at ease in strange surroundings, and that she was ready and able to see the patient as a person rather than an illness. Secondly, she had developed her role as the liaison between the hospital and welfare agencies outside. As the Almoners' *Yearbook* for 1935 stated 'Where an almoner is employed she is usually found to be the chief link between the hospital and the outside agencies, public or voluntary, dealing with every aspect of the prevention of disease.' Like the psychiatric social worker in the mental hospital she came to represent the 'outside' world within the hospital.

Yet, in spite of some important developments before the Second World War, it is really in the post-war period that the outlines of a genuine medico-social work specialization can be discerned. This development is based on a more secure understanding of social work in general, of the almoner's varied specialized roles and of the highly complex institution in which most almoners work, the hospital. A number of almoners have been employed in local health authorities since 1929, and a few are beginning experimental work with general practitioners, but the vast majority of almoners are hospital social workers.

The significance of the hospital can most easily be appreciated by considering three related questions: what has the patient come to, what has he come from, and what has he come for?

The person who is formally admitted into hospital is thereby inducted into the role of hospital patient. Yet some of the characteristics of this role may already have become familiar, since the 'patient' may have been taking for some time a sick role. Parsons[5] has usefully defined the elements of this role as (i) exemption from the social responsibilities of normal day-to-day roles; (ii) the sick man cannot be expected to recover simply by his own, unaided efforts; he requires care and treatment; (iii) the sick role does, however, entail its own special responsibilities, since the occupant of the role is expected to get well as quickly as possible and to seek appropriate help and to co-operate with the helpers. The role of hospital patient obviously includes all these characteristics, but it has in addition its own special emphases. Perhaps the most obvious of these is the element of submission. The patient is often admitted at short-notice and in a manner that must sometimes appear arbitrary. He has to face the fact that experts have judged his condition to be serious enough (on medical or social grounds or both) to warrant the use of scarce and valuable resources upon him. He is taken out of his family and is, for a short or long period, no longer a man who works at a particular job, returns home at the end of each day, and is a member of certain recreational groups. His care is now in the hands of a large number of skilled people who play highly specialized roles towards him and each other. Even when these roles have an overt emotional content it tends to be of a generalized kind which is not specific and personal to the patient (e.g. semi-flirtatious behaviour between nurses and male patients). Yet his body is handled and his bodily wants are met in a way that may have no parallel since his infancy, when such behaviour was accompanied by displays of parental affection. The patient has to consider the interaction between all that is being done for him and to him and all that he feels and believes is happening inside himself. He has also to face the fact that his role of hospital patient implies membership of a new group, those who occupy a similar role in any given ward or hospital.

So far we have viewed the patient as a sick person, facing illness or disability in a strange, often impersonal world. Yet the hospital has an overridingly positive objective. It is an institution waging a dedicated war against death, decay, sickness and damage, which requires constant vigilance and the application of increasingly specialized treatments. This leads to greater division of labour and emphasizes the gravity of decisions about treatment, and the care and technical skill necessary in their application.

Within this organization, which seems staffed by people in a constant, if controlled, hurry and which often appears cruel, inadvertently or by design, the almoner may seem the odd person out. She is not concerned with direct nursing care and her task does not seem all that specialized. In the past she might have spoken of her special role in humanizing the hospital, but the whole hospital should be engaged on this. She claims now to help the patient with some of his feelings about illness, operations, etc. but again this is a task she should come increasingly to share with the doctors. Yet her work will probably never be as scientifically based as theirs. Such considerations affect her status in the hospital world and she can in this respect be compared to the general medical practitioner of whom Professor Titmuss has written: 'He is the indeterminate man; the man who is not sure of his place in the scheme of things; who is uneasy because he has to spread himself so widely and has no special role to perfect; no special skill by which he may achieve status. . . .'[6]

It is not simply that the almoner's role in the hospital often appears peripheral. In some important respects she is attempting to fulfil functions which, though they would make the work of the hospital more effective, are often resisted by hospital staff because of their emotional implications. The almoner is concerned with the feelings of the patient, and these are very often avoided by hospital staff because of realistic and fantasy fears about them. Menzies has recently depicted the work of the nurse as arousing strong and mixed feelings: 'pity, compassion and love; guilt and anxiety; hatred and resentment of the patients who arouse these strong feelings; envy of the care given the patient'.[7] These feelings are avoided partly by the division of the care of the patient into numerous parts. The almoner's function runs counter to this, since she is often attempting to see the patient as 'a whole person'.

Yet despite the tensions, almoners have a range of legitimate social work tasks that assist the hospital in achieving its objectives. They have from time to time attempted to describe and clarify them. Miss Cummins, for instance, who was the first almoner at St. Thomas's Hospital, saw the almoner playing a part in removing obstacles to the patient's successful treatment, while in 1903 the newly formed Hospital Almoners' Association set its members three aims: 'to reduce the number of casualty patients: to interview patients to discover if the doctor's advice can be satisfactorily followed: to encourage thrift'.[8] In 1939, the Institute of Almoners suggested that the work of the almoner could be divided into three main groups: '(1) co-operation with the medical staff, including reports on a patient's home circumstances and history, action to deal with home difficulties and to help the patient carry out his treatment, and arrangements for convalescence, surgical appliances, etc. (2) Co-operation with outside bodies and (3) administrative work, including ensuring the smooth working of a contributory scheme.'[9] More recently and successfully Snelling[10] has examined medico-social work and described ten functions. These can, broadly speaking, be divided into three main groups— education and research, general policy, and direct service to, or on behalf of, hospital patients. The first includes the almoner's contribution to the teaching of other hospital staff (including doctors[11] and nurses, and students, both professional and pre-professional social science students and those from other disciplines, e.g. speech therapy). The second (policy) covers the maintenance of an effective social work department and any contribution to the development of the hospital, so that it might meet the patient's needs more effectively. The third category can be divided into a number of basic components: social work help with problems relevant to the commencement, success or cessation of medical care; appraisal of the patient's situation to assist the doctor's diagnosis or decision on disposal; help to patients who are responding to illness and the hospital experience by a disturbance in their social functioning and, finally, help to those in some kind of difficulty in using medical or other social services.

We have seen something of the nature of the hospital as a social institution and some of the changing ways in which almoners have defined their functions. Does the almoner still seem 'the odd person out'? The answer would appear to be, 'No'. The almoner is not the doctors' handmaiden, though identification with these powerful figures often seemed the best means of securing her own identity: she participates in fulfilling the objectives of the hospital. She enables the doctor to carry out his roles of diagnosing, treating and disposing by obtaining information about the patient and offering her professional opinion on its significance. She assists the hospital staff and patients by attempting to understand and to give help to those who are having difficulty in accommodating to the role of sick person. She helps the relatives of the sick person whose difficulties in adjusting to his changed role are hindering his full acceptance of it. If we recall some of the characteristics of the sick and hospital patient roles it is clear that they will constitute different kinds of threat to different personalities in various situations. Linden, for example, in a study of geriatric patients[12] has referred to four kinds of possible reaction to the hospital. The patient may straightforwardly recognize the hospital *vis-à-vis* himself and not deny its character by identifying with the staff; he may react with a neurotic transference on certain staff members, with a 'recessional' transference whereby the whole hospital is accepted or rejected as a good or bad object or with a 'sociological' transference, whereby the groups to which he belongs in the hospital have disturbed relationships with other individuals or groups. For some patients the legitimate withdrawal from home may be experienced as a threat because it allows them to indulge previously resisted wishes to withdraw and escape from difficult problems at home. For these patients the phenomenon of 'A Home Away from Home'[13] may be particularly alarming. Patients with only a tentative sense of their own identity will be threatened by the absence of key figures who mirrored back a consistent picture of the patient. Others may be frightened by the hospital's invitation to dependency because it seems to question their own sense of adequacy.

Some of the implications of this can be seen in the case of Mr. L., who was admitted to hospital for an operation for thyrotoxicosis. He was 38 years of age and a general foreman in a machine manufacturers. He had been referred by the ward sister who felt that he might require help because he had been out of work for three months. This, however, had not been discussed with Mr. L. and when the almoner introduced herself he wondered why she had come. He said that he had no problems and that he and his wife were very independent people. The almoner asked him about his work and Mr. L. talked about it at great length. He liked to be working, and he stressed how efficient he was compared to the others at work. The almoner wondered how he felt about returning to this job and Mr. L. said that the doctors had not been sure about this; they had talked about convalescence, but this depended on what *he* would decide.

In the next interview Mr. L. complained that the nurses fussed around him and would not allow him to do anything to help. He was the one who usually looked after people, but he never helped anyone unless they asked and he did not believe in fussing. He had nearly died when he had been informed that he could not leave hospital for two or three weeks after the operation. The almoner said that this was hard for him, but his job now was to be a patient and to help others with the work they were trying to do. For the first time Mr. L. seemed to be listening to what the almoner said.

In this case the client clearly felt that his competence and adequacy were being threatened. He had thought of himself as the helper and it was difficult for him to accept help. The almoner could have discussed with him some of the clear though implicit references to herself: Mr. L. said he would not help anyone who had not requested assistance, but this was precisely what the almoner was attempting to do in his case. Instead, the almoner used her knowledge of what seemed to be Mr. L.'s characteristic way of handling stress and posed the problem as one of a job to be done, something challenging to be attempted.

Some patients, then, will have difficulty in entering a sick role. Others will find it an attractive role which is hard to leave. Yet, for most patients the sick role is essentially temporary: it is in fact one of the important aspects of the role that the occupant strives for recovery and hence the abandonment of the role. This may become a particular problem at certain stages (e.g. convalescence) and for particular age groups. Adolescents, for example, who are struggling with problems of independence as they move towards a full adult status may find difficulty in relinquishing dependency once they have allowed themselves to experience it fully as hospital patients.

Roles, as we have seen in chapter two, essentially imply reciprocity, and the almoner is concerned with facilitating not only the doctor–patient relationship, but also the relationships between patient and relatives. Some relatives have difficulty in allowing their son, husband etc. to play a sick role. Mothers of young children,[14] for instance, may feel guilty that others have to nurse and care for their 'damaged' children, and may attempt to avoid this by blaming the nursing staff for alleged failure to exercise proper care.

We have, so far, spoken of the sick or patient role in a rather generalized way. Yet the person is not simply sick, but sick with a particular disease. This, again, has role implications. A patient may, for instance, be transferred from hospital to a terminal care Home and thus have to face the fact that he is not simply a patient, but a dying one. Obviously, this must create problems for his relatives as well as for the patient himself.[15] The almoner will also be concerned with the patient who is failing to fulfil some aspects of his role in the hospital, with the deviant. Here we see the almoner in her essentially Janus-like role, since she will try to help the patient to obtain satisfactions from a more effective performance in a patient role and also the hospital staff to modify their expectation and behaviour towards him. She is, in fact, the 'odd person in', who is certainly of the hospital at the same time as she works with staff and patients and also with relatives who come into the hospital, as she originally came herself, from outside. She is concerned to facilitate effective role-taking and role-making in the interactions between staff, patients and relatives, not by providing a general service for every hospital case, but by offering a casework service to those who cannot fulfil their roles unaided.[16] This, of course, does not imply that the almoner has no interest in the quality of the hospital's general service to all patients. Bartlett, a leading American teacher of medico-social work, has recently stressed the contribution that almoners could make to its improvements. 'Much has been made in social work of the need for social action to influence programs through legislation. But the opportunity to influence policy, standards, and the nature of the service from within the program has not been sufficiently recognised by either medical or other social workers.'[17] The almoner is concerned with hospital policy in general, both because her social work requires certain minimum conditions for its effective operation and also because she is the *hospital's* social worker.

The Rentons.

Some of the implications of these general views of the almoner's functions within the hospital will now be considered in the light of a case illustration, Mr. and Mrs. Renton.

21. 2. 60.

Mr. Renton was admitted from Casualty in an extremely ill condition. He was found to have cancer of the lung with a poor prognosis. Mr. and Mrs. Renton ran a family business and the doctor referred Mrs. Renton to the almoner to discuss some of the implications of the diagnosis for its future. They had been married for over 30 years and had no living children. Mrs. Renton had had a number of miscarriages and her only child (a girl) had been killed in a car accident when she was five. This was 20 years ago and since then at Mrs. Renton's request they had not had sexual intercourse.

24. 2. 60.

Mrs. Renton was interviewed by the almoner. She was a dark, strong featured woman, with a 'hard' appearance. Her manner was controlled in regard to her own actions and controlling towards the almoner. Her immediate request was for precise facts about her husband's diagnosis. The almoner responded with facts about hospital and nursing care, help available in the patient's own home etc. Mrs. R. assumed that her husband would die shortly and she discussed a number of possibilities—giving up the business they had worked so hard to create in order to nurse her husband; placing him in a nursing home near the hospital and returning home to look after the business. The almoner tried to help Mrs. Renton to express her own feelings—what did she feel herself was the most bearable plan? Mrs. Renton burst into tears and said 'I wish I were dead.' The almoner sat quietly while Mrs. Renton cried, remarking that it sounded like a long sorrow. Mrs. Renton seemed surprised at her own outburst and said it was the first time she had cried. She quickly recovered and said she always had great difficulty in sharing her feelings. The almoner said that perhaps Mrs. R. wanted to be sure the almoner was understanding correctly what she was feeling. Mrs. R. nodded. She spoke of her fears of cancer and went on to express considerable guilt about the way she had treated her husband. She praised his goodness and his self-sacrificing nature; he never made demands upon her. She also vented considerable hostility against her sisters who never helped and the 'negligent' G.P. (Mrs. R. had been dissatisfied with his attention and had persuaded her husband to see a consultant who had previously treated her for gallstones). The almoner said that Mrs. R. was trying to face a very dreadful thing, and it was so dreadful that it must seem someone must be to blame. Mrs. R. said that she wanted to think about that: she always had to think things out. She accepted the almoner's offer of a further interview.

In this recorded extract we can see that Mrs. R. responded to the almoner's warm interest in her feelings as the wife of a man who was likely to die shortly of cancer. She expressed some of her guilt concerning his illness and indeed his married life with her. She was able to lessen some of her controls and to move away from the pressure to make an immediate decision about the business. She had begun to consider her actual feelings in the situation and her fears of cancer. What she might be able to face with further help is the fear of her inability to cope with the situation and the impact of the illness on her own conception of herself. To help in this interview the almoner gave Mrs. R. appropriate information about the services available, since without this Mrs. R. could not come to a reasonable decision. Yet by informing Mrs. R. she focused attention on the social problem rather than engaging in a discussion of the medical diagnosis. She allowed the interview to progress slowly, but gave several leads to the client in an attempt to help her express her feelings. These were ultimately followed and then the almoner helped the client by recognizing some of her feelings about the fact that she had broken down and cried. Mrs. R. went on to try to handle her feelings of guilt, and the almoner recognized at the end of the interview that she and Mrs. R. had done as much work as they could at that time. Mrs. R. clearly indicated that she wanted to go away and think over what had been said.

26. 2. 60.
Letter from Mrs. R. to the almoner, thanking her for their discussion. She said that she had continued to think about her problems and could hear the almoner's calm and logical voice as she thought things out. She had tried to cry, but could not. She thought it had helped to put things into words; she was frightened of boring her friends and of becoming dependent upon them.

In this letter Mrs. R. shows clearly that she has continued working on her problems after the interview with the almoner. She uses her recollections of the almoner, in fact, to help her play the role of the other in a debate within herself, and it is not only the almoner's words that have been 'taken in' but her attitude and her responsiveness to dialogue. Yet Mrs. R. was unable to cry again, and we are reminded of the importance of the real presence of a responsive person in helping us to experience and face previously unacknowledged feelings.

27. 2. 60.

Mr. Renton was responding a little to drug treatment. It was decided that he should have radio therapy to his head and neck. The prognosis was later extended to about a year. From 27. 2. 60. until discharge on 10. 4. 60. Mr. Renton received a number of visits from the almoner and these were summarised in the following way.

Mr. R. was at first too ill to talk very much and interviews were kept very short. Gradually, his own personality and his ways of coping with life in general and his illness in particular became apparent. He appeared to be a mild man, with a marked lack of aggression. He had struggled to keep going in the last few months without complaint, but had finally resigned himself to dying, showing consistent concern for his wife. In fact he seemed persistent in subjecting his needs to hers.

At first he found it difficult to accept the almoner's concern and he tended to change any conversation about himself to less threatening subjects, such as hospital procedure. He became emotionally distressed at any mention of his wife. Gradually, however, he was able to talk of his physical discomfort and his wish to die, to have it all over and done with. He said he had given up hope for the future, but could console himself because he had made provision for his wife.

As treatment continued he became more alert and he was able with encouragement from the almoner to begin to face the prospect that he would not die immediately. He discovered with her his renewed wish to live and then his fear that the improvement would not last. However, he began to make plans and the almoner encouraged him, sometimes going through each phase step by step.

Meanwhile Mrs. R. was receiving help through her own interviews with the almoner. She told the almoner about her strong feelings of being unwanted which dated from her childhood. She recalled how astonished she had been when an attractive girl friend of whom she had been very fond died suddenly, leaving her the unattractive, unloved one alive. She was next able to express a strong fear of recurring, incapacitating headaches, and her inability to cope with them. The almoner suggested that it was very important for her to control what happened to her, and that it must seem very frightening if she could not control things. This lead Mrs. R. to talk of her fear of possible mental deterioration in her husband and in herself. She responded to the almoner's realistic consideration of the facts.

The decision to give Mr. R. treatment and thus prolong his life was a shock for his wife. The almoner recognised that this would mean prolonged uncertainty and sacrifice for her. Once Mrs. R.'s feelings about this had been expressed she was able to move towards planning in the light of the new prognosis. At first, Mrs. R. determined that she would devote herself quietly to her husband and give up her participation in a full social life. The almoner questioned the realistic basis of this, suggesting that Mrs. R. might well feel she ought to act in this way as a return to her husband for loving such a person as she felt herself to be. Mrs. R. was able to work towards a more balanced outlook giving weight to her own needs as well as being able to modify aspects of her previous way of life in her husband's interest.

27. 4. 60.
Final interview. Mrs. R. gave the almoner a present. She seemed to be more relaxed and confident in herself and encouraged by Mr. R.'s unexpected progress. She reviewed past events clearly and thought that she would be better prepared to face the next crisis. She was extremely grateful for casework help which she saw as a new kind of experience. The almoner emphasised the part Mrs. R. had played.

The case of Mr. and Mrs. R. illustrates a number of important features of medico-social work. Firstly, much of the work is short-term. This emphasizes the importance of establishing realizable goals with the client without seeming to rush him into a quick decision. Secondly, work is best carried out through co-operation between the medical and the social work personnel. Thirdly, one of the most important aspects of hospital life is that of uncertainty and change of plan. In this case Mr. and Mrs. R. had first to accustom themselves to the death of Mr. R. and to deal with the wish that it was in fact already accomplished. Then they had to readjust to the fact that death had been postponed. In working through these problems of role they were helped to recognize some of their full dimensions by the almoner's encouragement of the expression of feeling and her ability to stay untroubled in the midst of considerable feelings of aggression and death.

Finally, the case helps us to see the significance of a particular illness to one particular family. The illness threatened the equilibrium of a marriage that had since the death of an only child maintained a compensating satisfaction in a combined and successful business. For Mr. R. the impending death was at first acceptable, and Mrs. R. initially worked on the assumption of his death. Mr. R.'s continued existence as a person with a terminal illness, in fact, made Mrs. R. face some of her feelings about her premature assumptions of his death and his illness. The illness seemed to signify her husband's disintegration (physical and mental) and her own, and also to question her own ability to control herself and the situation. The almoner's calmness and her response to Mrs. R. 'as a whole person' were important aspects of the successful handling by Mrs. R. of these problems. The almoner's work with her client proceeded at a pace that did not threaten Mrs. R.: a focus was maintained without the client feeling restricted, and the almoner helped Mrs. R. to build her strength on a real basis, encouraging her to explore the situation realistically. Many aspects of Mrs. R.'s personality and of the marriage were deliberately left uninvestigated and some aspects were only partially treated. Thus, Mrs. R.'s aggressive denial of her husband's sexual needs was not taken up for consideration, though Mrs. R. was helped to channel some of her aggressive, masculine drives on to the consideration of the situation facing her husband and herself.

THE MEDICAL TEAM

In the Renton case we saw co-operation between the almoner and the doctor. Working with other hospital personnel is a characteristic of medico-social work, and almoners place considerable emphasis on the hospital team. As in other branches of social work it is sometimes difficult to avoid the impression that the idea of the team is used as a means of changing rather than describing the real situation. Quite often the team simply does not exist and the almoner has an important task in securing co-operation from hospital personnel. This is as important a part of her work as direct casework with patients or rather the former is often a crucial aspect of the latter.

Mr. Leonard had a successful operation for the amputation of his right leg. However, his post-operative behaviour on the ward proved difficult and the sister 'phoned the almoner and said that Mr. L. should be seen. 'He's being most unhelpful. He's one of yours alright.' The almoner called at the ward sister's office as soon as she could. Sister hoped that she had come about Mr. L., but doubted what the almoner could do. She supposed the almoner would make it out to be a childhood problem, but there was nothing they could do about that on the ward. People had to be treated as adults. The almoner asked sister to help her by explaining the kind of problem Mr. L. was creating. She said she could see that sister was doubtful whether anyone could do anything. Sister said his behaviour was most aggravating. He kept on playing the nurses off against one another and he was verbally very cruel to the other patients. Sister said that she could cope with most things but she just hadn't the time to work this sort of thing out. 'We're very busy you know.' The almoner commented with a laugh that she was probably making sister feel even more pressed for time: sometimes perhaps sister wondered which was worse, the almoner or the patient she came to see. Sister laughed and seemed to relax. She sat down and the almoner said that Mr. L. was obviously quite a worry to sister. Sister agreed, and she and the almoner discussed the patient for a short time. Later the almoner saw Mr. L. and had a series of interviews with him. His behaviour was largely an attempt to avoid facing the implications of the operation. He was being sadistic to others because he was afraid of facing his feeling that others had been sadistic to him. He was also avoiding the depressive feelings that normally accompany loss whether of a loved person or a physical part of oneself. The almoner helped him, firstly by showing him where he was attempting to be sadistic towards her and pointing to some possible reasons for this. Later she supported his gradual approach to face his depression and sustained him through a period of 'mourning' for his lost leg. During this period she also saw the ward sister from time to time, helping her to prepare for possible changes in Mr. L.'s behaviour when he became depressed and to see his increasing quietness less as improved behaviour and more as a sign that he was beginning to face some very painful problems. The help Mr. L. received from the nursing staff was an important factor in the ultimate success of a piece of casework.

In this case the almoner gave direct help to Mr. L. by avoiding the role of victim that he wished to force her to play and asserting her role as a helping person who was not afraid of Mr. L.'s hostility and could help him to understand it. She also helped the ward sister, though it could not be said she became her caseworker. She recognized the anxiety behind sister's rather brusque, controlling attitude and tried to establish effective communication with her by showing that she could see that some of the feelings towards Mr. L. sometimes overflowed on to those who might try to help him. She did not rush to interview the patient, but spent some time with the sister encouraging her to give her view of the situation.

On other occasions, of course, it is the medical staff who create problems that hinder full co-operative work by the team.

Take, for instance, Dr. K. who asked the almoner to see Miss B. who kept on coming to out-patient clinic with minor complaints. 'She's a complete neurotic. I think she needs a good talking to. You see her and I don't want any of this "supportive" stuff. You try and stop her coming to see me. She keeps on coming.' The almoner said that she would be interested in seeing Miss B. but the doctor was rather tying her down to a particular course of action. Why did he feel so sure that a good talking-to would work? The doctor asked what the almoner meant by 'tying her down'. He was not the sort of man who just issued instructions, but nonetheless he wanted the damned woman seen. The almoner said that she did not want to complicate matters, but she thought that they should try to see what she should do for the patient. The doctor became more angry and said that surely the almoner could manage to do that much for herself. The almoner began to feel angry, saying that she had not made an unreasonable request, adding spontaneously that she was not Miss B. This remark brought the argument to a stop and the doctor began to laugh. He said he could see that Miss B. did make him angry and what annoyed him most were her continual demands for advice. The almoner had by now become calmer and she and the doctor were able to discuss the crucial features of the case, using what had occurred between them to increase their understanding of the kind of feeling Miss B. aroused in others.

In this case the almoner attempted to establish a working relationship by refusing to carry out the doctor's fiat and standing by her position in the face of his anger. The almoner naturally experienced the force of the doctor's criticism and began to feel and show her own anger. No one would advocate this as a 'technique' to be applied in every situation of this kind, but by showing an immediate human reaction the almoner stimulated a response from the doctor which eventually helped them both to understand both their own situation and the patient/client's.

These two illustrations emphasize the team-*making* aspects of the almoner's work. They show that casework in a multi-disciplinary setting is not a simple, once-for-all acceptance of the 'limitations' of an agency, but a matter of the continual refurbishing of the worker's intentions and the extension of her abilities in facilitating the work of others. She has to recognize hostility, apathy and misplaced enthusiasm in herself and in others, understand their significance and mitigate some of their more disabling effects. In some ways she can be considered as one of the hospital's most sensitive mechanisms for feeding back to its personnel information that will correct, maintain or enlarge the ways in which a particular patient is being treated. This means that she will at times appear to be siding now with the patient and now with the doctors, and in the face of misperception she must hold up for herself and others a consistent picture of her place in multi-disciplinary practice and facilitate the imaginative and appropriate use of her knowledge and skill. As Bartlett has suggested, 'Multi-discipline practice is a way of thinking, of keeping ideas related; a way of feeling, of readiness to share; and a way of doing, of adding one's contribution to that of others so that something larger emerges from the combination. It is a constant interweaving of all these phases of professional activity.'[18] The almoner has an important part to play in encouraging the development of this kind of co-operative work, but it is not, of course, her exclusive concern. Like the caseworker in any setting she must appreciate that those who are not social workers can often gain an imaginative and just view of a situation intuitively, immediately and sometimes almost gratuitously.

Miss Geraldine M.

The following case illustrates two important aspects of the work of an almoner: help to patients who are in difficulty over management of their affairs because they occupy the role of hospital patients, and help through referral to other agencies once hospital care has terminated.

Miss M., aged 48, was in hospital for six weeks during which she had chemotherapy for thyrotoxicosis. She had an illegitimate son, John, aged 10. She referred herself to the almoner on her first day in hospital to clear up a point in regard to her National Assistance. She was an ambulant patient and the series of four interviews took place in the almoner's office. The first interview has already been discussed in chapter one.

Miss M. came before her next appointment was due with another query relating to her National Assistance. She took up some time during this interview in a recital of her troubles with the Assistance Board again. She had been having some investigations of her physical condition and recited her conversation with the doctors in great detail. The almoner felt the object of this was again to stress her worth by showing how well disposed they were towards her.

The almoner related this to the little Miss M. had told her of her past circumstances and her illegitimate son John. This led to a great flow of words. She said what a wonderful child he was, how he had not passed into a grammar school, but she did not mind this because she realised there were other opportunities open to boys these days and she felt it was because he had had such a lot of upset owing to her different illnesses. She then spoke in rather less detail of these other illnesses and this brought the subject back again to John. She said she was only waiting for the day when he would grow up and be able to go out to work, and she could lean on him.

The almoner indicated that she could see how she would need some support in this very difficult period in her life and that perhaps she felt she was not getting it now from anyone. This led again to a spontaneous rush of words about her sisters and her mother. Apparently the whole family felt that it was a tremendous disgrace for her to have an illegitimate child. The father was a ship's engineer who had died before he could marry her. Her mother had been apparently bitter about it, and Miss M. felt that in all these years she could have helped her very much more than she in fact had done, e.g. she had refused in the beginning to look after John when she was coming into hospital this time and it had taken a great deal of persuasion by an outside authority before she would consent to this. John is happy with his grandmother and therefore she is glad that he has gone there. The almoner tried to give Miss M. an opportunity to expand on the mother's attitude, but she was not willing to take it and turned instead to talking about her sisters.

The four of them are married, all to men in very good positions. One is divorced but has a very comfortable life because she has three sons who support her. One sister has two children and lives abroad with her husband. She has another sister who takes very little notice of her. She spoke most of all of another sister who is married to a doctor, and spent a lot of time telling the almoner how they took holidays abroad and what a beautiful home they had etc. In all this, her own feeling of inferiority and partial rejection by them came through clearly. She was concerned to say she could go to live with this sister, but did not wish to because their household was conducted in rather a haphazard manner and she liked order. She has stayed there before for several months, but found herself doing all the housework as they were without a maid at that time. Also she felt that John was victimised compared with their own children.

At the end of this interview, she said she had found some relief in talking, and was able to expand on this to the extent of saying that it was because she knew whatever she told was confidential and that the almoner was detached from the situation. A further appointment was arranged.

Miss M. clearly wanted to see the almoner again, but found it necessary to excuse her request for help by presenting a query about National Assistance. It might perhaps be considered that this 'masked' her real problem or was a superficial symptom of a deeper problem. Yet if we consider what she first discussed we see that in fact it expresses a *miniature* of one of her main problems— feelings concerning her lack of worth. She was unsure that the almoner would want to see her 'in her own right', so she produced a query and talked about her treatment at the hands of other helpers. The almoner did not relate this to what the client was feeling about her present interview, but connected the importance of the doctor's good opinion to Miss M.'s feelings about her illegitimate child. Miss M. found this a helpful remark and began to express her guilt concerning the effects of her ill-health upon him. The almoner apparently made little comment about this, but widened the focus of the interview by asking about the support Miss M. might expect to receive at the present time. This led the client to talk in some detail about her family, giving particular emphasis to the disgrace of her child and her ambivalent feelings towards her mother. In general the client presented herself as someone unsure of her own worth and usually victimized or insufficiently helped by others. Anxiety is, of course, a general feature of her medical condition, but in this case it would appear to be complicated by long-standing personality and family problems. These are given some emphasis in the following interviews.

3rd Interview.

Again she came in with a query relating to her National Assistance and the almoner stressed to her that, if she appeared to find talking about her feelings about her past and present circumstances helpful, she was very happy to see her on that basis, as that was part of her function in hospital and also that it could have a benificial effect on her medical condition as the doctor had himself suggested.

Quite spontaneously, she went on to tell more about her early life. Her father had been a man in a good position and all the children had been given a good education and high ambitions. It seemed that money and social status were the goals held up to them and she feels she is the only one who has not achieved them. The almoner asked her whether she felt other things could be as important as the ones she had mentioned.

She then began to talk about a letter she had received from her mother and how disappointed she was that her mother had not come to see her in hospital and very rarely visited her at her bungalow.

She felt that her mother always had this hard and unfeeling attitude towards her and had never in fact been like a mother to her at all. She enjoys being in hospital because everyone here is so kind and it is more like a home to her than any other place has been. The almoner wondered if she could think of any reason for her mother's attitude and she said that it was because she had always been her father's favourite and her mother had always been jealous of this. She described how her father would always stick up for her against her mother and how when he died it was she who had been by his bedside and she whom he had asked for. She felt that her mother had never been able to forgive her and that her mother had felt that she had taken her father away from her. She resents her mother for her lack of affection towards her, but at the same time realises that she has also strong positive feelings towards her mother. She described with some emotion how intensely she wanted her mother's affection and how she had never stopped trying for it and how in a way she had done more for her than any of the other children, and yet her mother had never responded and there seemed no way that she could get through to her. The almoner asked whether she felt her mother had ever helped her in any way and she said she was very fond of John and although she appeared at times to resent having him yet she would do all she could for him. The almoner tried to help Miss M. to look at her mother as a person with problems of her own and as someone who wanted to love her daughter probably as much as she wanted to love her mother.

Miss M. was quiet for a little while and then said very thoughtfully that she had never been able to express her feelings towards her mother to anyone like this before, in fact she had never been able to talk of her mother in this way. She realised that she had wanted John in order to have something of her own to love which she felt she had never had. The almoner tried to show her John as a person, too, who needed freedom to develop in his own way as she had needed it, and that by demanding too much from him, she might lose the love that he had to give her. She remarked that perhaps leaning on him was not such a very good idea after all, that she would have to face the fact that one day he would want to get married and would owe his first allegiance then to his own wife.

She was again quiet for a little while and then remarked that she thought she might go to live with the sister who was divorced. Apparently this sister had asked her to go and live with her before, because she was very lonely and felt that she could give her the comforts that she did not have in her bungalow.

The almoner wondered what Miss M. felt about this and helped her to express some of her feelings towards the sister, remarking that Miss M. seemed to have found it helpful to look at some of her feelings towards members of her family. She also wondered if Miss M. had considered whether she would like to be put in touch with a voluntary social work agency when she left the hospital. Miss M. was not sure about this, but remarked that the social worker was kind to suggest it. Perhaps there were others worse off than she was; what would her sister think? The almoner suggested that Miss M. would not find it easy and reminded her of her feelings about being humiliated by the N.A.B. and how she always had to bring some query or other to 'justify' her approach to the almoner. The almoner said that perhaps Miss M. would think it over: the almoner wanted her to feel there was someone to whom Miss M. could turn for help if she herself wished to.

In this interview the almoner began by attempting to show Miss M. that she did not have to bring a practical query as an excuse for coming and that a discussion of her feelings was perfectly appropriate within the hospital setting. This seems to have encouraged the client to talk about her feelings towards her mother in what was apparently a new way. This showed the almoner some of the main springs of Miss M.'s personality development, but her attempts to help the client to delineate both her mother and her son as 'real people' should not have been expected to succeed in such a short space of time. The client was rather hurried towards facing this reality. The almoner recognized that the client required help over a longer period than her hospital stay and suggested referral to an appropriate social agency. This suggestion should, however, have been considered more carefully within the context of the interview. The client had said that she had unburdened herself of her feelings as she had never done before and the suggestion of referral is likely to signify in terms of unconscious fantasy that some of her communications to the caseworker have been so frightening or so bad that the almoner thinks she should take her problems elsewhere.

4th Interview.

Miss M. called to see the almoner the day before her discharge and argeed to referral, rather too enthusiastically in the almoner's opinion. Miss M. said she was sure things would be better and she thought that perhaps she had been a bit silly in some of the things she had told the almoner. The almoner said that now Miss M. was going she wondered perhaps what the almoner thought of her. Miss M. laughed this off. She said goodbye to the almoner in rather a rushed way. Leaving a box of chocolates on the table on her way out she shut the door quickly behind her. The almoner followed and said that she wanted Miss M. to know how grateful she was and that she felt Miss M. had been able to work out some of her problems.

Miss M. contacted the voluntary agency soon after her arrival at her sister's home town. She appeared to be very depressed and to feel she was making no progress. She wondered how the almoner was getting on. She said the almoner had helped her while she was in the hospital, but now she was outside things were very different. The worker asked how she felt the almoner had helped and Miss M. mentioned the talks she had had about her mother and about John, but now she felt helpless. The worker said that she felt sure that Miss M. had been helped and she wanted to help Miss M. to build on what she had accomplished with the almoner.

In this case the almoner attempted to help Miss M. with her lack of self-value by asserting her continuing interest in her 'in spite' of what she had done, by showing that she was interested in Miss M.'s feelings on certain important topics and by helping her to review herself in roles other than those of patient and applicant for help. She encouraged the client to consider herself in the light of values other than that of social status and economic achievement and implicitly valued these other qualities in Miss M. It might perhaps seem at first sight that the client's problems were explored in a way that was not really relevant to her medical care and treatment. Yet the questions the client were asking were concerned with managing the transition from her valued hospital role to those roles she would have to play in the outside world. How could she support herself when she felt humiliated by the National Assistance Board? How could she resume her role as John's mother when she seemed to need a dependent role herself? To help her to answer these questions the almoner endeavoured to give her support in a way that was not humiliating, and to review the others in her environment towards whom she might play a dependent role. She helped Miss M. with her own feelings as a mother by considering with the client her own relationship with her mother, conveying that mothers were 'real' people with problems and needs as well as high expectations.

The almoner also attempted to help her client through referral to a family casework agency. This should certainly have been considered, but insufficient attention seems to have been paid to formulating the kinds of problem with which Miss M. might expect some help. The almoner's understanding of the case was far from complete and, though the outcome of her own contact with the client was beneficial, it could be argued that it might have been handled more purposefully. This general criticism applies to the treatment of the question of referral also. Referral is a complex process, which has been given insufficient attention by social workers.[19] This is surprising in view of the fact that most social work is referred either from other disciplines or from other social workers. In considering referral it is important to acknowledge its significance to the client, and to the worker, and to appreciate some of the resulting difficulties in the handling of the process. In the case of Miss M. there is little direct evidence about the attitudes of the social workers to the referral. The almoner has seen it as a means of meeting the client's need for a dependent relationship and appreciated some of her client's feelings on being referred. Apparently her client felt 'bad' and rejected and the almoner discussed this with her to an extent. At her first interview in the family casework agency, Miss M. expressed her depression and her feeling that the help she had received was no longer sustaining her. The 'good' she had received from the almoner was, as it were, still in the hospital. The family caseworker was able to acknowledge that Miss M. had received some real help from the hospital: Miss M. did not have to deny this as the price for receiving help from her new worker.

THE ALMONER AND THE GENERAL PRACTITIONER

The almoner works mainly in co-operation with doctors within the hospital, but sometimes she accepts referrals from general practitioners. In a few specialized and research settings an almoner is attached to a group of doctors in general practice. This is a new development in medico-social work which has direct relevance for the recent growth of social work in local authority health and welfare departments.[20] The first interview with Mary (aged 14) illustrates the kind of work an almoner might do in a case referred by a G.P.

> *Nov. 1960.* Mary was referred for help with choice of employment after she left school in July 1961.
>
> *Medical Situation*
> Diagnosis: Lympheedema praecox—a glandular dysfunction; origin not fully understood.
> History: Persistent and gross swelling of both legs since 1957. Left rather worse than right. Investigated in Department of Child Health 1958, and advised to wear elastic stockings. Treated in Department of Plastic surgery 1958–9, and followed up by that Department since then. Child's health has never been good—attacks of broncho-pneumonia regularly every winter in addition to usual complaints. Also subject to boils, septic fingers and urinary infections.
>
> *Referral.*
> Had made up her mind to be a nurse and very upset when surgeon disapproved. Second choice was hairdresser or beauty parlour technician. Family doctor disapproved of this as she would be standing all day. Mother wanted her to go into an office and was prepared to pay for commercial training. Mary's reaction had been that nobody was going to make her do anything she did not want to do. Mother and daughter getting very angry with one another. Mother and surgeon also at cross purposes over question of elastic stockings. Family doctor thought that any plan which depended on co-operation between mother and the hospital was bound to fail—which was why he had not referred child to almoner at the hospital where she attended Out Patients.
> The almoner sent a letter to mother asking if Mary might come for interview after school. Mother replied to say she would bring her.
>
> *1st Interview.*
> Mother and daughter arrived promptly. They were very alike in appearance, short and heavily built but with good skins. Very light brown hair and quite attractive features. Both had the same habit of pulling down one corner of the mouth and raising the opposite eyebrow as a preliminary to any reply.
> The almoner thanked Mrs. B. for taking the trouble to accompany her daughter, but suggested this might not always be necessary. Mrs. B. replied that of course she would always come with her. Mary

almost shouted, 'You never let me do anything by myself.' This started an argument between the two about unsuitable friends, coming home late from youth clubs, being too tired to attend in school and then doing badly, the importance of a good start in life. The argument consisted of accusations by the mother and vociferous denials by Mary. The almoner intervened in the argument at the stage of 'having a good start in life' to raise the point of the referral.

Mrs. B. started off again with her ideas of what would be best for the girl, that she should stay at school for another year and take English and Arithmetic, also shorthand and typing at O level and then go to commercial college for six months. Mrs. B. worked for a firm of chartered accountants where she was supervisor of the clerical and machine operator staff, and thought she could get a job for her daughter without difficulty. Mary meanwhile was keeping up a chorus of 'Shan't stay at school.' 'Shan't work in an office.' 'Nobody else's mother is as fussy and interfering.'

Eventually Mrs. B. came to the end of her resources whereupon Mary commented, 'that's all now, she's got that off her chest,' and the almoner asked her what she would like to do by way of working. She did not know, but hastened to add she was not going to be pushed around by anybody so the almoner need not think she was going to interfere.

The almoner suggested that as one had to work for a living it was worth getting something as enjoyable as possible and using any help towards this end that was available. One source of help was the Youth Employment Bureau who would be visiting the school shortly and there might be something the almoner could do if she would tell her what sort of things she had in mind. Mary replied 'Nobody wants me to do anything I want to do—he laughed at me when I wanted to be a nurse, and Dr. D. says I can't be a beautician.' The almoner said it must be hard when her suggestions were treated in this way and she asked what sort of qualities and qualifications she considered people needed to be nurses. Mary mentioned all the obvious ones which she considered she had in good measure. The almoner wondered about passing exams, and showed her two exam papers from the hospital finals; and physical strength. She agreed that she was no good at familiar work where people had an advantage over her, but she was good at new things when they all started together, but perhaps she might not be able to take the exams. It would be like not being able to take the 11+ and then it would all be wasted. No—perhaps nursing was not a good idea—but did the almoner think her legs were never going to get better? The almoner said Mary was obviously worried about her legs and it was important to find out what she could manage. She asked how much she could walk about without getting pain and how much better they had got in the last year. The almoner said that it was a quarter of a mile from the office to the operating theatre and back, so what did she think about a job where she would be running about or standing all day. Mary grunted —that's the worst of grown ups they catch you out all the time. Almoner wondered if there was anything at all that she liked doing.

Mary volunteered that she had a 35 millimetre camera and belonged to the camera club at school and at the youth club. She knew that there were photographers who worked in hospital and did the almoner know anything about it. Almoner suggested she went to the Youth Employment Bureau and got their leaflet on the subject, also that she asked the schoolmaster who ran the camera club if they would be learning to develop and print their own films. If G.C.E. was a basic requirement for that job would she feel any differently about staying on at school? Mary said she would see.

Arranged that almoner should speak to Youth Employment Officer for her school, that Mary should call at the Bureau and that almoner should meet her again in a fortnight.

Next Day.

Long discussion with family Doctor. Mary had been to see him and now wants to be an almoner. He had explained that would mean a long training, but why not concentrate on clerical work perhaps with a view to being in an almoner's office. She had seemed quite interested in this proposal. Family doctor agreed that any plan for girl would involve treating mother as well, but admitted he could not see where to start resolving the problem.

Telephone conversation with Youth Employment Officer—newly arrived in this district so unable to make constructive suggestions, and gave impression that she resented Almoner having anything to do with the case. She would be visiting school at Christmas so agreed to postpone almoner's second discussion with Mary until next term, by which time she will also have seen surgeon again.

Letter to surgeon in time for Mary's appointment asking if there were any special points to be considered in choice of employment. This letter was not acknowledged—an almost unprecedented occurrence for that department. This interpreted by almoner as confirming family doctor's statement that mother antagonised the surgeon.

The almoner was asked to help over Mary's choice of employment, but it is clear almost from the first moment of contact with her that the almoner is witnessing some crucial aspects of Mary's whole life. Her mother will not allow her to have a separate interview and cannot tolerate a discussion of her daughter's viewpoint until she has given her views. Clearly, the almoner is cast in the role of mother, but she attempts to avoid this by suggesting the realistic problem they might work on together—Mary's choice of work. This is, of course, limited both by her intelligence and by her illness and these limitations have to be discussed in a way that does not emphasize the discouragement Mary feels her own suggestions about work have already received. The almoner is not as successful in this part of the interview, since she leaves Mary feeling defeated by an adult's cleverness. This is of considerable importance to Mary's sense of her own value and of her own control over her life, since she must feel that her illness has really put her in the control of others more knowledgeable than she is. However, she seems to have obtained a good overall impression of the almoner judging from Mary's identification in wanting to become an almoner herself. An important part of the almoner's work on cases like this revolves around her knowledge of the social services and the way she interprets them to the client so that he or she might use them more effectively. In this case the almoner both encouraged Mary to seek help herself on technical details and also paved the way for her approach by direct contact with the Youth Employment Service.

What plans might the almoner make on the basis of the information she had? Mary is attempting to equip herself for an adult role in society, but she is handicapped by a particular disease and by a mother who seems to want to keep her in the status of a minor, dependent and cosseted. Her mother has apparently antagonized others who have played a helping role towards her, but, once she has been allowed to voice her opinions, she can 'allow' her daughter some discussion with the almoner. In fact, the interview seems almost to have been two interviews, the first with mother and the second with Mary. What requires testing is how far Mary can feel that what is discussed and decided in 'her interview' is also acceptable to her mother. The almoner has started to differentiate herself from the mother, and it remains to be seen if she can tolerate this person 'different' from herself and yet forming a relationship with Mary. The attempt to separate mother and daughter was unsuccessful and should probably not be repeated, since a willing separation is likely to come at the symbolic climax of helping rather than at its circumstantial beginning.

THE ALMONER AND THE LOCAL AUTHORITY

Comparatively few almoners work in a local authority setting, but their casework is of considerable importance in view of the general extension of local authority social work. Of particular interest is the problem of the identity of the function of a social worker in a local authority health service. There is no general Act of Parliament to administer, as in the Child Care Service, and arrangements or health services vary from authority to authority. Yet our society is gradually extending its care for the handicapped, even if some groups of handicapped people (e.g. the blind) seem able to evoke a greater response of sympathy and help than others. The general social function of a welfare service for the handicapped would be to express a just concern that all the handicapped should participate as fully as possible in the life of our society. This necessitates entry into the different worlds of each main kind of handicap and facing whenever necessary the handicapped person's shame and withdrawal, fear, hostility or denial. The functions of the welfare officer would seem to consist in carrying out the policies of his department in the light of this general attitude, which would be consistently held and not subject to the ambivalence often characteristic of social opinion towards the handicapped. The kind of work envisaged can perhaps be seen in the case of Mr. W.

George W. (aged 40) was referred to the local welfare department by the police who had received telephone calls from neighbours. The male welfare officer called at Mr. W.'s home and discovered the following information: the client lived with his mother (aged 70), a vigorously active woman who looked after her son well and was indignant that neighbours could have thought she needed help. Mr. W. suffered from T.B. hip; he had been admitted to hospital for an operation, but had discharged himself because he hated being on a ward. He had two brothers who were happily married and lived outside the locality. The officer expressed understanding of Mrs. W.'s feelings and these were in fact soon overcome because she was relieved that someone had come to talk about her son. She admitted that he had been depressed recently and supposed that some neighbours might have become worried about this because a man had recently created a great deal of disturbance in the neighbourhood before he had been admitted to mental hospital. She then told the officer he could go up and see George in his room.

Mr. W. was suspicious at first, but responded to the officer's interest. His hip was extremely painful, though he had carried on working until his recent admission to hospital. The worker asked what plans he had for any further treatment. Mr. W. looked very resentful and the worker said he was not there to persuade him to return to hospital, but he did wonder how long Mr. W. could continue like this. Mr. W. said that he had been very afraid of being cut open and went on to talk of his fears of madness. The worker asked if he had been in touch with any psychiatric services, but Mr. W. said he had not. The worker suggested that perhaps Mr. W. would like to be put in touch with them, but the client retorted that he thought the officer had said he had not come to persuade him to go to hospital. After further conversation about his work record in the past the officer agreed to call again in a fortnight's time.

This contact began well and some aspects of the situation can already be seen. The client is suffering considerable pain but this seems preferable to admittance to hospital which is associated with cutting open and thus exposing what is really (internally) wrong with him. This internal 'badness' seems to be equated with madness, and it is the realization of this which causes the worker to swerve away and mention the psychiatric services. This confirms the client's fantasy that his 'inside' madness frightens people away when they see it. Mr. W. appears to lose some faith in the worker.

In the interviews that followed, however, the worker, who had been able to see the loss of *rapport* in a supervisory session on the case, began to help Mr. W. to face some of his fears. Mr. W. had a basic fear that he was a failure; he seemed to be highly intelligent, but he had failed his degree examinations and ever since had followed occupations that did no justice to his capacity. He was afraid of illness and sudden death and he felt abnormal because he was unmarried and because of his disability. The worker maintained a consistent interest in Mr. W. and was not alarmed by his increasing despondency. Mr. W. complained of his loneliness, but blamed himself for this: he would use his friends until they would give no more. He reacted to the worker in much the same way and the worker helped him by showing that, though he could only give Mr. W. an hour a fortnight, within that hour he used all his attention and ability to help him. Gradually Mr. W. responded to the worker's concern and showed some relief that his pattern of using his friends had been broken without the loss of the worker's regard. The worker encouraged Mr. W. to talk about and later to test out some of his intellectual capabilities and continually mirrored back to his client a confidence in his potentialities. At the end of the sixth visit Mr. W. himself introduced the subject of hospital treatment. He was later readmitted to hospital where he underwent a successful operation. He required a great deal of help after this, but both he and the worker could derive confidence in later discussions by looking back at this accomplishment and trying to assess what had made it possible despite all the obstacles.

NOTES

[1] Gray, Dr. C., 'Treatment of Phthisis: State or Charity?', *Charity Organisation Review*, July 1902.

[2] Quoted in Cummins, A. E., 'The Selection and Training of Hospital Almoners', *Year Book of the Hospital Almoners Association*, 1933.

[3] Snelling, J., 'Social Work Within Medical Care', *The Almoner*, Vol. 15, No. 3, June 1962.

[4] Rees, H., *A Survey of Hospital Almoning*, Institute of Almoners, 1941.

[5] Parsons, T., *The Social System*, Tavistock, 1952, pp. 436–7.

[6] Titmuss, R. M., 'Science and the Sociology of Medical Care', *British Journal o Psychiatric Social Work*, Vol. III, No. 4, 1956.

[7] Menzies, I., 'A Case-Study in the Functioning of Social Systems as a Defence against Anxiety: A Report on a Study of the Nursing Service of a General Hospital', *Human Relations*, Vol. 13, No. 2, May 1960.

[8] Quoted in Marx, L. C., 'Early Days', *The Almoner*, Vol. 6, No. 8, Nov. 1953.

[9] Quoted in Edminson, M. W., 'The Middle Period, or Episode Two, 1914 to 1939', *The Almoner*, Vol. 6, No. 8, Nov. 1953.

[10] Snelling, J., op. cit.

[11] See also Ullman, A., 'The Role of the Social Worker in Teaching Fourth-year Medical Students', *The Almoner*, Vol. 12, No. 10, Jan. 1960; McNicol, J., 'The Role of the Almoner in the Teaching of Medical Students', *The Almoner*, Vol. II, No. 11, Feb. 1959.

[12] Quoted in Roberts, E. L. and Lindsay, J. S., 'The Mental Hospital: Structure, function and communication', *British Journal of Medical Psychology*, Vol. XXXV, Part 2, 1962.

[13] Title of a chapter by Coser, R. L. in Apple, D. (ed.), *Sociological Studies of Health and Sickness*, McGraw-Hill, 1960.

[14] For a fruitful discussion of the reactions of a particular group of mothers see Woodward, J., 'Notes on the Role Concept in Casework with Mothers of Burned Children', *The Almoner*, Vol. 14, No. 2, May 1961.

[15] For a general discussion of casework in this situation see: Player, A., 'Casework in Terminal Illness', *The Almoner*, Vol. 6, No. 11, Feb. 1954. Pearson, N., 'Casework in Terminal Illness in Great Britain', *The Almoner*, Vol. 6, No. 4, Feb. 1954. Birley, M. F., 'Terminal Case', *The Almoner*, Vol. 13, No. 3, June 1960.

Notes

[16] One of the most frequently debated issues in almoning has, of course, been concerned with the systems by which cases are referred to almoners. Does the almoner take work referred from doctors and other hospital staff, or does she attempt to see all admissions or all patients suffering from certain diseases? For a discussion of these issues see: Bate, H., 'Referred Work Only', *The Almoner*, Vol. 10, No. 8, Nov. 1957.

[17] Bartlett, H., 'Frontiers of Medical Social Work', *The Almoner*, Vol. 15, No. 6, Sept. 1956.

[18] Bartlett, H., *Social Work Practice in the Health Field*, National Association of Social Workers, 1961, p. 73.

[19] A useful beginning has, however, been made in *The Family, Patients or Clients— A Study of Co-operation in Social Casework by Almoners and Family Caseworkers*, published for the Family Welfare Association by the Faith Press, 1961.

[20] See Shaw, L. A., 'The Need for Social Casework in the Setting of a General Practice', *Case Conference*, Vol. 1, No. 5, Sept. 1956; Dongray, M., 'Social Work in General Practice', *British Medical Journal*, Nov. 15th, 1958; Clyne, M., 'Almoners in General Practice', *The Almoner*, Vol. 14, No. 9, Dec. 1961; Collins, J., 'Looking a Gift Horse in the Mouth', *The Almoner*, Vol. 16, No. 4, July 1963.

Chapter Six

CASEWORK AND THE PROBATION OFFICER

CASEWORKERS often describe their 'clients' in general terms as 'people who come to a social agency for help'. They place a high value on ideas of self-determination and acceptance, as we have seen, and they aim at regulating their work to the client's own pace of learning and change. In supervising offenders, however, the probation officer has to work within the time limit of the probation order (between one and three years) and with 'clients' who (if they are over 14) have consented to probation only perhaps because of a more frightening alternative. How far can the probation officer be characterized as a caseworker? Can a helpful and significant relationship develop between the officer and probationer through what is frequently described as casework in an 'authoritarian setting'?

The probation service still appears somewhat divided about its identity. Some officers see themselves as caseworkers who, as it were, simply happen to work in a court setting; some prefer to think of themselves as court officers, while others echo the suspicion of casework voiced in a study of the service still in popular use, 'it is the element of friendship in probation or in any kind of social work that produces results, not "case work" '.[1] Some of these opinions reflect the historical development of the probation service which began in the voluntary work of the Church of England Temperance Society. The first police court missionary was appointed in 1876 and statutory recognition came with the Probation of Offenders Act in 1907. The service, thus, had a dual origin in voluntary missionaries who 'believed in the supreme importance of the individual to God, and (for whom) the parables of the lost-sheep and the prodigal son were ... casework manuals',[2] and, secondly, in the position of statutory officers of the court.

126

This twofold origin created some tension within the developing service and probation officers were sometimes concerned to reconcile a helpful, 'friendly' approach with their official status. A probation officer in 1915, for example, stated that 'Unbending the official attitude must be done at the right time in the right way. An attempt at a nearer approach to some people may be misunderstood and invite familiarity. This must be avoided at all costs.'[3] One way out of this dilemma was to consider the probation officer mainly as a source of referral to other agencies. This seems to be suggested, for example, in a publication of the National Association of Probation Officers in 1935: 'There are two good rules for a probation officer to follow in coping with his work: one is to avoid giving money, and the second is to consider whether there is another agency already existing to perform the service which he is asked to render.'[4] Such an approach was in accordance with the Probation Rules issued ten years earlier which instructed that in the case of those under 16 the probation officer 'shall endeavour to secure his connection with some organisation for the care and protection of the young, such as a Sunday School, club, association of boy scouts or girl guides . . . and other similar movements'. (Rule 43, 1925).

Before the Second World War the probation service maintained an existence apart from the rest of social work. Since the war increasing emphasis has been placed on the common elements of casework and within this context the work of the probation officer has come to be seen as casework within a particular setting, the 'authoritarian' setting of the court. Thus, the Morrison Committee on the Probation Service declared in 1962 that 'To-day, the probation officer must be seen, essentially, as a professional caseworker, employing, in a specialised field, skill which he holds in common with other social workers.'[5] Yet the nature of this and other specialized fields has not been fully explored. Some probation officers are convinced that it is insufficient to describe their work as casework in an authoritarian setting, since some at least of their methods differ from those used in other casework agencies.[6] A considerable bulk of probation work is, of course, not concerned with offenders. In 1960, officers in England and Wales dealt with 25,892 matrimonial cases in which it was necessary to see both partners and a further 17,506 in which only one partner was seen. Pollard has recently suggested that 60 per cent of all marital cases come to the probation officers on the initiative of the client.[7] Other probation officers have described their work directly as a form of psychotherapy.[8] Some have no hesitation in referring to their probationers as clients, whilst others agree with the Morrison Report that 'when applied to an offender who has been placed on probation this term (client) is "inappropriate since it obscures the disciplinary aspect of probation by suggesting that the offender's approach to the social worker is wholly voluntary"'.[9]

Perhaps the most economical and useful description of the probation officer is that he is the court's social worker. In pursuing social inquiries, for instance, he is contributing to the court's work by presenting the results of his social work investigation. It is in the interests of both the court and the offender that the decision on disposal is based on all the relevant facts and attuned as far as possible to giving the offender the best chance to reform. There are, of course, special features in the probation officer's appraisal; he does not give the court his 'raw' diagnosis, but attempts to communicate its content in a manner appropriate to the purposes of the court; in this, as in many aspects of his work, the caseworker in the court acts publicly in a way that has few parallels in other forms of casework. Yet it is precisely because he is the court's social worker that he can appreciate the significance of these special features. A characterization as the court's social worker can be applied to each aspect of the work, to supervisory duties in connection with the Children and Young Persons Acts, to aftercare (which is increasing in range and importance), to matrimonial work and even the comparatively large amount of miscellaneous and voluntary work. (For example, in 1960 probation officers in England and Wales saw, 11,830 cases categorized as 'advice concerning difficult children'.) The work of the probation officer clearly covers a wide range and there seems to be no end to the process of accumulating more work as the service develops. In this chapter it will not be possible to illustrate each kind of work, but special aspects have been chosen because of their significance for the discussion of the functions of the probation officer.

CASEWORK WITH THE PROBATIONER

The probation officer is essentially involved with the personnel and the purposes of the courts. The personnel are judicial, law-enforcing and custodial and the probation officer is brought into contact with them not least because he often acts in the role of mediator between the offender and society. He has also to establish his own separate identity and functions, and this often constitutes one of the crucial problems of the setting. One extreme solution is for the caseworker to submerge his own separate identity with that of the other personnel of the court, whilst the opposite extreme can be found in the probation officer who unconsciously encourages his clients in their defiance of authority or who splits himself off from the rest of the court so that his own relationships with the client can remain 'uncontaminated' by authority. The officer's task in establishing his own professional identity is sometimes complicated by the unconscious projections and defences of magistrates and police. Some magistrates, for example, seek to avoid making a considered decision in each case by placing whole classes of offenders on probation, while police officers sometimes adopt attitudes which encourage various confused ideas about probation. Yet, in spite of these and other tensions, the probation officer remains the court's social worker no matter how ambivalently the court personnel may feel towards him nor how incorrectly it perceives his functions. It is in fact part of his task to help magistrates etc. to allow him the conditions for good work, at the same time as he learns to appreciate and value in them processes and roles which are not, and should never be, those of the social caseworker.

The court and its personnel pursue certain broad purposes, the protection of society and the reform of offenders in the light of the principles of justice. How does the work of the probation officer accord with this? It has been suggested that in fact 'the probation officer belongs to a team, each member of which has a different function—the Police have the duty to catch criminals, Magistrates to administer justice, Clerks to advise on the Law and keep the records. The probation officer alone is concerned primarily with the welfare of the individual'.[6] Elliot Studt in a recent survey of the field of corrections in America[10] refers to the teamwork obligations of workers in that field. The concept of 'the team' is attractive to social workers, as we have already seen in chapter five, and in some ways they might be described as a profession in search of a team. At first sight the idea of the court as a team appears somewhat fanciful. Are the strategies employed by each group of personnel part of the same 'game'? Can these strategies, in fact, be sharply divided from each other? Should the probation officer sometimes see his task as that of a 'contest' with other personnel, in which he pits his knowledge and skill against theirs in much the same way as lawyers struggle against each other in the court? Such questions indicate that the idea of a team cannot easily be applied to the courts, but we should also recognize that the courts are also expected by society to extend mercy and the chance of rehabilitation to an increasingly wide group of offenders. In fulfilling this social function the courts are assisted by the probation service which becomes part of 'the team' by attempting to understand the offenders on whom the court wishes to make a decision or on whom a decision has already been made.

The court is concerned to protect society, but it is also charged with showing mercy and offering to the offender where appropriate the chance of rehabilitation in his own eyes and in the sight of society. In extending this opportunity to the offender the court may make a probation order and thus originate a period of casework help. This has three main characteristics. It begins with a court order made after the offender's consent has been obtained (if he is over 14); the order imposes a time limit on both probation officer and client and, thirdly, it lays down certain broad injunctions. These characteristics will now be considered in more detail.

The offender's consent can often seem to be a mere acquiescence in the face of a feared and unknown alternative. It is frequently dismissed by commentators as a mere Hobson's choice. Alternatively, it is suggested that virtually no client in any social agency is 'free from compulsion, since it is the pressure of their needs and their inability to meet them unaided which oblige them to seek help'.[11] Both views require examination. The dismissive approach suggests that because a choice is made in very restricting circumstances it is not a choice, or that because of the pressures of the situation it is not a decision that the '*client*' has made. Yet much of the early stages of probation may well be concerned with helping the client to explore and stand by the meaning of the consent which he undoubtedly gave. The second view, that no client is free from compulsion, rests on a confused idea of motivation. To say someone is 'obliged' to seek help through pressure of need is simply to point to the fact that someone is strongly motivated to

receive help. It is not to support the contention that their purposeful action was somehow unavoidable. The offender like any other
applicant *could* refuse help; the probationer like any other client
has gone some way towards accepting (albeit with many reserv-
ations and unresolved doubts) a commitment.

The following case extract illustrates the importance of the
probationer's consent:

> The court had made a probation order for two years in the case of
> Roger D. aged 17 for breaking and entry into a number of factories.
> The probation officer was able to see him for a short time im-
> mediately after the court hearing.
>
> Roger sat on the edge of the chair and smiled nervously. The
> officer suggested that perhaps he was wondering what it was all
> about. No, said Roger, a few of his friends had been on probation
> and he knew what it was like. The officer wondered what picture of
> probation he had. Roger smiled and said he didn't really know; it was
> difficult to say. He supposed he would have to report and all that.
> The officer said that the order that had just been made concerned
> Roger, and he would like to explain what it meant. Roger said that
> the judge had said it all. The officer explained that the order really
> concerned both of them and he wanted Roger to know what it was
> all about. Roger sat back in his chair and seemed a little more
> relaxed, but he kept looking at his watch. The officer explained the
> order and asked what he felt. Roger said, it was alright, but he knew
> it all anyway. What was the use of going through the motions? The
> officer remarked that he could see that Roger was feeling angry at
> having 'to go through the motions'. Roger thought it didn't really
> matter, he had to come and listen. The officer said that Roger was
> feeling that he had to submit to whatever the officer decided to do,
> but that was not in fact what he had chosen. He repeated his ex-
> planation of the order and hoped that they could work some of these
> things out. They would have to stop now, but he arranged to see
> Roger in a week's time.

The probation order imposes a time limit on the casework
process. Such limits are not, of course, unknown in other agencies.
Many clients in hospital have in fact to receive some help in a very
brief period of time, though the actual time limits are often unknown at the beginning of the case. Some agencies have attempted
to set a time limit in agreement with the client on the exploratory
phase of casework. This has been a particular feature of those
agencies in America that have been influenced by the Functional

School of Casework. In probation, however, a fixed period is imposed on officer and client alike, though it is always possible for application to be made to the court for the order to be discharged before its term has run. The time limits imposed by the order have at least two general consequences for casework with the probationer. Firstly, it emphasizes the importance of setting a goal which is realizable within the time in hand. Secondly, the time limit itself can be studied and used as an aid in helping the probationer.

The case of Maurice D. (40) illustrates the first point. He had been placed on probation for theft in connection with his bouts of drinking. The fifth interview took place when the officer called at his lodgings to discuss Mr. D.'s failure to keep a job.

> Mr. D. said that he would like to say how much he had thought about the last interview. He was sure his present troubles were to do with his past. He knew his sister would have told the probation officer all about it, but he would like to explain himself. The officer said he would be interested to hear. Mr. D. explained that he had been brought up in a household containing his mother and father, his maternal grandmother and three sisters. His father had been wrapped up in his work and was seldom at home. Mr. D. was sure that if his mother was alive he would not have committed the offences. He used to be terrified of his grandmother who had been blind but had always been convinced he was doing something wrong. He recalled how his sisters (and particularly the one with whom he was now lodging) used to belittle him. The probation officer began to ask questions about Mr. D.'s childhood and both officer and client were soon involved in a long and detailed recital of past history.

It is possible to see Mr. D.'s account of his past as a way of avoiding the hard unpleasant facts of the present. Clearly, a knowledge of the past is relevant and often essential, but it is always important to reflect on the reasons why a client chooses to talk of his past, to emphasize now this and now that aspect of its many facets. As Mr. D. spoke he revealed many problems which could have become the focus for work with the officer—Mr. D's lack of opportunity for full identification with his father, his unsatisfactory super-ego development in so far as his actions seem to have been guided not so much by his own views of what should be done, but by what pleased his mother or saved him from his grandmother's rebukes. These are problems of considerable com-

Casework with the Probationer

plexity and the probation order is for one year. If the officer is to help Mr. D. to some achievement, however small, within that period it is essential to come to grips with some of the problems in the present (work, drinking, lodgings), though these will always be seen within the context of his own history.

In some ways, of course, the decision to make a probation order of a particular duration is an arbitrary one, and both officer and client may have to struggle in order to accept it. It is important that too much is not expected and that the length of time required before some agreement is reached with the probationer as to the particular objectives of the work is not underestimated. The establishment of the officer's helpful intent in the face of a considerable negative transference from the offender's remote and recent past may be a lengthy process. Some writers have spoken of the aim of probation in rather global terms. Minn, for example, has suggested that 'by the time the period of supervision has been completed the person should be self-dependent'.[12] This is a large aim and one wonders what self-dependence would be for a man like Mr. D. It is perhaps preferable to consider self-dependence not as a direct aim, but as the by-product of a process which aims at helping a person to solve certain problems, whilst learning to live with aspects of their lives which it would be optimistic to describe as problems.

Mrs. F. (46) an intelligent middle class woman recently widowed, was placed on probation for two years for shoplifting. After a period of resentment against the probation officer, Mrs. F. formed a warm attachment towards her. Towards the end of the probation order she told the officer of the long afternoons she had spent in some of the larger London stores. She would stay until nearly closing time and then buy something, usually not anything she wanted, and then come home. She was firm in her belief that she would not steal again, but the probation officer said that if she ever felt like it she was to get in touch with her. Mrs. F. did not respond immediately to this, and spoke about some of the things she had talked of previously and of how much more there was to talk of. Later she recalled a book she bought for her young niece, a story for every day of the year and once you had finished, you could always start again at January 1st. 'It was comforting but exhausting and also somehow frightening—it could go on for ever.'

In this extract the client is clearly struggling with feelings about

133

the fact that the term of probation is nearing completion. She has perhaps been testing herself out by spending long periods in the shops, but the officer shows alarm at this rather than emphasizing its positive aspects; she offers the possibility of further help in a limitless future. This possibility does not help Mrs. F. to try to work out an essential feature of the function of the probation service, its time-limited characteristic. This is, more often than we have perhaps appreciated, a positive factor which can be used to help the client come to terms with all that it represents. In order to achieve a helpful use of time, however, 'one must first have come to grips with it in oneself, otherwise the limitations it introduces as a therapeutic agent are unbearable and what the therapist cannot bear in and for himself, the patient cannot learn to bear either'.[13]

The third characteristic of casework with the probationer (that it begins with an order laying down certain broad injunctions) is often referred to as the most important aspect of probation work. The subject has been widely discussed under the heading of 'casework in an authoritarian setting', and it requires special treatment.

CASEWORK IN AN AUTHORITARIAN SETTING

'Probation officers must never forget that they represent authority and so to inadequate parents are a reminder that society expects them to shoulder their responsibilities. . . .'[14] There are perhaps three main aspects of authority that should be distinguished in any discussion of the subject in relation to social work. We should ask, what is the social worker authorized to do by the agency and by his or her training; what does the client authorize both implicitly and by specific consents; and how does the client perceive the worker and the agency, (for which authority figures in the client's past do the agency and the worker stand?)? If this threefold classification is adopted it will be apparent that the quotation at the beginning of this section embraces too large a version of authority and perhaps confuses the clients' perceptions of general powerfulness with authorized power. Probation officers do not 'represent' authority in this way; they are authorized to secure the probationer's adherence to the general and particular conditions of the order and to take action if the probationer fails. An examination of the conditions will show the extent of the officer's authority.

The general requirements of a probation order usually take the following form: the probationer is required to lead an honest and industrious life and/or be of good behaviour and keep the peace; to inform the officer at once of a change of job or address; and to keep in touch with the officer in accordance with his instructions, allowing home visits if the officer wishes. In addition special requirements can be imposed; for example, that the probationer is not to associate with particular persons or that he should receive medical treatment. In some respects these conditions do not appear onerous, but they impose restrictions that an adult would not have had to observe since he was a child. His minority status is perhaps emphasized by the fact that the general requirements are vaguely defined and that a great deal depends on the definition given by his probation officer. On the other hand, the officer will interpret them in the light of the individual offender's needs and show that this interpretation springs from his concern for his client and not from a desire to wield arbitrary power. If the conditions of the order are broken a great deal still depends on the officer's judgment, since he will try to assess the significance of the breach of probation before deciding whether it should be reported to the magistrates. The probation officer is formally given authority over a probationer by the court's order and the client's consent, and in the event of a serious and meaningful breach of the order the probation officer may have to bring the probationer before the court and prove his case. Yet the exercise of authority is tempered by the discretion allowed to the officer and by his concern to use his authorized powers for his client's benefit.

Grace, aged 9, was on probation for persistent truancy from school. She had two younger sisters and a brother of 3 years of age. Her father was a man of changing moods, usually showing extreme anger or a love that could deny the children nothing. Grace was brought before the court on a charge of truancy: she often stayed away from school to go to the cinema, with money pestered out of a rather ineffectual, depressed mother or wheedled out of father. Clinical examination showed Grace to be of high intelligence, and she was placed on probation for two years. At first, she was very silent in her interviews and the probation officer provided drawing materials and encouraged her to draw and talk about what she was drawing. (The aim of this was more effective communication and not an attempt at play therapy). Gradually Grace became more relaxed and the truancy lessened considerably. Grace became more assertive with the probation officer. She began to miss her interviews with the officer who warned her that if this continued she would inform the magistrates that a breach of the order had been committed. Grace still failed appointments and began to stay away from school again. The officer informed the magistrates and the magistrates decided that the original order should continue in view of the officer's report on previous progress.

In the interview after the hearing Grace was her old withdrawn self. The officer suggested that Grace had not really believed that she would be brought back to court. Grace said nothing. The officer said that it might look as if they were both back at the beginning again, but Grace knew really that she was not a frightening giant person (giants had figured in the more recent drawings), though she did mean what she said. She had brought Grace back before the court because what happened to Grace mattered to her. Grace smiled slightly.

Many details have been omitted from this extract (including some interviews with parents and the content of Grace's own interviews) in order to emphasize the use of authority. This was a case in which the main focus of work was on the child. The officer found the father extremely elusive and the mother used what energy she had in simply maintaining the existing pattern. Work with Grace was, however, still family-centred, in the sense that Grace's problems could only be understood as those of a child trying to learn ways of living and of loving in her particular family. What seems to have been helpful in the probation officer's approach?

Grace's problem of authority was clearly important. In her family there was no one who could help her to develop inner control by presenting a reasonably consistent authority which enforced orders because of a concern for the child. Authority figures in her home were either powerless or arbitrary; they could nearly always be manipulated and in fantasy must have appeared as fiercely destructive or as already destroyed. The probation officer played the role of a sympathetic, encouraging person who understood that Grace might well be afraid of her, possibly treating her as an arbitrary, frightening, powerful figure. The officer gave her a means of communication that she could use and gradually Grace came to feel safe. She then began to test out the officer, obviously working out whether or not she could manipulate her as she did mother. The officer maintained a consistent attitude and held Grace to the order and thus to reality. In reporting the breach the officer had to face the fact that Grace might have been sent to an Approved School, but she was also able to report to the magistrates on the good progress achieved. When she saw her after the hearing she spoke about some of Grace's possible feelings. This was important, since her objective was not simply to control Grace's behaviour: it was to help her by means of a relationship with a person, who had some authority, to reconcile her own feelings that authority was either arbitrary power or something that could easily be manipulated. The probation officer represented authority only in the sense that she was sometimes perceived by Grace as one of her own authority figures. The probation officer used her fairly limited authorized powers in order to help Grace. After the resolution of this phase of help it may well be that Grace will herself authorize the probation officer to help in other aspects of her life. The most important generalization illustrated by this case is that the exercise of authorized power can be itself a helpful measure for the client. In this respect it is impossible to agree with those officers who see 'the central problem for the probation officer in relation to his clients (as) the reconciliation of the authoritative and the therapeutic aspects of his work'.[6] The probation officer like other social workers will not, of course, always be able to help people. Some will find it difficult, if not impossible, to take help from someone vested with authority, yet we should not make the distinction between the 'authoritative' and the 'therapeutic' aspects of the work too emphatically. The probation officer does not try to help, on the one hand, and, on the other, behave in an authoritative manner. He often tries to help through the exercise of some of his authority.

This authority can be helpfully exercised in two main ways:

(i) by demonstrating that a person in authority can be helpful, understanding and not punishing, destructive or possessive;

(ii) by setting limits in order to relieve internal and external pressure through the provision of support, and to help the client towards greater self-control.

The client comes with certain experiences with figures of power and authority in the distant and in the very recent past. He may have had cruel or inconsistent parents or no one who helped him through the exercise of their authority, and he has certainly had recent experiences with police, magistrates etc. The probation officer may very easily appear just another in a long line of 'bosses and bullies'. Gradually, the officer by his attitude, by the way he treats his client will try to demonstrate his difference from them. He still has authority, but he will try to show and prove that he can be trusted, can come to be accepted as *an* authority for the particular client.

One of the ways of helping from a position of authority is to set limits to behaviour. Take the following case:

> Mr. B. (20) was placed on probation for three years, being convicted on a charge of carnal knowledge of a girl of 15. A baby was born to the girl and B. was made liable under an affiliation order. The probation order carried the special requirement that B should reside where directed by the probation officer. B's history indicated that he had had an unhappy childhood, having had poor health and living with an extremely promiscuous mother. He was said, however, to be capable of good conduct when under strict supervision.

B has had several changes of home and has twice changed his name. At the time of conviction he was living with a man, Mr. Z, who was hoping to develop B's powers as author and wrestler.

At first, the probation officer was concerned to break the relationship between Z and B and to ensure that B did not see the girl. He came to appreciate, however, that this double 'embargo' placed too great a strain on B, who was allowed to see the girl and encouraged to prove himself and to plan for marriage in two years' time, if this is what they both wished. Meanwhile, Z moved to another part of the country and asked the probation officer for permission for B to join him. The officer recorded his interview with B on this subject:

> Upon being advised of Z's letter B at once made it clear that he had no wish to join Z. At the same time he was sensitive enough to wish not to offend Z and asked that when I wrote I would make it appear that I was forbidding the association. I advised B to be practical and to face up to reality so that he might now decide to make the final break. He would not consent, however, and asked for permission to spend Whitsun with Z. It was again pointed out that quite apart from renewing a dangerous association he would be wasting money he really owed to the girl: the arrears were now £16.

Shortly afterwards the following meeting between B and the probation officer was recorded:

> I saw B standing on a street corner not far from the office and learned from him that he had not intended to call upon me. In the short time it took to walk to his 'bus stop I was able to tell him that I was not at all happy about his present attitude, which was one of impudence as well as indifference, and I instructed him that, come what may, he must report Friday next when his future would be discussed at length. He was asked to think over his present position in which he was virtually homeless, hopelessly in arrears in his affiliation payments and liable to be recalled to Court for that failure and, having ignored a recent instruction to report to me, was endangering his freedom under the Probation Order. His future prospects looked bleak indeed and his present attitude gave me little confidence in his future.

These two extracts illustrate different ways in which probation officers might try to control behaviour, to set limits. Clearly, the officer in dealing with B's association with Z is focusing attention on an important problem. B has had experiences which have made him unsure of his identity and of his potentiality to evoke love and affection. It is possible to view his relationship with the girl both as a search for affection and for reassurance about his masculinity. He seems to have had no stable masculine model in his life, and this emphasizes the importance of the probation officer. B is still in some conflict about Z. He wants to break the relationship but seems to be ambivalent. The officer attempts to ally with the part of B that wants to break away. He attempts (in both interviews) to influence B not by forbidding, but by pointing out the consequences in reality—the consequence to B and to his plans for the future. In the second interview, however, he makes more personal charges against B, stating that he is impudent, etc.

From these two interviews we can, I think, draw some conclusions about setting limits and making rules in casework:

(*a*) we often attempt to influence clients by pointing out, and helping them to grasp, likely consequences of their intended actions;

(*b*) these are best seen in the light of reality to which both officer and client are subject rather than as personal orders to the client;

(*c*) if rules are made they should obey certain conditions. They should be based on the knowledge that some other way of satisfying need is available (in a sublimated or modified form); their purpose should be explained; and they stand best chance of success when they can be used to support one side of an ambivalent feeling. It is, however, important to appreciate, and help the client to grasp, that rules in this context are applied to behaviour and not to feelings. The probation officer in the interviews above could usefully have explored Mr. B's feelings about the officer's attempts to control his behaviour and to encourage him to learn to control it more effectively himself.

So far, we have considered the probation officer as the court social worker and as a caseworker in what is often described as an authoritarian setting. Are there any general statements that can be made about his clients? Perhaps the most positive judgment that can be made on the present state of research into the causation of delinquency is that it encourages a multi-factor approach. This is in accordance with the heterogeneous nature of crime, which can cover a vast range of behaviour from the trivial theft to the calculated murder. Consequently, no useful generalization can at present be made about the offender as such. The probation officer cannot expect offenders to reveal similar characteristics of personality, heredity or environment. Sometimes it is the material environment that will seem to provide the predominant pathogenic force. At other times the probation officer will wish to concentrate his efforts on building-up the offender's means of coping with his impulses and in such cases the probationer may need 'a living rather than reliving experience'.[15] Yet, there is one important generalization that can be made about the probation officer's clients in so far as they are also offenders. They have all been subject to the processes of law, to arrest, arraignment and sentence. In no other branch of social casework do we have to meet and help people who have been so publicly exposed and so formally punished. We may in other fields encounter people who have fantasies of this nature, but nowhere else do fantasy and reality so nearly coincide. Take, for example, the man of 40 placed on probation for a sexual offence against a young girl, who says to his probation officer on their first meeting after the court:

'Well, what are you going to do for me? I've had my punishment, the publicity, the court and now I'll have to face you every time. How can I live it down?' The officer says that he is there to try to help the man to leave all the past behind. Mr. C would report to him every two weeks and he would be very pleased to talk over things that might be worrying him.

The officer in offering help tried to present some kind of contrast to the man's recent experiences in court. Yet it might have been more useful before talking of the future to (so to speak) stay with Mr. C. in the present and help him to assimilate what has been going on by first of all explaining and recognizing his feelings. In that short extract Mr. C. presented a number of possible openings:

'What are you going to do for me'—is the officer seen as just another in a series of officials Mr. C. has recently encountered, who have encouraged him to feel in the hands of, and subject to, people? 'How can I live it down'—what does Mr. C. want to live down? Who makes him feel most ashamed? Mr. C. is also reacting to a situation in which he is given the status of a minor—an adult who has to report regularly to someone in authority. One way of dealing with this uncomfortable situation is to define it exclusively in terms of a painful procedure to which one simply has to submit, making it clear at the same time that no good can come out of meetings with the officer. Thus, the client admits he is controlled, but his definition of the situation quite effectively controls the probation officer. Mr. C.'s method is in fact commonly employed by those who are afraid of what meetings with a caseworker might disclose. Such clients are, however, emphasizing one of the general functions of the probation officer (the control of a probationer's behaviour in order to prevent further crime) at the expense of the other general function (extending help to the offender to rehabilitate himself in his own eyes and in the sight of society's representative).

CASEWORK WITH MARITAL PROBLEMS

Historically, it is possible to identify three separate approaches to the problems of helping marriage partners. The first approach, that of emphatic intervention and advice can be illustrated from the following comments of a woman probation officer earlier in the present century: 'When I get them together it is just a matter of tact and advice. If there is a question of persistent infidelity or real brutality I do not attempt to hinder the girl from obtaining what redress the Court can give her.' With other cases the welfare of the child was her 'strongest card'.

> Out of my Police Court experience I draw a picture of the child's probable fate if bereft of mother or father in the way they contemplate; I point out, too, their own probable fate. The temptations to which each will be subjected, and the accumulating responsibilities that may ensue. I relate cases where prison has been the ultimate consequence. And when I have got them in a frame of mind to try again, I try and get them better rooms. If it is mother-in-law, I go and see her and talk to her as a mother myself with a grown-up son and daughter. If it is domestic training, I go down to their home on a Sunday morning and show her how to cook a cheap and simple meal. . . .[16]

This shows the brisk concern of the convinced activist in human affairs and it is perhaps not surprising that the next phase in the development of casework with marital problems showed a marked reaction. This was the stage of neutral clarification, as we can see from the following quotation: '(Marital casework has) developed slowly from an early idea that legal separation of husband and wife should be avoided at all costs, to the present technique of pointing out the various paths open to both parties and leaving them to decide the course which they will follow.'[17] We are now entering a third period in which emphasis is being given to the task of understanding the nature of the marital relationship. This approach avoids the two extremes possible under its predecessors (too much help aggressively applied, on the one hand, and too little help, on the other), and is based on a fresh attempt to understand each marriage in the light of certain psychodynamic principles. These three phases, it should be noted, probably succeeded each other in the temporal order noted here, but it would, of course be impossible to say whether any approach was held by the majority of officers at any particular time. Nor should it be assumed that the progression has simply been an uninterrupted progress from inferior to superior forms of help. Each phase has made an important contribution within the service and, as a theorist of the present psychodynamic approach has stated, 'Technique cannot be considered without reference to the setting in which it is practised.'[18] In fact, the handling of marital problems should be based both on a study of the nature of marital relationships and on a clear view of the function of the agency offering the help.

A fruitful view of the marital relationship can perhaps be based on an exploration of some relatively simple ideas. In the first place, it is important to look on a marriage as deeply purposive. This is partly a question of acknowledged expectation (sexual satisfaction, a reasonable home etc.), but of greater importance are the unacknowledged purposes in all marriages, including those that seem to be unsatisfying or unsatisfactory. The application of this idea of purposive behaviour to most aspects of marriage has been economically expressed by one of Snow's characters in the novel, *Homecomings*.* At one point in this book Lewis Eliot reflects on his 'unsatisfactory' marriage to a mentally disturbed woman:

> There was a lot of chance, I knew, in human relations; one cannot have seen much unless one believed in chance; I might have been luckier and got into a relation less extreme; but, on the whole, I had to say of myself what I should have said of others—in your deepest relations, there is only one test of what you profoundly want: it consists of what happens to you. (p. 49).

What kinds of purposes do we envisage when we talk of marriage in this way? Clearly, one of the most important purposes is the establishment of a relationship in which one can love someone of the opposite sex and be loved by them in return. Marriage is thus concerned basically with difference (one loves someone who is different from oneself, sexually and in many other ways) and with giving and receiving in a relationship of close, physical intimacy. The idea of loving and being loved requires, however, a further dimension if it is to be rescued from sentimentality. Dennis,[19] in a recent review of the sociological evidence on the state of marriage in contemporary Britain, has pointed to an apparent contradiction between the growing popularity of marriage and an increasing inter-changeability of role between men and women, together with a tendency to find some of the main satisfactions of marriage (e.g. sexual fulfilment) outside its boundaries. He suggests that the explanation of this contradiction is to

* Published by Macmillan, 1956.

143

be found in the fact that marriage alone offers the adult in our society a relationship in which he can be accepted and involved *as a whole person*. This sociological observation can be applied to the main purpose of marriage and we can speak of the ability to love and be loved as a whole person. The psychoanalytical approach can help to deepen this idea. A 'whole' person is not simply the person seen as he presents himself in all of his relationships (or as many as we can humanly grasp at one time), but also those aspects of his personality which he regards as bad, destructive and worthless and which he struggles to disregard or to disown. In marriage:

> these rejected, disowned parts . . . are very often projected on to the other partner, who just as often accepts them and uses them in accordance with his own inner needs. . . . The crucial, and from the standpoint of offering help, the positive aspect, is that in marrying, the partners have also attempted to 'make contact' with and to love these disowned aspects of themselves.[20]

Marriage is a relationship in which the partners can enjoy the closest physical and emotional intimacy since their own infancy, and it marks at the same time the final stage in their evolution towards social maturity—the establishment of a separate and in some senses exclusive 'household'. Because of this it engages the personality at the deepest levels and Oscar Wilde was essentially correct in observing that 'marriage is hardly a thing that one can do now and then'.[21] The personality is deeply engaged in a number of important areas. In the first place the individual is confronted by another whose responses to his personality and to his body must impinge on his own conceptions of himself and on his body-image. Secondly, his relationships with his parents are involved both in the active present and also in a reactivated form. Some of the inevitable feeling involved in establishing an independent 'household' can perhaps be best illustrated by reference to Desdemona's speech to her father in the first Act of Othello:

> My noble father,
> I do perceive here a divided duty:
> To you I am bound for life and education;
> My life and education both do learn me
> How to respect you; you are the lord of duty,—
> I am hitherto your daughter; but here's my husband
> > Act I, Sc. III, 182–7.

Such feelings of divided loyalty may fairly easily be admitted, but feelings arising from the reactivation of early childhood experience are bound to be more difficult to appreciate. 'At both conscious and unconscious levels, husbands and wives transfer on to each other feelings for the important people of the past, and unresolved conflicts from these earlier phases of development are thus likely to be stirred into life again.'[22] This is particularly important in view of the concept of the 'whole' person advanced earlier. Marriage represents a stage in social maturity, but it is also an institution in which each partner wishes to feel safe enough to express childish aspects of their personality without this resulting in destruction of themselves, their partners or the marriage.

So far we have been considering marriage mainly from the point of view of the individual partner. It is, however, the interaction between the partners that gives each marriage its own individuality. In considering this interaction we have moved from a position of assigning blame to one partner or the other, through categorizing a marriage in terms of the personality of each partner (e.g. a dominant woman married to a submissive man), to a position in which we examine the ways in which partners 'collude' with one another in maintaining a certain kind of marriage or ways in which their respective definitions of their roles 'fit' together to form a certain kind of unity. This 'fit' is often difficult to discern, but it can be found in many aspects of the day-to-day lives of married people. Take, for instance, the case of the couple who maintained an unorthodox way of transferring money from husband to wife. Each Friday evening the husband would return home from the public house with a sum of money in his wallet. He and his wife would go to bed, but when he was asleep she would get up and take the money from his jacket. Neither of them spoke about this arrangement to the other and yet the sum of money was always the same. Here we can see an illustration of the concept of 'fit', and also of the way in which one couple played out the theme of giving/taking which was mentioned earlier as one of the most important aspects of marriage. This man and woman had complementary needs in relation to giving and taking; he had difficulty, it would seem, in giving and she in receiving, but both could tolerate a situation in which one stole from the other.

These, then, are some of the psychodynamic notions recently used and developed (particularly by the Family Discussion Bureau) in understanding the marriage relationship. In some ways they are quite simple ideas, but their simplicity has probably been exaggerated by the necessary brevity of this account. They are not offered as a final solution; indeed, their application often leads to a depressing realization of the complexities of any marriage relationship. They constitute, however, a useful beginning. Marriages are complex and 'men and women are infinitely ingenious in their ability to find new ways of being unhappy together',[23] but the ideas outlined in this section provide some means of beginning to grope towards their understanding.

These ideas have been developed largely in a specialized agency with considerable resources in the way of psychiatric consultation and a trained staff. This agency has, however, also been concerned with helping social workers in other settings (e.g. probation officers, psychiatric social workers etc.) to apply this understanding to their own work. We should consider, therefore, not only this psychodynamic approach to marriage, but also the different settings in which it is to be applied. In our present context this is, of course, the probation service.

Matrimonial work in the probation service consists partly in conciliation cases at the request of the courts and partly in work with people who come directly to the probation officer or indirectly through referral (e.g. by the police). A recent study of the matrimonial work of the probation service suggested that there was little difference between the two groups in regard to success achieved in the conciliation attempts. Referred cases were as likely to be successful as direct applicants for help. This perhaps encourages us not to make a rigid demarcation between the two groups, but, from the point of view of function, it is important to discern the nature of any differences.

In so far as the probation officer is concerned with matrimonial cases referred by the courts (either when the wife applies for a summons or when the couple have appeared at a hearing of the domestic court), his position as court social worker suggests that such work is properly part of his function. In fulfilling this function, however, it is important that he distinguishes clearly between his own task and that of the magistrates, and between a social work and a legal process. The applicant referred from the court may well feel cheated or forced into a position in which he may find himself agreeing to what he does not really want. In such circumstances the officer must carefully regard and respect the client's legal position and make it clear that he is neither giving legal advice nor appraising the applicant's grounds for a summons: his task is to discover what marriage problems exist, what solutions have been attempted, and how far the applicants have considered or are prepared to consider alternative plans. He must seek authorization for conciliation directly from the applicants.

The actual procedure of investigation and of conciliation has traditionally consisted in the probation service of single interviews with each partner and then a third interview in which they are seen together. The assumptions underlying this procedure of a fair hearing and a judicious pronouncement appear legal in character, and it is questionable how far such a procedure is conducive to the understanding of the marriage necessary either for a legal decision if the case came to court or for conciliation.

How far does the role of the probation officer as a court social worker also apply to the considerable body of matrimonial work with cases that come directly to the probation officer? It seems that the general social function of the officer is similar to the one he fulfils in the supervision of offenders—he offers on behalf of society a second chance; he and the institution he serves are there to conserve and protect. As probation officer he occupies a special place in matrimonial work, standing at the point at which couples appeal for help to those they feel are in authority outside the marriage. However the matrimonial case reaches the probation officer the immediate issue is often one of action, impressive and public. In trying to help such marriages the probation officer holds the balance, not in the sense of assigning blame, but as one who stands for the marriage: he is not blind, like the figure of Justice, since he attempts to see the good and the bad, the destructive and constructive forces. He persists in the effort to understand the marriage and represents society's concern at any implied or actual marriage breakdown.

In this section an attempt has been made to present some important ideas about the psychology of marriage and the function of the probation service in marriage conciliation. Much work has still to be done since we are only at the beginning of our understanding in each of these areas. A particularly fruitful line of inquiry would be one concerned with the place of religious faith in both client and caseworker in each kind of marital counselling.

It is interesting to note that in Pollard's study[24] 40 per cent of the (560) probation officers regarded a strong religious faith in the officer as an important factor in the success of matrimonial casework.

The following case extract will illustrate the growth in the understanding of a particular marriage by a probation officer as he attempted to fulfil the functions of his agency.

April 1962

Mrs. Frank came to see the probation officer one Monday morning on the advice of the police. She had gone to the police station in a panic on Sunday evening after her husband had stormed out of the house, flinging down the carry-cot containing their six-month-old baby whom he had been unable to console. He had also struck his wife and she had a black eye as a result.

Mrs. Frank was a small woman, discretely and neatly dressed and displaying an outward appearance of considerable composure. The officer asked her to tell him what had happened. 'It's all finished, of course; all broken-up and what I want you to do is to help me sweep up the pieces.' This sounded rather like a prepared speech to the officer, who asked Mrs. Frank what she thought he could help her to do. She was silent for a moment and then said her mother had mentioned something about a separation. The officer explained the legal position. He said he could see Mrs. Frank wanted to do something about the situation; perhaps it would help her to see what she might do if she told him what had happened. Mrs. Frank described the scene as the culmination of a series of quarrels which had been getting worse since the baby (George, named after his father) had arrived. There had been tension after the arrival of Edwina (aged 3), but this last baby had seemed to make things much worse. She said she did not care if Mr. Frank came back or not, but he'd left them without any money. He'd put on his jacket as he went out and his money was in it. The officer suggested Mrs. Frank must feel very angry at being left to cope and yet perhaps she missed Mr. Frank also. Mrs. F. said she could manage very well on her own: her mother had managed on her own and so should she, but what was she to do about money? She had nothing. The officer said that it seemed as if she somehow felt she *ought* to be like her mother, though she wondered if she could. Perhaps she felt her mother had been through a great deal for her. Mrs. Frank launched herself into a long account of her mother's struggle to bring up her two brothers and herself despite the apparent efforts of her father to sabotage her work. She described her father as a weak man who attempted to assert himself by occasional outbursts of temper. It was only when he was in a temper that he gave the children the impression that he was actually there. His fits of temper became more frequent and more violent and in the end the parents separated when Mrs. F. was about 14. Mrs. F. said she could not recall ever feeling for him and concluded by suggesting that the probation officer could see that she had not a very high opinion of men. Without waiting for any comment she wondered why she had been saying all this. She had come because she wanted some action and all they were doing—or rather all *she* was doing was talking. The probation officer said that Mrs. F. was concerned about what she had been saying, and that perhaps her low opinion of men extended also to himself, since it looked as if he did not know what he was doing. Mrs. F. fixed him with a critical eye and asked if he did. The officer said that Mrs. F. was feeling angry. Mrs. F. interrupted with an emphatic denial. The officer said that the idea of anger was perhaps upsetting to her and wasn't this perhaps an important factor in the present situation? Mrs. F. said nothing, but sat back in her chair a little. The officer said that Mrs. F. did want something done and he again described the legal position about application for a summons. She must make the decision, but he thought that she might also like to consider other ways of trying to solve the problem. Mrs. Frank said that the officer ought to see her husband: it wasn't fair that she should have to go through all this. The officer said he would very much like to see Mr. Frank. He explained the confidential nature of the interview, but Mrs. F. brushed this aside, saying that the officer should do what he thought best. She seemed by now to have lost a great deal of interest in the interview. The officer said that it was also a question of what she and her husband wanted. Mrs. F. seemed to brighten a little at this and it was arranged that the officer would write to Mr. Frank. It emerged that Mrs. Frank knew that in all probability her husband would be at his mother's.

Three days later Mr. Frank was seen by the probation officer. He was carelessly dressed in rather bright colours, and his attitude at first was one of bravado. He wondered what 'the little woman' and her mother had been concocting now. The probation officer said he could see that Mr. F. felt he was being called to account, but he felt unsure what had been said 'against' him. In fact, the officer had only seen his wife, and he was there to try to see if Mr. and Mrs. F. wanted to do anything except attempt a separation. The notion of separation seemed to disturb Mr. F. He enquired what would happen to the children. The officer said that this seemed to worry him quite a lot, and Mr. F. expressed considerable guilt at the harm his actions might have caused them. He had called to see his wife, but, though she let him in (her mother was out) she would not let him console George whom he could hear crying upstairs. In the end, he had to leave the house in a temper because he could not stand the sound of the child crying. The officer asked Mr. F. what he thought it was he could not stand and Mr. F. replied that it was all so sad, but whatever one did there would always be a child crying somewhere. The officer admitted that this was so, but this did not mean one should not try to do something where one could: sometimes one could get others to help as well. He said he could see Mr. F. was doubtful and perhaps he was doubtful whether anything could be done about his sorrow for the marriage. Mr. F. laughed at this, but agreed to the suggestion that the officer would see Mr. and Mrs. F. separately for a few interviews and then when they knew how things were going a little better they would all meet together. He said he would see Mrs. F. and suggest this, but Mr. F. said they had talked about it already and had hoped the officer would see them.

On the basis of these abbreviated reports of two quite lengthy interviews, what could be said about the quality of this particular marital relationship and about the officer's use of function?

We aim at an appraisal of a family or a marriage in dynamic terms, and this requires an assessment of the operation of past and present forces as well as some idea of the effects of changes in task necessitated by the natural development of the family. In the case of the Franks we can see a marriage influenced by the past experiences of each partner. Mrs. F.'s childhood, with its denied feelings of love towards her father, is evidently a factor in the present situation, as is her close identification with her mother. We have no information about Mr. F's. childhood, but we should make some conjecture about his difficulty in allowing babies to be sad. This clearly influences the present, but it is perhaps also a reflection of the unsatisfactory way in which his own depressive feelings and fantasies were handled in infancy. In terms of the family's own natural history, as it were, it seems possible that the partners were able to maintain a fairly satisfactory marriage until the birth of their first child, and that the crisis really emerged with the birth of their son. This was probably unsettling to each partner. The male child seemed a rival to father who shows some signs of doubt about his manhood (of the two he in fact seems more 'maternally' concerned about the children). For Mrs. F. the male child 'doubled the dose' of masculinity in the family and perhaps made it more difficult to avoid facing some of her feelings about her father. One way of dealing with this would be to identify more firmly with her mother and this would, of course, have repercussions on the husband. Both partners show concern about aggression. Mrs. F. has difficulty in expressing acknowledged aggression, though the interview shows that she can express hostility in a quiet, but effective way. Once she had expressed it, however, she seemed to 'collapse' and to become a 'tool' in someone else's hands. Her husband was obviously concerned about the harm his aggression had caused, and his wife, according to his account, managed to confirm and perhaps increase his guilt by refusing to let him make reparation to George and by provoking him to lose control once again.

Yet this is to concentrate on the negative aspects. Mr. and Mrs. F. also had positive feelings towards each other and positive purposes when they married. She chose to marry a man who would represent the aggressive and the depressed part of herself, which she denied. He married someone who would help him to express the maternal aspects of his personality and to work out the problem of controlling his feelings.

The situation thus appears complex even on the basis of information from two interviews. To help his clients, the probation officer has attempted to explain and carry out the function of his agency (the court), which is there to decide on the legal issues of separation and also offers the opportunity for the couple to think again and to think out the action they propose to take. Thus, the officer in his interview with Mrs. F. does not, as it were, hurry her away from the idea of action (of doing something). He twice made her general legal position clear. He encouraged her to consider her feelings about her contemplated action rather than express an opinion on the chances of her success in court. With Mr. F. he has attempted to distinguish his reality from the 'conspiracy' he seemed to expect. He holds the marriage up as a focus for both Mr. and Mrs. F., and offers a positive statement of the function of the agency—it could make a decision on separation, but it could also help them to think out some of the problems in their marriage.

A beginning has been made in this case. Each partner has expressed some feelings about certain aspects of the marriage, and the probation officer has shown that he can express some of their unexpressed feelings for them. Yet it is only a beginning. The work of marital counselling is complex and in most cases there comes sooner or later for worker and for client a stage at which all that seems to have been accomplished is a depressing and paralysing demonstration of the fine details of complexity. The endurance of this depression, the ability to hold the examination of the marriage steady in the face of apparent chaos, often proves the turning point in marital, and perhaps all, casework. To go through this experience, the probation officer can rely on the function of the agency which persistently faces the clients with the choice—shall we work at our marriage with the help the courts provide or shall we attempt the legal remedy also available? He can rely also on his own patient attempt to understand the 'wholeness' of the marriage and to help the partners to understand it in their own way.

NOTES

[1] Glover, E. R., *Probation and Re-education*, Routledge & Kegan Paul, 1949, p. 262.

[2] Newton, G., 'Trends in Probation Training', *British Journal of Delinquency*, Oct. 1956.

[3] Crabb, W. C., 'Probation Officers and Probationers: Their Relation towards Each Other', *Probation*, June 1915.

[4] Mesurier, L. (ed.), *A Handbook of Probation*, N.A.P.O., 1935, p. 58.

[5] *Report of the Departmental Committee on the Probation Service*, (Morrison Committee) Cmnd. 1650, March 1962, p. 23.

[6] See e.g. 'The Distinctive Nature of Probation Work', *Probation*, Vol. 9, No. 2, June 1959.

[7] Pollard, B., *Social Casework for the State*, Pall Mall Press, 1962, p. 80.

[8] See e.g. Golding, R., 'A Probation Technique', *Probation*, Vol. 9, No. 4, Dec. 1959.

[9] Morrison Committee, op. cit., p. 24.

[10] Studt, E., *Education for Social Workers in the Correctional Field*, Council on Social Work Education, U.S.A., 1959.

[11] King, J., *The Probation Service*, Butterworths, 1958, p. 11.

[12] Minn, W. G., 'Probation Work' in Morris, C. (ed.), *Social Case Work in Great Britain*, Faber, 1954, p. 135.

[13] Taft, J., 'The Time Element in Therapy' in Robinson, V. ed., *Jessie Taft: A Professional Biography*, Pennsylvania Press, 1962, p. 175.

[14] King, J., op. cit., p. 96.

[15] Grossbard, H., 'Ego Deficiency in Delinquents', *Social Casework*, Vol. XLII, No. 4, April 1962.

[16] Mrs. Sansom, 'Woman who makes Happy Wives', *Probation*, July 1928.

[17] Minn, op. cit., p. 143.

[18] Woodhouse, D., 'Some Implications for Casework Practice and Training' in *The Marital Relationship as a Focus for Casework*, Family Discussion Bureau, 1962.

[19] Dennis, N., 'Secondary Group Relationships and The Pre-eminence of The Family', *International Journal of Comparative Sociology*, Vol. III, No. 1, Sept. 1962.

[20] Woodhouse, D., op. cit.

Notes

21 *The Picture of Dorian Grey*, London, 1890.

22 Pincus, L., 'The Nature of Marital Interaction', in *The Marital Relationship as a Focus for Casework*, op. cit., p. 22.

23 Introduction in Eisenstein (ed.), *Neurotic Interaction in Marriage*, Tavistock, 1956, p. 15.

24 Pollard, B., *Social Casework for the State*, Pall Mall Press, 1962.

Chapter Seven

CASEWORK AND CHILD CARE

THE child care service in its modern form was established in 1948. Its immediate origins and the history of social service on behalf of children are by now familiar, but it should be emphasized that the Children Act, 1948, was the direct product of general social concern for children deprived of normal home life. A department of the local authority was to act like 'a good parent' to these children. In some ways this function had been previously fulfilled by Poor Law Authorities and by Voluntary Societies, but in 1948 a new emphasis was given to the continuity of care based on a recognition of the particular needs of individual children. These needs, moreover, were not to be met simply from the resources of one department; the Children's Department would require, like any parent, the use and co-operation of other services. At the same time the importance of the child's own family was recognized. A Home Office Circular (8th July 1948) stated that 'to keep the family together must be the first aim, and the separation of a child from its parents can only be justified when there is no possibility of securing adequate care for a child in his own home'. Since 1948, the service has largely been concerned with attempting to establish its general identity and with working out special problems in helping children, foster parents and natural families.

The main difficulty of the child care officer in regard to the general function of the service seems to revolve around the problems of acting like a good parent at the same time as a great deal of responsibility is shared with other people, who may themselves be parents or parent substitutes. Freeman, for example, has argued that a parental role is not feasible for the local authority for a number of reasons. These include 'the precarious legal position of the local authority, the uncertainty of how long a child will remain in care, the enduring strength of family relationships, the division of responsibility within local authority administration'.[1] He suggests that the local authority should adopt instead a role of 'temporary guardianship'. Clare Winnicott has expressed the difficulty in another way. 'The worker . . . embodies society's sense of parental responsibility towards the child who looks to her for just this. If a worker fails to embody the parental function of the agency to the child, the child's needs will not be met. The worker does not of course *become* the child's parent in the day-to-day relations which are concerned with his care and management, but she is the over-all caring parent behind the parents and the foster-parents, supporting their relationship and preserving continuity and reliability.'[2] Another writer asks if 'instead of aiming to become mother substitutes, might a more professional attitude be more appropriate? Such an attitude might be defined as one of unpossessive involvement?'[3]

These terms are all used in the attempt to say something important about the role of the worker in the Child Care Service, but each constitutes only a partial interpretation. An alternative approach is to consider that the social function of the Child Care Service is to administer the appropriate legislation and its subsidiary administrative regulations, but the spirit in which this is done is informed by our judgment both of the broad purposes of such legislation and of the best knowledge of child development available. This spirit or set of attitudes would be composed largely of the partial interpretations already offered, such as 'good parents', 'temporary guardians', 'non-possessive substitute parental care', etc. These terms on their own appear much too general to be useful to the caseworker in the child care service. Indeed, too much general talk about guardians, 'good parents' and possessive/non-possessive parental care could become actively misleading, since such terms are likely to be indefinitely blurred by fantasy. The set of attitudes I have referred to would certainly include the following:

(i) We accept responsibility for pursuing the welfare of each particular child as long as this is legally prescribed and appears justified in his own interests;

(ii) we try to ensure that he partakes as fully and realistically as possible in the experiences we provide which have as their objective his growth towards physical, emotional and social maturity;

(iii) we accept that his welfare cannot be achieved without considering his feelings about his own parents and securing as far as possible their co-operation in plans necessary for his future.

This is not an exhaustive list, but it illustrates the argument that we need to clarify our specific attitudes towards the care of children.

The present interest in the general function of the Child Care Service has arisen because of the problems and discoveries made in the course of the operation of the new service. The complex and enduring ties of children to their families, the changing demands made on foster parents now that the old concept of 'the fresh start' has been abandoned, the challenge of so-called preventive work—these have all contributed to changed and changing views on the work of children's departments. Yet an important part of the problem arises from the emotional factors, of a conscious and unconscious kind, involved in such work. There are, for example, considerable feelings of guilt about taking children away from their natural or substitute homes; unconsciously this is the equivalent of stealing children because of envy, and feelings of worthless emptiness. Once children have been removed they are 'given' into the care of others, who in their turn will unconsciously and sometimes consciously react to the child care officer as the person who gives and takes away their new children. Within the context of these fantasies the child care officer often attempts to work with children, foster parents and natural parents. Whether the strains of her work are thought of as conscious or unconscious, whether or not we wish to acknowledge the symbolic features of her work, these aspects, both negative and positive, enter her relationships because they are inseparable from her functions.

We shall now examine some of the casework problems that arise in the Child Care Service. Attention will be given to casework with children and adolescents, with foster parents and with families.

CASEWORK WITH CHILDREN

Caseworkers have always been used to making plans for children, but it is only recently that they have, in this country at any rate, paid much attention to making plans with children and to establishing their specific roles in a situation in which the child has already formed strong relationships with others. It is helpful in considering these problems to think in terms of casework with children. In the Child Care Service a considerable amount of emphasis has been placed on the child's relationships with foster parents, natural parents or staff of residential homes and it has been assumed that the child care officer should consider these as primary relationships with which her own work should not 'interfere'. However, children may require a considerable amount of detailed personal help from the child care officer and I have elsewhere suggested[4] that this can be considered in three main ways: helping children to prepare for, and absorb, the good and bad features of important events; helping them to develop new relationships and repair damaged ones; helping with problems of conflict. Each of these categories will be illustrated by a case example followed by discussion.

Rosemary, aged 10, had been in care for four years, but the child care officer had only known her for two months. Rosemary's foster home had broken down because of the illness of the foster mother, but a new home had been found in a fairly distant authority. Rosemary wanted to say goodbye to her mother who was in a mental hospital. She had visited her once before.

Rosemary was very silent during the car journey. The child care officer wondered what she was thinking about. Rosemary said 'nothing'. The child care officer asked about the new foster home; Rosemary had recently been on a week-end visit. Rosemary said it was very nice, but it had taken a long time to get there. The worker asked her if she knew that part of the world. Rosemary said she did not. Worker said she would soon make friends there.

In the waiting room at the hospital Rosemary was silent. The worker asked her if she had been before. Yes, about a year ago, but her mother had had to rest. Rosemary started to cry. The worker said that Rosemary would not want her mother to see her crying. Rosemary stopped crying and went to look out of the window. She asked why her mother was such a long time coming.

In this incident insufficient attention has been given by the child care officer to one of the most important principles of casework with children, always consider the child within the context of his existing family relationships, whether he is physically living with

Casework and Child Care

his own family or not. Rosemary in the situation described above is probably worrying both about her mother's condition and about the problem of going to live a long way from her mother. She also has the problem of trying to find some way of controlling her feelings when she actually meets her mother. These are the problems present in the situation with which she requires help rather than those that she might face when she moves from the district. How might the worker help her?

Firstly, more could have been done on the car journey to prepare her for how she might feel when she arrived. Secondly, the worker could have attempted to express some understanding of what the silence was about—sadness, fear of expressing any feeling in case control broke down. In showing an understanding of what she might be feeling the worker could also have helped the child by saying that such feelings were natural in the situation. The worker was hindered by her brief contact with Rosemary before the visit and she would not be maintaining contact when Rosemary left the district. Yet this meeting and the parting from mother was an important episode in her life which could have been handled in a way that encouraged her own emotional growth. Instead, the worker assumed the role of 'an ordinary adult' and she did not help Rosemary to act towards her in any other way. The interview in fact illustrates a common tendency in work with children: 'where children are concerned, the temptation of the adult, or one might say his conscientious compulsion, is to take too much responsibility or none at all'.[5]

Sometimes, of course, it is not possible to talk directly to a child about his problem. The following is an example of work with a younger child.

David (4) had been in care since he was 6 months old. His first foster home broke down when he was nearly three because the foster father became ill. He was placed with his new foster parents, Mr. and Mrs. L. when he was 4. They found him extremely withdrawn. Recently a number of toys had been smashed and David had said Joy (the L.'s own child of 6) had done it, but Joy had denied this. The child care officer decided to see David on his own. She asked Mrs. L. to bring him in from the garden. Mrs. L. did so and then left him with the worker.

David stood by the door. The worker started to build with some bricks. She said she knew David was probably afraid of her, but she

158

was not just the lady who took children away. (She had removed David from his first foster home.) She went on playing with the bricks and said that she was going to tell David a story pretending the bricks are people. David then came nearer. The worker said that Mr. and Mrs. L. wanted her to tell David this story. One of the bricks was made into a boy and other bricks into a mummy and daddy and their daughter and the first foster parents. The worker told the story of the first mummy and daddy who could not look after the boy anymore. David took them and put them under the rug. The worker said they had gone away, but they still thought about the little boy and wanted him to be happy, so perhaps they should not be hidden right away, because they want him to be happy with the mummy, daddy and daughter.

In this case the worker was attempting to help David to form some relationship with his new foster parents and she used an indirect form of communication. She attempted to distinguish her role on this occasion from that in the past and also demonstrated some of the difference. The use of bricks and the telling of a story does not mean that in some unspecified way David was expected to play out his problems, but simply that toys and games often provide a very useful way of communicating with a younger child about the things that worry them. In the case of David the worker was careful to link what she did and said with Mr. and Mrs. L., and she focused on the problem of forming new relationships by using her knowledge of David's past and attempting to show him that the pieces fitted together. It was important that the worker also included the foster parents in her plans for helping David with his problem, but in this instance the worker was probably correct in deciding that as the person who could 'fit the pieces together' she was in a good position to supplement the help the foster parents might give.

Gerald (10) had been fostered with Mr. and Mrs. G. since he was 5 years old. His mother, who had appeared spasmodically over the years with numerous unfulfilled promises, was now making a firm effort to make a new home for him. The G's had agreed, after some persuasion from the worker, to allow the mother to visit Gerald in their home. The worker called for the mother at the end of the visit and then visited the foster home the evening of the same day. The G's were angry because Gerald was very upset. The visit had gone very smoothly with Gerald behaving politely but rather coldly towards his mother. Now he was crying and saying he would have to go home. When the G's asked why he was crying he said because he would miss Whisk (the G's dog). The worker said they were all feeling wretched. The G's agreed and wondered if it had served any purpose at all. The worker said that the mother had been upset, too, but that the worker would try to help them decide how to do what they all wanted, to make Gerald happy. She told Gerald that he was feeling he did not know which way to turn, but he had not to make up his mind all at once.

In this difficult situation the worker attempted to help, partly by recognizing the feelings of all those in the situation. She acted partly as an interpreter to others (e.g. of mother's feelings) and she will probably continue by helping the G's to see Gerald's conflict, which was potentially in existence from the beginning of his fostering. The child care officer may well decide to work directly with Gerald on this problem, and one of the most helpful aspects of her approach to him will be to show that she can 'contain' the strains of the different interests in the situation as she also helps him to deal with his considerable conflict in loyalties. In adopting this role it is hoped that the child care officer will 'mirror back' this unity to Gerald.

In the cases so far considered, we have seen some of the problems of child care officers as they carry out their statutory duties of visiting children in foster homes and maintaining continuity of care as the child's environment changes. In pursuing these functions the child care officer should recognize how powerful she seems to children and the actual rights and duties she has in particular situations. She also embodies in her attitude and in the way in which she helps children to express feelings in a situation and to develop ways of controlling them, the three important aspects of child care summarized earlier in this chapter.

CASEWORK WITH ADOLESCENTS

In working with adolescents we approach a situation more closely resembling that of working with adults. Yet if we treat these two situations as identical we are likely to miss the specific characteristic of adolescence, its place between childhood and full adult status. Adolescence is a period when the earlier phases of infancy are recapitulated and the adolescent is again working through the early crucial anxieties—can he love and be loved, can his goodness survive the attacks of his badness, is he an individual, distinct from others, though with some attributes in common and some ties of relationship with others? These anxieties arise in connection with his own family (or substitute family) and outsiders. The adolescent still needs his parents as he begins finally to establish his identity apart from them.

Peter (16) came into care on the desertion of his mother at 12. Father showed only occasional interest in him, but Peter settled in a foster home and made a good relationship with a woman child care officer who left the area just after he started work at 16. He was transferred to a male officer whose first interview was largely concerned with complaints from the employers that Peter had been missing from work on several occasions. This was his third job in very quick succession.

The child care officer asked Peter to come into the office. (The previous worker had attempted to prepare Peter for her departure.) The child care officer introduced himself and said that Peter had usually seen Miss Z. Peter said nothing and then added, it was all the same to him. The worker said it was not easy meeting new people. Peter replied, in an apparently carefree tone, that it didn't matter to him whom he met. The worker said that Peter probably expected him to say something about his job. Peter said that it was not fair. They never gave him time to settle to a job; they move you on if you cannot do it the first time. There is always someone looking at you to see if you've done it alright every five minutes. Well, he wasn't going to have that. He was getting angry and looked at the worker in a defiant way. The worker acknowledged the anger and said it probably looked as if he was another in the line of people checking up on what Peter did. Peter said nothing, but seemed to relax. The worker said it would take some time for them to understand one another, but he was sure the problem at work could be solved. Peter would have to have a job, but perhaps they should talk about the kind of work. What sort of work had Peter's father done? Peter launched into a story of a father successful at everything he touched, a man who could do anything and for whom Peter would do anything.

In this interview the worker has begun to discern some of the dimensions of the problem. Peter seems, at the beginning of the interview, to be denying any feeling about the former worker, though it has some resemblance to the earlier 'desertion' by her mother. This aspect is not, however, taken up by the worker. His concentrated on the problem of work, recognizing Peter's anger and at the same time making it clear that he would have to work. This is an aspect of casework with adolescents that is of some importance. Adolescents should be helped to see that adults care sufficiently for them to set some limits and to have clear expectations of them. One of the ways of showing such care is to allow the expression of anger and resentment at these limits at the same time as they are firmly though not inflexibly held. Peter began to show that his problem about work was connected with the impossibility of 'competing' with an omni-competent father. He also expressed resentment at the constant supervision, which the worker discussed in terms of Peter's expectation of the officer's role. It is possible that this supervision was an aspect of Peter's relationship with his father, and that Peter had split off the negative feelings connected with it in order to preserve the image of the perfect father. This might be discussed with him later, but perhaps the most important aspect of the work with Peter would be the way in which the worker helps him to deal with his immediate problem in his job. As they discuss alternative jobs or how Peter might control his feelings of anger, the worker will be helping him to participate in a helpful relationship with a man who is not threatened by, or threatening to, Peter's desire to become a man himself. In this way he may be helped to work out a real picture of his own father and of his own masculine roles.

This case might have come in other circumstances to a probation officer and it might well have been dealt with along similar lines. In work with other adolescents casework in the child care service has special features. One important group are those children admitted to care at an early age who go through adolescence whilst still in care.

Jennifer (15) had been in care since she was 2 years old. She had lived in residential homes, but had been with her present foster parents since she was 14. Her foster mother asked the worker to see her because she was spending her wages at the weekend and had to borrow fares etc. the rest of the week. The worker told Jennifer that the foster parents were worried. Jennifer replied that she was not, and she did not know what all the fuss was about. It was *her* money, wasn't it and she'd had to work hard for it. The worker agreed it was her money, and said it probably was difficult for Jennifer to see why anybody was concerned, but she and the foster parents were. She asked what Jennifer really wanted to spend her money on. Jennifer said she did not know. The worker said it was difficult with so many things to buy and one was not sure if one could save up or not. Jennifer said she did not want to save and asked what the worker spent her money on.

This seems to be a case in which some kind of educational role might be undertaken by the worker. Jennifer said she did not want to save, but she expressed some interest in the worker's spending habits even if this was formulated as a fairly aggressive question. Jennifer has not had much opportunity to learn about spending, and the worker, once she has gained her interest, may well be able to teach her. Yet such teaching must be based on a firm grasp of the symbolic value of money. Money signifies independence and control, but to a deprived child it may also signify love and thus constitute a challenge to their sense of inner worth. Do they deserve these tokens of love, have they sufficient inner resources to retain these good things? It is in the exploration of such questions as these that the special aspects of casework with adolescents in care will become apparent.

CASEWORK WITH FOSTER PARENTS

In selecting and helping foster parents the child care officer is called on to undertake a task that is unique in social work, even though to achieve her objectives she uses some skills common to social work. For example, similar skills in making an appraisal of a family during a home visit are employed by the probation officer who has to complete a pre-trial report.

There is still considerable uncertainty about the most effective ways of selecting foster homes and about the roles the worker should adopt once the home has been selected. Part of this uncertainty is connected with the functions society expects the child care officer to fulfil in this area of her duties. Society expects the child care officer to judge the suitability of foster parents and this virtually means judging their adequacy as parents. The worker is also expected to continue to judge this adequacy once the homes have been selected and to help foster parents to continue the effective care of other people's children. It is not surprising that in the face of such expectations the child care officer has not always been clear about her role.

In selecting foster parents it is important not to claim to be able to predict too much too soon. As we shall see in the discussion of prevention it is dispiriting and disruptive to set one's goals too high. If we think, for example, that in one or two interviews we shall learn much about the unconscious motives of foster parents we are deceiving ourselves. There are two features of selection which seem of paramount importance. The regulations direct the child care officer's attention to them when they state that the home must be suitable to the *needs* of the *particular* child. This entails that the worker should form as clear an idea as possible of what the child needs and his characteristic ways of handling stress and relating to people. The same questions must be asked of the foster parents. Useful evidence may be found in references and other sorts of information, but the most important evidence arises in the course of the worker's interviews with the prospective foster parents. In appraising how they respond to her as a newcomer into their lives, how they react to her presentation of the different aspects of fostering, and how they show their own needs, the worker will obtain an essential view of their possible future response to a foster child.

Consider, for example, the application for a foster child from Mr. and Mrs. T.

The child care officer arrived at their house and Mr. T. let her in. He expressed surprise that he had received no letter from the worker asking him to come to the office for a formal appointment. He seemed satisfied with the explanation that it was sometimes difficult to plan interviews in advance.

The worker persuaded Mr. T. to finish his meal which was going cold on the table and they talked generally for a while. Mr. T. apologised for his wife's absence; she worked and did not get home until later. When Mr. T. had finished his meal he showed the worker the rest of the house. The worker was struck by its uniform drabness. Mr. T. again mentioned the worker's unexpected arrival and suggested with a laugh that it was a good idea to do this as it showed just how people really lived. The worker reassured Mr. T. and said that at present she was not especially interested in how often the cleaning was done. This put Mr. T. at his ease and they began to discuss fostering. The T's had been married 6 years and were unable to have children. They both felt marriage was 'made' by children.

The worker broadly outlined the nature of a Children's Department, and Mr. T. seemed able to appreciate the differences between long-stay and short-stay foster children and adoption. He said that initially they had considered that their financial circumstances would have prevented their being accepted as foster parents. The worker said that finance was of some but not major importance.

Mrs. T. arrived and the worker went over some of the main points already discussed. Mrs. T. said she thought children made a marriage, cemented it and provided something to work for. The worker was conscious of the ease with which the T's talked. Mr. T. had expected something more formal and had said to the worker—'You ask the questions and we will give the answers.' The worker replied that this was not the prime purpose of their preliminary discussions. The T's said they both appreciated these things took time.

There are a number of important features in this interview. Mr. T.'s view of the likely role of the child care officer loses some of its uncertainty from the beginning. He tried to form and test a modified view by expressing uneasiness about inspection and his own merits as a possible foster parent (the reference to financial inadequacy may well have a wider significance). He expected a formal interview, almost a kind of question-and-answer examination, but he seemed to be able gradually to respond to a different interpretation of the worker's role and his own reciprocal relationship. It would, however, be of considerable importance to test whether his response was a real recognition of this different interpretation or a kind of deferential reversal before authority. The T's both seem to appreciate the various aspects of fostering, but again the worker would in the next interview try to see what difference her explanations made to their plans, what further thoughts or modifications they entailed in the eyes of these applicants. Finally, it is noticeable that they both see children as 'cementing' the marriage. Does this mean that the marriage is in need of a bond and that a foster child is seen as a last chance? In exploring this important area the child care officer will obtain valuable impressions if in addition to asking questions she attends to the ways in which the foster parents participate in the process of selection. How far does this appear to be a joint activity in which each plays a complementary but distinct part? In the record of the interview we read that 'They *both* appreciated' . . .: the worker should re-examine the raw material on which this statement and others like it might be based. How in fact does this couple come to and express agreement? It is in pursuing such questions which arise from a consideration of the process of the interview that she will obtain a clearer picture of this marriage.

In the selection of foster parents the child care officer must come to a decision as to the suitability of any particular home. This involves collecting 'evidence', reviewing it and making a judgment. These are activities which social workers sometimes find difficult, and we have seen in the previous case that workers can become uneasy when applicants refer to their inspectoral role. Yet the child care officer is continuously reviewing and judging a foster home even after it has been selected. Her statutory responsibility to do this is clear and most foster parents are aware of this aspect of her visits. One of the most important elements in the work the child care officer undertakes with foster parents is to be found in the way she helps foster parents to experience her 'reviewing' activities as mutual and supportive, based on the assumption that they both want the foster child to grow up happily.

Take, for example, the J. family, who had just received Jimmy (8) as a foster child. The worker visited.

12. 4. 60.

Mrs. J. was very positive that everything was going well. It was hard work, of course, and he had them up very early in the mornings. The worker wondered if it was harder work than Mrs. J. had expected. Mrs. J. gave an emphatic negative and asked the worker if she would like some coffee. The worker said she would. When Mrs. J. returned the worker said she was very pleased that they were happy. Mrs. J. smiled and the worker mentioned that it had been the experience of the Department that children often behaved badly after an initial period in a foster home. Mrs. J. said she was sure that they were going to avoid this and this was why they were giving him so much time.

In this interview the foster mother seems to have some difficulties in coming to terms with the worker's role in the situation. She sees her as someone from whom any worries have to be hidden and who has to be placated (with coffee). She cannot accept as helpful the suggestion that she is not finding fostering quite as she expected. The worker tries to help her to anticipate problems and to give her some reassurance that such problems are to be expected in the nature of things. In the following interview the caseworker made a more determined (and successful) attempt to show Mrs. J. that worry and some negative feelings towards Jimmy were understandable and that she could admit to them without fear of condemnation by the worker.

10. 5. 60.

Mrs. J. was looking very tired and seemed rather depressed. The worker commented that she had just been talking to a member of staff in one of the Residential Homes about a child that had been worrying her. Mrs. J. began to show some interest. The worker said that they had not been able to solve the problem there and then, but they had both felt better for talking about it. Mrs. J. said that it was funny but she had been worrying a bit lately about Jimmy. He was telling lies and this made her so angry and she knew it wasn't good for him if she was angry. It made her feel ashamed. She entered into a discussion of Jimmy's 'bad' behaviour.

ADOPTION

The adoption work of the child care officer can take three possible forms. Under Section 38 of the 1958 Act the child care officer visits the prospective adoptive home as the local authority welfare officer. In many cases she acts as *guardian ad litem* for the courts and in this position is brought into contact with natural and adoptive parents. Thirdly, Children's Departments increasingly act as adoption agencies themselves, and the officer is thus concerned with placing children in homes with a view to their adoption. In each of these roles the child care officer is concerned, to a lesser or greater degree, with fulfilling statutory requirements, helping others to see and come to terms with them and with the strains and stresses of the situation, judging the present performance of those who would take on the role of adoptive parent and making some kind of prediction for the future. This work bears some similarity with that undertaken by the child care officer in fostering, but there are some important differences. In judging the suitability of foster parents the child care officer decides whether or not they are likely to be able to look after a child, responsibility for whom is shared with the agency. One of the most important questions she will ask herself is, how are these applicants likely to work with a child care officer in the future? In adoption work this question is clearly irrelevant. The child care officer is concerned with the adoptive and sometimes also with the natural parents until the court order symbolizes the fact that society now regards the child as 'belonging' to the former. Yet, the adoptive parents can never be the child's natural parents and one of the child care officer's major problems is to decide if their present playing of the adoptive parents' roles constitutes reasonable ground for predicting how they would handle their child's inevitable questions about his identity and status.

It is not possible in the present work to illustrate each facet of the child care officer's functions in relation to adoption, but extracts from the case of Roger Dunster will illustrate some of the main problems.

Mr and Mrs. Brookside, in their middle forties, applied to the Children's Department as prospective foster parents. Investigation led to their approval as foster parents, and the following extract from the first interview is important in the light of future events.

Mrs. Brookside is a very talkative woman. This proved to be a very long visit and it was not necessary for the child care officer to try to discover anything about Mrs. Brookside's background because she was so forthcoming about her history. She was far more communicative, however, about her husband's life and what she had done for him. It seems that she has done everything possible to find his family. He was an illegitimate child brought up in a Children's Home. She said that he never made much comment about this and when they were married 30 years ago he wondered whether Mrs. Brookside would change her mind about marrying him when she knew he was illegitimate. He had always said very little about this but she was certain that it was on his mind and as soon as many of her family responsibilities had ended she took it upon herself to find out about his parents. It seems that she has turned Somerset House upside down and travelled over the country to do this and was eventually lucky in tracing his mother and various sisters. He had been thrilled at the time and has tended to be much more contented since he has found a family. Because of this Mrs. Brookside realises the importance of family contacts for children and commented on how there could be no substitute for a child's own family. These investigations had taken her the best part of ten years.

The officer gained the impression that Mrs. Brookside has the right ideas, but that she finds them extremely hard to put into practice, and that in effect in some ways she has failed her own family. Her eldest daughter Barbara was married at the age of 17 because she was already expecting a child. She is waiting for a divorce to come through, but at the same time is living with another young man in another part of the country, whom she hopes to marry the day after her divorce is made absolute. The child of the first marriage is a little boy called Roger now aged nearly five. It seems that Mrs. Brookside and her husband have the greater part of the care of Roger although he has been passed backwards and forwards from one to the other in a very unplanned sort of way. Mrs. Brookside said she was sure that the right place for Roger was with his new parents, but it was clear that Barbara is rejecting Roger completely and that he is developing into a very disturbed little boy. She thought that it was almost some form of mental cruelty really that was inflicted upon Roger by her daughter. She has been considering taking Roger back again to care for on a more permanent basis and has been wondering whether or not she and her husband should not apply to adopt him if her daughter is willing. At the moment her daughter's fiancé is considering applying to adopt him but Mrs. Brookside believes at the back of this is his wish to please Barbara.

Several short-stay foster children were successfully placed with the Brooksides, but in January 1963 they applied to adopt Barbara's child, Roger. The child care officer visited. The Brooksides have had a great deal to do with the care of Roger when he was small. Mrs. Brookside told the officer that she looked after him until he was nearly two years old but held back a great deal of feeling for him as she felt he was returning to his mother which was his rightful place. She had encouraged and helped her daughter to assume care of Roger but she rather doubts now that this was the wisest thing. From what she said it seemed that Roger had been rejected by her daughter Barbara completely. There is another child of her daughter's marriage who is spoilt and idolised. Since the birth of this child Roger has been excluded and repressed according to Mrs. Brookside.

Roger has been living with Mrs. Brookside since February 1962. She has had a great deal of difficulty with him, his speech was and is extremely backward and babyish and he is having to attend the speech therapy clinic. For some time there was excessive soiling and wetting, although it has been cleared up gradually. Mrs. Brookside found Roger very timid and she says it is not very often that he behaves as a really normal boy should. He has been under constant observation of the Medical Officer who, according to Mrs. Brookside, also has highly commended her for her care of the boy. Both she and her husband wish to adopt Roger because they feel there is no place for him with his real mother and stepfather and they want to give him the security of their own home.

Her youngest daughter Hazel now aged 13 has shown some signs of jealousy. Once again Mrs. Brookside has given this a great deal of thought and seems sometimes to come up with the wrong answers making complications when none exist. As far as Roger's mother is concerned she and her husband are going abroad for 2½ years. Mrs. Brookside feels that this will help in their adopting Roger as it will give him chance to stabilize without any contact at all from their daughter.

The Child Care Officer summarized her impressions in the following words:

Both Mr. and Mrs. Brookside are well known to us as they have been vetted as foster parents. Mrs. Brookside has shown an ability to deal with difficult foster children but also seems to be a fairly emotional and sometimes rather unstable woman. It has sometimes seemed that in her determination to deal with the difficulties of foster children she has wanted to prove to herself that she can cope with these difficulties and that her failure with some of her own older children is not really her fault. She is certainly very anxious and I should imagine has been somewhat interfering in the lives of her children. She has tried to be intensely honest with her children and has followed this on with Roger but the consequence is that she tends to over-estimate what any child can emotionally take and tends to impose too much upon him. Her husband is much calmer and gentler in temperament and though Mrs. Brookside says she defers to him, one gets the impression that it is she who takes the decisions in the family. Mrs. Brookside has great verbal ability and gives every sign that she knows all the answers. She has discussed the possibility of adoption with Roger and says that he knows what this means and what it implies. She says that he will continue to know of his adoption and that he is bound to know that his new sister is in fact his mother. It has already been decided that he will call her Barbara. I have no doubt that Mrs. Brookside is being completely honest about this, but I am sure she experiences a great deal of difficulty in coping with the outcome of information like this which she gives to the children.

What have we learned about the Brooksides so far? Mrs. Brookside has dominated the scene and we know little about her husband. This is unfortunate in view of the adoptive child's sex. Mrs. Brookside seems to have a good understanding of the needs of the deprived child and she certainly managed the situation of her husband's deprivation to good effect. She has apparently helped short-stay foster children and she has clearly played a large part in Roger's upbringing already. She seems to need to prove her goodness and also to treat children as if they were capable of making adult choices and carrying adult responsibilities. The child care officer would wish to deepen and test her impressions and she has the opportunity to do this as she supports Mrs. Brookside in complying with the procedures and facing the delays and doubts of the waiting period. This 'supportive' work should be seen as a means of appraising how the prospective parents react to the possibilities of disappointment and frustration. Questions concerning the child's change of name, his own feelings and his mother's consent all provide opportunities for helping the applicants work out the implications of their new role and also for deepening the child care officer's understanding of the situation. The following interviews illustrate these aspects of the child care officer's function.

24. 10. 62.

Roger came to the door to let the child care officer in and after some hesitation decided he knew who she was. He announced that she was the person about the adoption to Mrs. Brookside. Their introduction was somewhat prolonged in that he immediately went off to fetch some guns and proceeded to play cowboys and indians around the furniture. He was quite attention-seeking, but Mrs. Brookside remained calm in the middle of this and gave him every encouragement to direct his energies elsewhere. The officer felt that his play was imaginative and was impressed by the difference that there was in him from the time when she first met him. His speech was certainly much more clear and he had gained enormously in self confidence. He eventually went into another room to play.

Roger is apparently in very good health and is continuing to grow rapidly. Mrs. Brookside often takes him up to see the Assistant County Medical Officer and he is very pleased with the physical progress that Roger has made since he has been with Mrs. Brookside. Roger still attends for speech therapy and from what Mrs. Brookside says there is a gradual improvement in his enunciation. He is far less babyish in his talk than he used to be.

Education: Roger has moved up to the X Junior School and Mrs. Brookside has noticed that he appears to have been affected by the change. She wonders if his present form-mistress understands the difficulties that he has had to overcome and thinks that she will visit the school to explain. Roger has occasionally been dreading going to school and it looks as though he might be being pressed too hard. It seems that his arithmetic is weak but his reading is well up to standard. He enjoys reading and Mrs. Brookside has been very pleased indeed by the obvious progress that he has made in this subject. The officer advised her to discuss this progress with the headmaster and to explain Roger's general circumstances so that the teacher can be sympathetic to him and help him in every way possible.

Adoption. Mother's Consent. The clerk at the Justices Clerk's Office had told the officer that he had written to Roger's mother but had received no reply. She told Mrs. Brookside this and she said that her daughter had been on holiday for three weeks with her. She was still prepared to give her consent to the adoption and no doubt would be seeing to this now having returned to her home.

Roger's Attitude to his Mother. The child care officer tried to discover from Mrs. Brookside if there had been any reaction from Roger to his mother visiting. She has explained to him what the position is and he is well aware that the person he calls Barbara is in fact his mother, but Mr. and Mrs. Brookside are intending to adopt in order that they can keep him with them for ever. It seems, however, that during the visit Roger had cried and said that he wanted to go home with his mother. Mrs. Brookside had been very concerned about this and her daughter had said that she was perfectly willing to take him if he wanted to come, but that she was not a bit certain about what was the right line of action. Mrs. Brookside has often in the past commented to the officer that Barbara and her husband completely reject Roger and are insensitive to his needs.

Mrs. Brookside had gone to the Assistant County Medical Officer to discuss this and the latter had advised very strongly that they should go ahead with the adoption and that to allow Roger to return to his mother at this point would probably be devastating and destructive. The Brooksides had decided to go ahead.

Mrs. Brookside however was wondering whether it would be worth while letting Roger go to his mother for his holiday. She was inclined however to think against this as she felt it would be undermining and would serve no useful purpose. The officer wondered if his reaction to his mother had been a test to see if Mrs. Brookside meant what she said when she had told him that he could live with them forever. She also said that it seemed a mistake to expect Roger at his present age to take the responsibility for such a decision as this; she felt it must be the adults who decided. Mrs. Brookside clearly needed a great deal of reassurance on the right course of action.

16. 11. 63.

Mrs. Brookside called at the Department. She told the child care officer that all the documents were now complete at the Magistrates Court and that it would only be a matter of time now before the hearing was set. She came in however to discuss whether or not she should change Roger's name from Dunster to Brookside. She was under the impression that the clerk at the Court House felt that to change his name might cause Roger a certain amount of distress and that she could perfectly properly leave his name as Dunster if she so wished.

The officer discussed this with her fairly thoroughly and pointed out various facts to her. It became clear during the discussion that Roger himself is expecting his name to become Brookside and it seemed to the officer that with a child as insecure as he is that this might undermine him even more should his name remain Dunster. She asked Mrs. Brookside what it was that she felt she would say to him when he was a few years older and was not able to understand why his name had not been changed. She said that her natural instinct was that his name should be Brookside and she had been rather taken off balance by the clerk's suggestion. The officer felt that although Mrs. Brookside sees complications in this adoption fairly clearly, to encourage her to allow Roger's name to remain as Dunster would be merely to increase them.

On this occasion she learned a great deal more about her daughter, Roger's mother. It seems that Mrs. Brookside herself is trying desperately hard to sort out why her daughter has been such a problem. She learned that after the birth of her baby, this daughter went off with the milkman, and although she is back with her husband, he cannot bear to touch her. This is not making for an easy relationship within the marriage.

Mrs. Brookside had the need to talk about this daughter from the time she was born and was clearly trying to sort out where she and her husband had gone wrong. She said it was only recently that she has felt at all close to her daughter and that even as a child she was extremely hard to get through to. She had always treated her eldest daughter *as* the eldest. Mrs. Brookside feels that her daughter could well do with psychiatric help. Her daughter's memory of occurrences within her childhood are distorted and she has recently told her mother of the nightmares that she used to have as a younger child.

The officer understood that Roger's mother and her husband were likely to go abroad soon. She has suggested however that if she does not go with her husband she would move down into this area. Mrs. Brookside said that she would be most concerned if this happened for Roger's sake but she feels that possibly she would be able to help her daughter.

The officer talked a little about what she would say to Roger as the reason why his mother did not continue to care for him. Mrs. Brookside has got this sorted out fairly clearly. She feels that her daughter is not really rejecting of Roger and in fact feels extremely guily about her lack of feeling for him. She had therefore decided that the story that she can tell Roger will in fact be the truth, that on her daughter's remarriage and with the birth of Trevor she and her husband were unable to continue looking after him and decided that he could return to the care of his Granny, who had been looking after him for the first three years of his life. Mrs. Brookside feels that she has been very lacking in foresight in that she allowed Roger to return to her daughter at the age of three and in fact tried to force her sense of responsibility for Roger when she clearly did not want him. She feels that part of the difficulty now is that Roger does not understand where he really belongs.

CASEWORK WITH FAMILIES

The child care officer is essentially involved in family matters in most of her work and it is, therefore, somewhat artificial to give her family casework separate treatment. When a child has been removed from his family the child care officer is concerned not only with the possibility of long-term rehabilitation, but also with the more concrete and immediate task of helping the parents to maintain contact with their child during and after the painful period of actual separation. The importance of the child's ties with his family even when physically separated from them has received some emphasis in recent research.[6] Yet, family casework in the child care service deserves special consideration in view of the new legislation which stresses the part local authorities should play in preventive social work. The term 'prevention' is familiar in social work writing; social workers sometimes feel they should be apologetic if they are not doing 'preventive casework'. How useful is this conception?

The idea of prevention has a long history as far as public provision for social welfare is concerned. It is possible to observe at least three stages in its development. Firstly, it was considered that people should be prevented from having recourse to dependence on such social provision as existed by the availability early in life of certain guiding influences. Thus, education was seen 'as one of the most important means of eradicating the germs of pauperism for the rising generation and of securing in the minds and morals of the people the best protection for the institutions of society'.[7] The second development came with such agencies as the Charity Organization Society in the second half of the nineteenth century. Prevention was now concentrated on providing a service which would meet social need in any given case so effectively that a second application for help was thereby prevented. The opponents of the Charity Organization Society at the turn of the century also advocated prevention, but this was seen as the 'arresting or counteracting of the causes of destitution so that it should not occur'.[8] This is the third development in the idea of prevention.

These different aspects of prevention can be seen in the very recent history of the Children's Departments since 1948. In this sphere there has been a change of practice from simply preventing children from coming into care (sometimes by helping to make alternative arrangements, sometimes not), to stressing the importance of avoiding the separation of the child from his family. Finally, we are beginning to say that we must prevent the conditions that threaten the existence of the family. A recent historian of the child care service describes this change in the following way: 'Preventive work should mean not only providing skilled help which will prevent the immediate separation of the parents and children, and enable the family as a unit to solve the material and emotional problem satisfactorily within themselves, but also the prevention of those conditions of personal and social failure which leave the family with no alternative but to make application to children's departments for the reception of the children into care or which eventually call for intervention by the court.'[9] This, of course, assumes that we can describe the conditions themselves in a way that is helpful for preventive action.

The quotation in fact represents our current enthusiasm for preventive work. The more enthusiastic we are, the nearer we come, in my view, to suggest that our aim is to prevent original sin. What, for example, could be more enthusiastic than the recent Ingleby Committee when discussing prevention? 'We have found it impossible to consider this question of prevention from a purely negative point of view. It is not enough to protect children from neglect even if the term neglect be held to include their exposure to *any* physical, mental or moral danger or deprivation. If children are to be prevented from becoming delinquent, and if those in trouble are to get the help they need, something *more positive* is required. Everything within reason must be done to ensure not only that children are not neglected but that they get the best upbringing possible.'*[10] This represents a powerful homily, but it contains not even the beginnings of a programme of action.

Now this kind of criticism can be (and sometimes is) dismissed as academic word play, but it has important implications for practice. If we believe (and we certainly often say) that social work is moving away from a residual and remedial function towards playing a part as one of our permanent social institutions, then it becomes important to establish, in this new context, goals which can be defined clearly and are, at least, within some possibility of realization. We simply cannot set goals if we think we are trying to do 'everything within reason' and if we imagine this itself constitutes a goal we will soon become frustrated. If we aim to do 'everything within reason', what have we against which to judge our efforts?

However, the subject cannot be left there. All we have seen, so far, are some of the ways in which the term prevention has been used and some of the difficulties. If we look at social medicine, the discipline from which the term originates, the notion which those connected with the social services have seemed to regard as unitary becomes analysable into component parts. Thus, it is customary in public health to distinguish three levels of prevention: *primary*, steps to obviate the development of the disease in susceptible populations; *secondary*, which is based on early diagnosis and prompt treatment once the presence of the disease is suspected; *tertiary*, which aims at limitation of the disability caused by the illness. Within this general scheme it is usual also to identify distinct processes through which preventive practices may be applied. Leavell and Clark, for example, identify five such elements, (a) health promotion, (b) specific protection, (c) early diagnosis, (d) limitation of the disability, (e) rehabilitation.[11]

This kind of differentiation of the concept of prevention is useful in any consideration of prevention in the field of the social services. The first two processes, health promotion and specific protection at once present difficulties. What is the kind of health we want to promote? The idea of mental health is notoriously difficult to define, especially if we allow ourselves to entertain some of the doubts expressed in a recent publication as to 'whether

* My italics.

we are dealing with a single continuum with positive mental health at one pole and a variety of mental disorders at the other, or with two separate continua',[12] (i.e. mental health—mental illness, mental health—? mental ill-health which is not mental illness.) It becomes difficult to see what is being promoted and by what means if, to quote another contributor to this volume, 'primary prevention encompasses actions, deliberative or otherwise, that maximise these social forces in the community which tend to encourage the full development of the human being as a rational, creative and self-actualizing organism'.[13]

Specific protection presents perhaps less of a difficulty. It is easy to point to the inadequacy of knowledge that would yield certain and sure protection, but preventive schemes in public health have not always been based on scientific knowledge. Part at least of Chadwick's public health programme was based on erroneous, let alone incomplete, theories. Eisenberg and Gruenberg have recently attempted to divide the psychiatric disorders of childhood into those for which there is convincing evidence that treatment is effective, those that have a reasonable likelihood of response and those in which the response is uncertain.[14] Yet our knowledge of what we are protecting people against and how we can protect them remains general and non-specific. A family background may consist of a dominant mother and a weak, ineffectual father and the outcome for children in such a family may, according to recent studies, range from no apparent effect to schizophrenia, alcoholism etc.

It seems that in the social services we should, for the present at least, concentrate on the three processes of early diagnosis, limitation of the disability and rehabilitation. Are there principles by which the casework of the child care officer can be guided to achieve such objectives in working with families? Three concepts may be singled out for special mention, those of focus of work, the family crisis and co-operation.

The families that call for 'preventive' work often exhibit many problems besides the failure to socialize their children, but no worker can define and solve all the problems, if only because there are definite limits on the material we can absorb and use. The focus of each worker is in fact supplied by the functions of the agency. Thus, the child care officer will be particularly concerned with parent–child relationships in the family. This entails a consideration of the real and fantasy relationships between the parents and their children and also of the relationships between the parents and their family of origin. It is her appraisal of these relationships that will focus the work and lead the child care officer to decide if the child or children are to remain at home and if and when they are to return after a period in care. If the worker decides that the child can be cared for effectively in the home, then she will give the parents support and practical help in relating constructively to the child. She will be protective of both parents and child, intervening in the mother's patterns of managing her relationships with the child by such behaviour as keeping him a baby, suppressing any expression of aggression and so on. If, on the other hand, the worker decides that the family problems are such that long-term care away from home needs to be considered, she may need to work towards this end with both child and parent. This is likely to be the case where there have been long-standing problems in the parents, or there has been no period of reasonably stable family life or where there is deep conflict over taking help. In this kind of situation the worker will attempt to help the parents to separate from the child, and the child to face the reality of what is happening in order to prevent a blockage in his movement towards maturity caused by having to maintain the pretence that his parents are dead, or he is so bad that they had to get rid of him.

On many occasions, however, this kind of preparation is not possible and children may have to be removed from their homes as an emergency operation. In such situations and in many others the concept of crisis is of some help. This idea, elaborated by Caplan and Lindemann,[15] assumes that an individual is usually in a state of relative equilibrium with his *milieu*, but that at certain times he is faced with problems that he cannot meet, and his equilibrium is threatened and perhaps breaks down. Sooner or later he deals with the problem, but sometimes his equilibrium has been re-established in a less healthy state than previously. The importance of this notion lies in the fact that at times of crisis a small influence exerted by a significant other may be sufficient to decide the outcome in a beneficial manner. No 'radical' change or exploration 'in depth' is attempted, but the person is assisted in a crisis in a way which may help him to face the next from a stronger position. This implies that the worker will attend to the crisis situation, helping clients to return to their former, more effective, role taking or, if this is not possible, to prepare for the acceptance of new or unaccustomed roles. Some families, of course, will be in states of relative equilibrium that are highly unstable.[16] Here the worker's task will be to attend to each crisis situation as she builds up her understanding of why these families find themselves in repetitive crises. As long as the worker remains open to the second part of her task, there would appear to be no reason for suggesting that crisis-focused work with families is 'superficial'.

Families in repetitive crises are, of course, usually the concern of several agencies and a co-operative attitude amongst social workers is a necessary condition of work coordinated to some agreed purpose. Yet this attitude is not automatically generated by the goodwill of social workers or the exhortations of their critics: it is created by collaborative effort. The following brief extract from the meeting of a coordinating committee[17] illustrates some of the problems involved.

The Devons Case

This case was reviewed by the co-ordinating committee, consisting of the Deputy Medical Officer of Health (in the chair), a probation officer, a child care officer, three health visitors, a woman N.S.P.C.C. visitor, a voluntary worker from a local family casework agency.

Health Visitor: This case was last reviewed three months ago and you may remember that I reported on some progress with Mrs. Devons. Well, I'm afraid that this has not been sustained. In fact, I feel very let down. I'm afraid that there's drink in this case and Mrs. D. has not been frank with me. I thought I had a good relationship with her, too, but I suppose I was mistaken. The general situation in the family seems much the same and I understand the N.S.P.C.C. have been visiting.

Deputy M.o.H.: Perhaps the N.S.P.C.C. visitor would like to make some observations.

Visitor: Well, what concerns me most is Mrs. D. I have visited on a number of occasions and I find her a . . . well . . . a disturbing person. It's the look in her eyes, you know. I wonder if the mental health worker should not visit. You know, these mental cases can do such worrying things and I'm worried about the children.

Child Care Officer: I would like to make a comment about the children. There seems to have been a distinct improvement in school attendance recently and I wonder if we are not taking too gloomy a view of the family. I have visited five times since the last review and on each occasion Mrs. D. has spoken warmly of the Health Visitor and seems to be building a relationship with the N.S.P.C.C. visitor. Could we perhaps try to see what it is that makes us despondent about this case and why there might be concern for Mrs. D's mental health? I wonder how we think she functions as a mother now compared to three months ago.

Voluntary Worker: I'm very concerned about the two eldest children, George (14) and Ethel (13). Mrs. D. has complained several times about them and they do seem to be getting out of hand. I have known this family on and off over several years and I confess they have me stumped. I just do not know which way to turn to help them for the best.

M.o.H.: There seem to be a lot of agencies concerned with this family. Is there any chance of reducing the number at all. I'm a great believer in one worker for one family.

Voluntary Worker: Well, if you remember, doctor, we did agree a little while ago to divide up the work with this family, but I have found it very difficult to keep to this. The problems in this family simply swarm all over each other.

Probation Officer: I was not very happy myself with that arrangement and I think we may all have felt guilty about violating it.

Voluntary Worker: I think 'guilty' is rather strong.

Probation Officer: Perhaps it is, but the point I wanted to make was that we ought to be more sure about what's going on in this family. I notice, for instance, that no one so far has mentioned my client in this case, Mr. D.

(General laughter)

Everyone seems to think that he doesn't count for much, but how *does* he fit into the situation?

Health Visitor: That's the trouble, of course. If he only played his part, but he's never in a job.

Child Care Officer: Yet the home seems to 'tick' over quite well when he is at home. I think the recent improvement in school attendance is primarily due to his being at home.

Health Visitor: But it's not manly for a man to spend so much time in the home.

General discussion followed on the attributes of the 'good' husband and father. It was finally decided to review the case in another two months.

It is difficult to convey briefly a meaningful impression of a group meeting such as this, but this short extract illustrates some of the difficulties of coordinating a joint policy for helping problem families. In discussion of the Devons case, workers are concerned to express their feelings of failure and frustration and perhaps to gain some 'absolution' from their fellows—these families *are* difficult and you are doing all that you can. The problems presented by the case are complex, but the group does not take advantage of the interventions of the child care officer and, later, of the probation officer to pause, to begin to build a coherent picture of the family. Some of the workers express their fears (e.g. the Woman Visitor's fears of madness, the Health Visitor's of being let down by Mrs. Devons), but they are not used to deepen the workers' understanding of the family by examining what they do to create such feelings in the worker.

In this chapter we have seen the child care officer in many different situations of inevitable strain and difficulty because they are at the centre of her functions. These functions revolve around the meaning for herself and her clients of the statutory provisions of the Service she represents. As she visits and interviews she is trying to ensure the care of children for whom she has assumed some responsibility, and this entails continual testing and judgment of situations and people against ideas of 'good' child care, which she holds as an individual and as a member of the Service. Her purpose in doing this is not simply judgmental (and never condemnatory), but partly to fulfil the social work objective of appraising where help is needed and how it might be accepted. In addition, however, the child care officer has the responsibility of acting if she judges that the necessary help will not achieve results in time to forestall grave harm to the child. She is entrusted by the community with upholding standards of child care at the same time as she helps foster parents and natural parents to interpret them in their own particular case and to achieve them. She is continuously involved in complex situations governed by fantasy as well as by reality. It is part of her function to understand the fantasies particularly connected with her work and her own roles (e.g. she may seem to be the omnicompetent, all-powerful mother who alone knows how to rear children or as the threatening person who actually tries to steal children). She must come to terms with these fantasies herself as she perseveres in her attempts at real, constructive help.

NOTES

[1] Freeman, J. W., 'The Child and the Local Authority', *Child Care*, Oct. 1960.

[2] Winnicott, C., 'Casework and Agency Function', *Case Conference*, Jan. 1962.

[3] Kellmer Pringle, M. L., 'Emotional Adjustment Among Children in Care', *Child Care*, April 1961.

[4] Timms, N., *Casework in the Child Care Service*, Butterworths, 1962, p. 41.

[5] Robinson, V. (ed.), *Jessie Taft: Therapist and Social Work Educator*, London, O.U.P., 1962, p. 229.

[6] See e.g. Kellmer Pringle, M. L. and Clifford, L., 'Conditions Associated with Emotional Maladjustment Among Children in Care', *Educational Review*, Vol. 14, No. 2, Feb. 1962. This reports research confirming the hypothesis that one of the conditions distinguishing the stable from the maladjusted child in residential care is the regularity and frequency of contacts with parents or persons outside the Home.

[7] Shuttleworth, Kay, *Fourth Annual Report Poor Law Commission*, 1838.

[8] Webb, B. and S., *The Prevention of Destitution*, Longmans, Green & Co., 1911, p. 224.

[9] Heywood, J., *Children in Care*, Routledge & Kegan Paul, 1959, pp. 179–80.

[10] Command 1191, *The Ingleby Report*, Oct. 1960.

[11] Leavell, H. R. and Clark, E. G., *Preventive Medicine for the Doctor in his Community*, McGraw-Hill, 1958, p. 21.

[12] Caplan, G. (ed.), *Prevention of Mental Disorders in Children*, Tavistock, 1961, p. 402.

[13] Bower, E. M., 'Primary Prevention in a School Setting' in Caplan (ed.), op. cit.

[14] Eisenberg, L. and Gruenberg, E., 'The Current Status of Secondary Prevention in Child Psychiatry', *Am. J. of Orthopsychiatry*, Vol. XXXI, No. 2, pp. 355–67, April 1962.

[15] Lindemann, E. and Caplan, G., 'A Program for Preventive Psychiatry', quoted in 16.

[16] See Wadfogel, S. and Gardner, G. E., 'Intervention in Crises as a Method of Primary Prevention', in Caplan (ed.), op. cit.

[17] In most local authority areas regular meetings of Co-ordinating Committees are held to discuss cases of child neglect. Local social workers from the statutory and voluntary social services concerned usually attend. For a review of the work of such committees see Rose, G., 'Co-ordinating Committees', three articles in *Case Conference*, June, July, Sept. 1957. Some interesting observations have recently been made by Olive Stevenson in 'Co-ordination Reviewed', *Case Conference*, Vol. 9, No. 8, Feb. 1963.

Chapter Eight

FAMILY CASEWORK

KNOWLEDGE AND METHODS OF WORK IN FAMILY CASEWORK

CASEWORK began in the voluntary social work agency which had as one of its original aims the strengthening of family life. In this country and in America family casework has been a seminal influence on the whole development of social work. Thus, the concept of family casework is ambiguous. It designates a particular setting for casework practice (the voluntary and, perhaps in the future, the statutory[1] family casework service) and also provides a description of casework in general (it is often said that case-workers should help people 'within the context of their families'). In this chapter an attempt will be made to elucidate the features of family casework as the specialized function of the general social work agency, whether this is envisaged as statutory or voluntary.

The general social work agency has a greater flexibility than many others, and can experiment more freely with new ways of discovering and meeting need. This is, however, a mixed blessing. Family caseworkers and their clients must often have been confused by the failure to define any function and misled by un-acknowledged assumptions that were in fact equivalent to defined functions. Flexibility serves as a possible basis for identity only when it operates within specified limits. Such limits can be found in the concept of 'the family as a whole', and it is suggested that this provides the core around which the family caseworker's functions can be built. The idea of service to the family unit and the encouragement of 'good' or 'healthy' family life provides a point of entry into the family and the beginnings of an agency pro-gramme that can be presented to the community. The family caseworker presents himself to the family as a worker in an agency concerned with the welfare of their family group. Whereas the probation officer's point of entry in probation cases must be the offender, the almoner's the sick person and so on. Concern with the family group also defines the family caseworker's special field of knowledge and some of the methods of work which he or she will use more frequently than workers in other settings. The family caseworker will not, of course, be concerned with all families, but only with those facing a particular crisis or with those prone to crises. Hill has offered a formal analysis of the family crisis[2] which shows some of the foci for the family caseworker's investigations and some of the family occasions on which her help may be required. He suggests that the family crisis is produced from the following sequence: 'A (the event) → *interacting* with B. (the family's crisis-meeting resources) → *interacting* with C. (the definition the family makes of the event) → produces X (the crisis).' He has classified 'the events' in terms of dismemberment (or loss of a family member), accession (or the addition of an unprepared-for member), and demoralization (or loss of morale and family unity).[3]

The family caseworker's knowledge of the family and her use of it in her work rests on an assumption about the fundamental importance of the family and the crucial nature of efforts to improve its functioning. As Waller has observed:

> . . . the family is important in the life of the individual because it gets him first, keeps him longest, is his major source of cultural imperatives, and prescribes them with emotional finality. It is important because it not only satisfies the wishes of the individual but it is instrumental in shaping those wishes into a form which only the family can satisfy. In our society the family furnishes the basic environment for personality. . . .[4]

The family caseworker helps the family to fulfil these lofty functions as she works with the daily problems of family life (budgeting, finding accommodation, coping with children etc.).

In order to understand a family problem it is important that the family is approached as a group interacting and reacting in love and strife or, in the words of Sumner, 'antagonistic co-operation'.[5] This was appreciated by an early social work student of the family, whose work has not perhaps been sufficiently appreciated. Helen Bosanquet stated that the parts of the family:

> are admirably fitted by nature to subserve each other's needs, and to supplement each other's efforts. The need of the weak for protection

finds its correlative in the pride of the strong in protecting: the clinging appeal of the child for affection elicits a response which might otherwise remain dormant forever. The authority which all adults like to exercise finds a beneficent outlet in guiding the action of immature wills; and children who weary when left to the caprices of their undisciplined natures, find strength and contentment in a rule which is autocratic without having the impersonal rigidity of external law. And the man, again, who would prefer solitude to the constant clashing at close quarters of his own will with that of another man, finds it completed instead of thwarted when its functions are supplemented by those of the woman.[6]

The family exists to satisfy the needs of its individual members (originally the parents) and to perform certain essential tasks from the point of view of society. Winch has developed a classification of the needs of individual family members in the following terms: autonomy—to be unattached; independence—to avoid domination and constraint; deference—to admire another person; nurturance—to help a weak person; recognition—to win the approval of others; succorance—to be loved and indulged.[7] From the point of view of society the family in modern urbanized society is the chief means of socializing children and maintaining the achieved socialization of adults. It is in terms of the satisfaction of these individual and societal requirements that the family caseworker judges the 'health' of the families with which she works.

In satisfying their individual needs the husband and wife evolve a series of interlocking role relationships which are later extended by the children and their needs. These relationships can be seen as divided into the nuclear family's three main systems, husband–wife, parent–child, child–child. In extended families, of course, each of the systems is complicated by the additional grandmother–grandfather dimension. The role relationships actually established at any stage in the development of a family are partly the product of the individual's previous personality development (people will bring to their marriage and their families a more or less extensive role-repertoire from which they can choose); partly the result of the demands made by the other partner in the role; and partly the result of modification induced by the family's changing task (socializing adolescents imposes different strains and evokes a different challenge from socializing the latency child) and the developing notion of the family's own identity. Moreover, families

do not live in a social vacuum and many of the internal transactions can be fully understood only when the definition of roles
current in the society (or subculture of the society) is taken into
account.

The family caseworker is, however, specially concerned with
the origins and resolution of family conflict. Spiegel has offered a
useful classification of the reasons for a breakdown in role com-
plementarity and of the steps that could be taken to restore it.[8] He
lists five possible sources of role conflict: cognitive discrepancy,
when one or both role partners are ignorant or unfamiliar with
the required roles: goal discrepancy, or a shift in the objective of
the role behaviour from gratification to defence or vice versa;
allocative discrepancy, or conflict over a person's right to the role
he wishes to occupy; instrumental discrepancy or the absence of
the necessary resources and, finally, discrepancy in cultural value
orientation. These conflicts are resolved by a number of different
processes, some of which are classified as manipulative and others
which come about through mutual insight. Among the former
processes Spiegel places coercing, coaxing, evaluating, masking
(the pseudo-mutuality described in chapter nine would be an
example), and postponing. The latter processes include role reversal, modification through joking, referral to a third party,
exploring, compromising and consolidating.

We have, so far, examined ways in which the family caseworker
might begin to understand the family as a group of interacting
individuals. The concepts that have been suggested can be summarized in the following diagram:

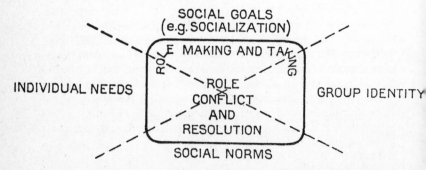

A knowledge of the family is required for casework in any setting,
but it is used more intensively and continuously by the family

casework agency as it responds to the client's request from or referral to a general social work agency. The family caseworker has a special responsibility in maintaining the connections between the internal world of the individual, the realm of family action and the wider society.[9] In his response the family caseworker uses methods which, though by no means exclusive to his setting, characterize his special approach. He has traditionally been more concerned than social workers in other agencies with the home visit, the request for material aid, the relationships between the family and the outside world and the multiple interview. These will be considered in detail below, but an attempt will first be made to illustrate the application of the concepts already noted in the case of the D. family.

The D. Family.

This family was referred by a health visitor to a family caseworker employed by a local authority for work with problem families. The problem was seen by the referring agent in terms of Mrs. D.'s relationship with her step-daughter, Rita. The family consisted of Mr. D. (33), Mrs. D. (21), his second wife, two children of the first marriage, John (10) and Rita (3) and Ronald (4 months) the child of the second marriage. John lived with his maternal grandmother, though his father had legal custody. The grandmother had 'rescued' John from his home because of his bad relationship with Mrs. D. The neighbours had complained about Mrs. D.'s treatment of Rita. *3. 6. 57.* Worker called. The house is one of a terrace block on a new housing estate. It had a small garden, carefully cultivated. The house was extremely clean, but very barely furnished. Mrs. D. was a youngish-looking person, with coarse features and an ugly laugh. She was very poorly dressed in contrast to the children, particularly the baby. She was carrying the baby and trying to feed with a bottle, but at once started by giving the worker a demonstration of R's 'odd' behaviour. She commanded R. to 'stand by the lady' and then smiled triumphantly when R. refused to do so and remained standing by her side. She said 'you see, she is all "Mummy" and will not go anywhere unless I tell her to, not even to her Daddy'. She complained about R's wetting and soiling 'which I will not stand from any child'. It was bad enough to have to wash nappies for the baby. R. presently asked to be put on the pot, and the mother rushed out of the room in a rage, shouting 'Who'd be a mother'. She several times hurled abuse at Rita when she so much as moved a limb.

The worker was struck by R's cowed behaviour and the automatic response to her stepmother's commands. She remained motionless in a chair when put there, looking at the worker with sad, intelligent eyes. She appeared to be well nourished and reasonably dressed, rather pasty faced, with straight straggly fair hair and blue eyes. Mother said that when R. had filled her knickers the previous day, she had put her to bed at 3 in the afternoon, leaving her there till the following morning, but added that of course she had taken some food up to her. She said her husband had disapproved of this treatment, but how else was she able to deal with it?

She said she had thought of leaving her husband with both children and taking herself to a great-aunt who had been very good to her. She regretted she could not give R. any love 'which was the right of every child' and at one point remarked, 'It is a shame really, she is such a pretty child.'

She said that only since meeting her husband had she herself known love and affection. He thought the world of her. She could understand his difficulties in not wishing to separate from R. after parting from John on account of her, for which she thinks he has never really forgiven her. She thought that if at least R. could be put into a day Nursery, that would be a solution of some kind. When staying with a paternal aunt during Mrs. D.'s confinement, she had been 'brought out of herself' and had seemed a different child.

Mrs. D. said that she had married her husband mostly so as to get away from her home as soon as possible. She had been an illegitimate child and had heard about this when she was 13. She had been brought up by her maternal grandmother in whose house she and her mother had lived, and her mother had told her she had not been able to stand her crying and filling her nappies which had made her mother want to hit her. She had thought for a long time that her mother was her sister and had called her 'Betty' and her grandmother 'Mother'. In later years she was hit several times for not calling her mother 'Betty'. She said she was raped by her grandfather when she was 10, and hit by him with a strap whenever she was 5 minutes late coming in at night. She had made repeated attempts to discover who her father was, and each time had been given different answers. Finally she had come to the conclusion that her mother did not know herself. Her mother seemed proud of having lived with several men. She said her mother had done her utmost to prevent her from reaching married status, and she herself regards it as some achievement that she has married the father of her child.

The worker remained almost entirely passive on this occasion, just listening to Mrs. D.'s story which she most willingly volunteered. She said she could understand her difficulties in giving

Rita love when she herself had so little love shown to her. She asked whether she would allow the worker to see her husband to hear his point of view before being able to decide what advice to give in the circumstances. Mrs. D. thought it would be quite easy for him to take off time, because he could make up for it.

9. 6. 1957. Appointment given to Mr. D. which he did not keep.

12. 6. 1957. Father to agency. He explained that he only had a few minutes since his pals were waiting for him in the van. The worker reassured him, and explained briefly the gist of her conversation with his wife and asked for his views. He is a slight, ill-looking man with haggard features. His talk was smooth and his intonation monotonous, and he used wide gestures as if he were trying to sell something. The worker noticed a difficulty in following questions, and he explained he was deaf in one ear because of a war injury. He has had a variety of jobs lately, selling carpets, vacuum cleaners and heating appliances, after giving up his work as a tool setter at X earning £15–20 p.w. because his second wife did not like being alone on his fortnightly shifts of night duty. He swept away the difficulties that existed by saying his wife tended to exaggerate. After the birth of her own baby, she had been like a cat on hot bricks with him and had been harried by Rita's demands on her. He made light of Rita's timid and frightened behaviour and said she was always like that with strangers. She was simply bored and that was why she wetted and soiled and tore pillow cases to shreds, and if the worker could get her into a nursery into the company of other children, everything would be all right. His wife used to have fearful tempers, but he had cured her by his firmness. He explained that she had had a shocking past and seemed surprised to hear the worker knew about it. He was adamant that he would not let Rita go. The worker said she appreciated his point of view and would investigate the possibility of admission to a nursery school. Having in mind Mrs. D's threat of leaving her husband and Rita she told him that he could always get in touch with her if necessary.

18. 6. 1957. Home visit without appointment. Mrs. D. opened the door with rather an apprehensive look which blossomed into a welcoming smile when she saw who it was. The worker noticed that whenever there is a knock at the door she looks as if expecting the worst. She had no teeth in her mouth and looked more spotty and slovenly than ever. Her husband, she said, was asleep upstairs, not having gone to work because he had overslept in the morning. She said at first it was nice to have him at home, but later remarked what a nuisance he was in the house and that she could not get on with her work. She said the worker's presence would be a good excuse to get him up. The worker explained she had come to have a chat with her, but she seemed ill at ease and insisted on getting him up.

Her husband came down shortly. He too was without teeth. He seemed slightly embarrassed on seeing the worker and hid this behind a manner of rather kittenish playfulness, but on the whole seemed more at ease than at the agency. The worker was surprised to hear a child singing and talking in the back and to discover it was Rita. Father was kindly and patient in dealing with her requests, whereas Mrs. D. just sat tut-tutting whenever there was a sound from her. She was markedly uncomfortable and whenever her husband left the room she found some excuse to get him back. In answer to the worker's question, she said she was afraid of saying anything and being taken to task by him after she had left. The worker mentioned the plan to get Rita into a nursery. She thought this would be a great help but that nothing but getting her out of the house permanently would make a real difference. Again she harped on the ill-treatment of Rita and how it would spoil her life. When her husband approached the room, she dropped her voice. The worker remarked that there might be an advantage in discussing the situation openly and in the presence of a third person. She agreed she would tackle her husband as soon as he came back into the room but did nothing. It seemed she was rather frightened of him and has to work herself up to a pitch, before she can put her case. In view of his placating manner with her, and his obvious preference for soft-pedalling difficult issues, her attitude seemed rather uncalled for.

After the husband had returned the worker made a start by saying that the solution they had discussed did not appear to be entirely acceptable to his wife. He pretended the worker was referring to the time that would have to elapse before Rita could be admitted to a nursery school. He spoke very suavely and with a great many clichés about how we could not expect things to happen more quickly. He used a torrent of glib talk to say very little and managed to side track his wife's gathering anger. The worker got him back to the real point at issue, which was the future of Rita, her happiness as well as his and his wife's. She stressed that any solution would have to be in the interest of all of them, and made no secret of the fact that this would not be easy.

At that moment, Mrs. D. found the necessary courage to explode. She said it was no good, she hated Rita and he would have to choose between them. He immediately tried to pacify her and it was he who then mentioned the possibility of Rita going to his sister's. In the ensuing conversation, Father convinced himself more and more that it would really not be difficult to let Rita go to his sister's—even though that would mean a break not only from Rita but from his sister as well. The worker pointed out these risks, but again he made light of them and said he was the sort of man who could be quite content with his own family and did not have to visit relatives. He could understand how his wife wanted to make a new start with a family of her own. He said that in a way he shared these feelings, and that he had sometimes wished they had not got Rita but the point was they had, and he had therefore expected his wife to accept the fact that she had 'got Rita for life'.

The more ready he seemed to let Rita go, the more Mrs. D. veered in the opposite direction. She now said it was no good, and would not be fair to her husband to allow him to give up Rita as well as John, but she herself could not alter either and she could not find any love for Rita, and the only solution would be for her and the baby to go. At this point she started to cry bitterly. She kept on repeating that but for the birth of her own baby she might have gone on loving Rita, but at the same time she admitted that her hatred of Rita had started before the birth of the baby. When she first came to Mr. D. as a house-keeper he had given her the chance of whether or not to keep Rita. At that time he said she seemed as fond of Rita as she was of her own baby now.

The worker said that they would have to talk at much greater length about the problem, and Mrs. D. said she would like to see the worker again.

19. 6. 1957. The local nursery school was approached and the case discussed with the head teacher. Apparently Mrs. D. had already been there to get Rita's name down and the teacher was appalled at Rita's condition—also the scratches on mother's face. Promised a place for September. Explained that they were trying to help by being maternal and supportive towards Mrs. D. who responded well to praise.

24. 6. 1957. Home visit. Mother worried about health of baby and asking for feeding instructions, hoping the visit would save her a walk to the Welfare. The worker explained she was not competent to advise, but reassured on apparently healthy looks of the baby and suggested she took him to the Welfare if she was worried.

She said her husband was going to phone the worker to ask whether she would go and see his first mother-in-law who was caring for John. Maybe she would also care for Rita. He had discussed the situation with his sister who had seemed willing to have her but had pointed out that this would mean a break between them.

On Thursday last week Mrs. D. and her husband had quarrelled again and she had gone to her mother's taking the baby with her and leaving Rita with a neighbour. She had left a note for her husband saying that she might be back at the weekend but might not come back at all. She described how he had been waiting for her to return, looking out of the window that evening, and she thought he had taken seriously her threat not to return. The worker asked why she had come back the same night, and she explained that there was no sleeping accommodation for the baby.

The worker then asked where Rita was. They were sitting in the front room and Mother explained that she had been in the process of changing her because she had wet her clothes. She got up and went into the back kitchen to collect her. There had been no sound from her and when she appeared she looked blue with cold, which Mrs. D. said was how she usually looked however warm it was. The worker gave Rita her keys to play with, and presently put her on her lap, where she quickly nestled herself. All the time the worker was talking with Mrs. D. who herself was making a fuss of the baby, cuddling it and kissing it. Worker asked her whether she sometimes felt like cuddling Rita and she said she did not.

She then suddenly announced she thought an exchange of house would be the ideal solution to all the difficulties. She thought she would be better able to show love to Rita if removed from this house and neighbourhood where everyone knew about her past. She felt quite sure it would make a difference to her feelings for Rita. While Rita was sitting on the worker's lap, she gave her a pencil and a piece of paper and she started to scribble and became quite animated. When her mother left the room for a moment Rita at once began to talk. This was the first time the worker had really heard her speak in conversation. She answered questions without any shyness, and laughed when she tickled her and continued to talk even when her mother returned to the room. Mrs. D. was surprised and said she had never spoken to people at the Welfare. Worker continued to fondle her and to talk to Mrs. D. at the same time, explaining that she was most willing to help with an exchange provided she and her husband could agree on what they wanted to do. She gave her praise for the way she was looking after the children from the physical point of view and stressed how clean and well-fed they looked. Mrs. D. said that to wash and iron for Rita was all she could do for her. The worker remarked that she had been interested in her husband's understanding of her when he had said that her conscience might worry her if she were to give up Rita. She reminded her that she was the only mother person Rita had known, and the satisfaction she might derive from making Rita into a happy little girl. She expressed herself strongly at Rita's wetting habits and said it was bad enough to have to wash nappies for the baby without having to cope with Rita's wetting as well.

When it was time for the worker to go she put Rita down and she went to stand by the side of her mother. Mrs. D. picked her up and started to fondle her and love her in her rough manner as she had previously done with her own baby. Rita responded by looking radiant and nestling against her mother gurgling with delight and Mrs. D. looked very happy. She insisted that the worker should take home some pinks which she had admired the previous week and told her to be sure and come again the following week. She said 'bless you' as she saw her to the door, still carrying Rita in her arms, and they both stood watching and waving as the worker got into her car.

The D. case shows in some detail a disturbed family group. Its identity is incompletely developed and it is in fact overshadowed by the first family and Mr. and Mrs. D.'s families of orientation. (Mrs. D. commented at a later date that Rita was cowed because she was afraid her mother would come and take her away.) Mrs. D. is clearly concerned about her right to be in the family and sees herself perhaps as someone who has stolen both R. and Mr. D. from another woman. She has certainly come between Mr. D. and his first son, but there are also some indications that Mr. D. colluded in this. The family appears to be meeting some social norms adequately—the house and garden are well kept. However, the inside of the home is bleak and comfortless, representing perhaps the members' feelings about the inner life of their family and themselves. The family appears to be failing in its task of socializing R. and only barely achieving the relief and management of tension amongst the adults.

The record of the case gives a much more complete picture of Mrs. D. and her relationship with R. than of other aspects of the family. Mrs. D. has brought many unsatisfied personal needs to the marriage and the family and these can be seen in R.'s problems. One of Mrs. D.'s greatest difficulties in dealing with her is that, for whatever reasons, she is so like Mrs. D.—she is dirty, she has not been given love, 'which is the right of every child'. Mrs. D. identifies herself strongly with R., but cannot satisfy the child's needs because they are her own. As a result of a deprived childhood Mrs. D. has not really the inner resources necessary for her mothering role. In many ways she would appear to be emotionally immature. Her ways of relating to Rita and Mr. D. (they are all for her or against her; she must go or some 'loved' person must go etc.) and her preoccupation with the themes of dirt and its control suggest what Renier and Kaufman have described as an anal character disorder.[10] Yet this must also be seen in relation to Mr. D. who seems to be letting her struggle with her problems of control etc. on her own. He mentions at one point that he has controlled her, but evidence of their behaviour together in the interview does not support this. Mrs. D.'s problems are presented primarily as arising from her relationship with R.—who has the right to be with father, or to be R.'s mother? How does the family attempt to deal with these problems? Mrs. D. attempts to coerce R. into behaving like a good child, while Mr. D. masks any series role conflict. R. herself still seems capable of response within a relationship, but this in its turn presents a rivalry situation with Mrs. D. There are many problems in this family, but continued investigation along the lines suggested will help to build what can be described as a family diagnosis. It is on the basis of this deepening understanding that help will be most effectively offered to the family.

The essential feature of help to this family will probably lie in long-term support and the acceptance of the fact that only slow progress is possible. In the beginning the worker may have to focus on Mrs. D., giving to her generously of her time and concern. As Mrs. D. responds to this (as she shows she can) it may then be possible gradually to include the other family members. It is important, however, not to do this prematurely. The worker in the recorded material seems in fact to have overestimated Mrs. D.'s capacity to share when she tried to show her what mothering R. might entail and how R. responded to it. The initial focus should remain on Mrs. D. for a considerable time, but, because of the nature of Mrs. D.'s identification with R., it is probable that in discussing Mrs. D.'s feelings as a child, implicit and helpful reference would be made also to R.

THE HOME VISIT

For a considerable period in the history of casework the home visit was largely taken for granted and no commentator seems to have considered it advantageous to describe or analyse the obvious. Until the late 1930's the home visit seems to have formed an unquestioned part of the process of fact-finding at the commencement of a piece of social casework. Its essential place in social casework can be seen in the early years of psychiatric social work. In the first year of the Mental Health Course at the London School of Economics in 1929/30, the Calendar stated that 'home visiting will form part of their (the psychiatric social work students) training'. One of the first articles by a psychiatric social worker stated that 'In a Psychiatric Clinic the task of the social worker is to help the doctor to gather the information necessary to diagnosis, and to carry out the part of the treatment which must be given in the home. . . .'[11]

Around 1940 there seems to have been considerable controversy amongst social workers about home visiting. Some social workers wished to emphasize the advantages (and status) of the office interview, whilst others saw the home visit as achieving objectives different from those of this kind of interview. The Hales, for example, in their essay on Social Therapy[12] in 1943 considered that the home visit established 'a really friendly relationship' and put the client–worker relationship 'on a much more matter of fact level'. Another writer in the same year suggested that 'No case front technique, however skilful can take the place of the less formal, more discursive contacts provided by home visits, though it must lay those firm foundations without which the latter may degenerate into mere conversation-making.'[13] It seems likely that, caseworkers had become self-conscious about, and possibly critical of, the verification function of the home visit and gave the visit the new more easily acknowledged purpose of friendly interchange.

The question whether the home visit was of any value at all was strongly put by Tod[14] in an article in 1950. He maintained that home visiting should not be an automatic part of the procedure of casework, but something to be decided in each case. He allowed that the visit might have value in checking the caseworker's first impressions, as a gesture of goodwill, or as a way of penetrating a confidence the client was not ready to make. On the other hand, it might help a client to avoid his problems in casework treatment, or neutralize his hostility which could be more easily accepted in 'the more impersonal atmosphere of the office'. Thus, the home visit was seen less as part of the procedure of investigation and more as an element in 'treatment'. This opinion, however, was not upheld by other writers at this time. In particular social workers with 'problem families' found that they had to begin offering their services on the doorstep.

A more recent factual study of the use of home visiting[15] suggested that 'reaching out' to the client by means of the home visit was experienced as a supportive measure and that the caseworker often obtained new information during her visits. It is, of course, easy to exaggerate the extent to which the client experiences the home visit in a positive light. A recent study of social work with families called attention to 'The "welfare" stereotype' and suggested that initially the worker was seen as a 'vague, rather threatening figure who had called on the family, evoking stereotyped responses and expectations'.[16] Sometimes, of course, the caseworker's visit evokes a more fearful and hostile reaction. In the case of Mrs. R. for example, the worker from a voluntary family caseworker agency, called at the home, having made an appointment by letter.

> Mr. R. was at home on his own. The worker introduced herself and explained which agency she came from. Mr. R. made no reply. The worker asked if the family had received her letter. Mr. R. said that indeed they had and he had thrown it on the fire. The social worker made no comment and Mr. R. said his wife had wished to 'phone to say she would be out, but by then it was too late as the letter had gone and the 'phone number with it.

In this home visit the social worker was certainly exposed to Mr. R.'s initial hostility, but because she was present in the situation she could demonstrate that this did not disturb her, encouraging Mr. R. by this response to enlarge on his reactions to social work help. In fact, he seemed to suggest that his feelings were more ambivalent than might at first have been obvious.

The home visit has special features of a positive and negative kind. It is, for instance, easier for the client to manipulate the worker, and the home contains innumerable sources of distraction from the business in hand. Yet the home visit should not be seen as entirely distinct from the office interview and the 'distractions' and difficulties can be seen as something more than irrelevancies. They are often a means of communication employed by clients who cannot refer to certain aspects of their problem verbally. Mr.

and Mrs. L. for example, never seemed able to remain together in the same room during the caseworker's visits. They would in turn find excuses (making tea, seeing to the children, getting some cigarettes etc.) to avoid a joint interview with the worker. They were splitting themselves off from each other because Mr. L. feared his wife's madness and Mrs. L. her husband's and her own aggression. The worker by her attitude, by her attempts to understand the husband–wife relationship, and by engineering some joint interviews was able to show the L's that dreadful consequences did not follow from renewed contact.

This illustrates one of the advantages of the home visit. The worker not only learns more, but, in some instances, is able to do more. The worker who visits a home regularly[17] is received *inside* the family and by her persistent endurance in the face of their dirt, anger, confusion, and emptiness is able to demonstrate that she is not overcome and destroyed. In the home visit the caseworker can use a number of different avenues of communication and can bring a 'difference' into the family. She may sometimes arrive or be called in at a point of crisis, but this is an opportunity for the worker to help the family to take in something of her attitudes and to learn from her actions. In the case of Mr. M. for example, the caseworker was called to the home at 10 o'clock one evening.

A family conference was in session with Mr. M's mother, Mrs. M. and Roger, the oldest son, aged 17. The worker had been called in because Peter (8) had stolen a watch from school. Mr. M. insisted on dragging Peter out of bed to explain his action. Mr. M. was shouting and from time to time Mrs. M. muttered that Peter would have to be put away. The worker had advised Mr. M. against rousing Peter from his bed. When Peter came down the worker said that everyone was feeling upset and unhappy and that went for Peter as well. Everyone proceeded to blame Peter and the worker asked why he had been called. What did the family want him to do? He suggested that there was a great deal of judging going on, and perhaps the M.s were afraid that they might be judged. Mr. M. protested that no one could judge him, but his mother told him to be quiet, that of course they were afraid. The worker said that the situation was not hopeless, though they might feel it was. He asked Peter for a short description of what had happened and suggested to Mr. M. that he went back to bed. Mr. M. had calmed down by this time and agreed. As the worker left, Mr. M. apologised for calling the worker out for something not very important. The worker said that it had been important and there was a lot of thinking to do on the problem, but none of them was at their best at that time of night.

MATERIAL AID

This topic has long puzzled and worried social workers. The granting of material aid has been seen as a relic of the paternalistic social work of the nineteenth century or as evidence of a less remote superficiality, that of treating symptoms and neglecting their cause. At the present time it is sometimes viewed as a necessary means of helping a family deal with its severe reality problems or establishing a relationship and thus paving the way for work on 'deeper problems'. It is nearly always treated as isolated from the main work with a family. Why does it persist as a worrying problem for the caseworker, especially since, comparatively speaking, the sums of money involved are often small? Caseworkers show no hesitation in spending a considerable amount of time with their clients and giving them a great deal of consideration and attention, but gifts in kind seem to constitute a different sort of giving.

As a first approximation to understanding the significance of material aid, let us 'take the role of the other' and ask what happens when clients offer caseworkers material gifts. The situations are not, of course, identical; the gift is frequently offered towards the end of a contact and is not given because the worker has requested it. None the less, there are sufficient parallels to make this a useful preliminary line of inquiry.

> (1) Mrs. W. knew that the (male) caseworker was leaving the agency. She rather awkwardly pushed a small paper bag across the table. It contained a handkerchief. She explained that it was 'not much', in fact she had got it in a sale. It might even have 'seconds' printed on it, she hadn't looked.
> (2) Miss T. (19) gave the worker a large bunch of roses in December. Her mother was somewhat disparaging of the gift, but later sent the worker a box of chocolates. The worker had discovered that one of Miss T's problems lay in her relationship with her father who had died recently. She felt very guilty about her hostility and spent large amounts of money buying flowers for his grave.

These two short extracts illustrate some of the complex feelings that can be communicated by a gift. The complexity can only be seen if the context in which the gift is offered is appreciated. Some of the context in case (2) is clearly apparent: the gift seems partly an attempt to bind the worker to Miss T. rather than to her mother and partly an indication that Miss T. is allaying her feelings towards the worker in the same way that she deals with her feelings towards her dead father. In case (1) the context is less clear, but Mrs. W. seemed to be apologizing for her gift and denying its value. This was mainly because she always doubted her own value and the goodness of anything she made or gave away. The gift may also be an indication of the value the client places on the worker and the service he or she has given and Mrs. W. might be expressing some of her resentment towards the worker because he was leaving the agency.

The caseworker needs to attend to the context in which the gift is offered so that she can assess the significance of its content and also of the act of giving. By offering a gift the client is attempting to initiate a new giving–taking role relationship. What significance might this possibly have? Obviously, it could be a way of expressing gratitude for help received or a means of playing a role otherwise denied, as, for example, in the case of the client who asked the worker to accept a present, saying 'I have no one to whom I can give'. On the other hand, the offer of a gift could be a sign of restlessness with being a client, always, so to speak, at the receiving end of the transactions. Sometimes, it seems, the client is asking how will the worker respond to this reversal of roles. In such situations the client is eliciting a response in the worker as a means of communicating to him more vividly what he feels as a recipient of help. At other times, the gift can be seen as a way of fixing a closer definition of the worker's identity or of masking hostile feelings towards the worker.

This brief discussion of the possible significance of the client's giving underlines one important aspect of the work of dealing with the client's request for material relief. The caseworker's attitude should be one of preparedness to view the request as purposive beyond the simple acquisition of a sum of money or an article of clothing, and the granting of aid as helpful over and above the effectiveness of a business transaction. In other words, the caseworker should not wish to split the giving of material help from the relationship of the client to the worker and to the agency he represents. The caseworker will not wish simply to grant a request (or refuse it) with courtesy and a mind blank to other possibilities. Yet, the material aid has also its economic significance as the social worker's knowledge of the working of contemporary society will demonstrate. Poverty is still a real problem in 'the Welfare State' and, whilst its alleviation is clearly the work of the large-scale services of Social Security and National Assistance, the casework agency has a part to play in alleviating some of the effects of poverty in the individual case. In order to fulfil this function helpfully and also avoid separating 'material needs, and the ways in which they are to be met, from human purpose and the development of being and relationship',[18] it is essential that the general social work agency formulates a clear policy for the guidance of workers and clients. The agency should decide that it is compatible with its general social function to grant certain sums of money etc. under certain conditions and for certain objectives. In the perspective of such a policy the caseworker's task in regard to material aid falls into line with the rest of his casework, which is aimed at answering the question, how can I help the client to use the services my agency offers?

Two Case Illustrations

(1) Mrs. D. (whose case has already been discussed on page 187) asked the caseworker for help with her children's clothing. The worker wanted to encourage Mrs. D. to take a more motherly interest in the children and to show her concern for Mrs. D. in a concrete manner. Mrs. D. had been very diffident in making the request and the worker had acknowledged her difficulty. She said that the agency could give some good second-hand clothing provided by people living in the city for 'people in temporary need'. Did Mrs. D. think she could qualify for this? Mrs. D. tended to withdraw her request, but the worker helped her to reach a decision and also involved Mr. D. He also was reluctant, feeling that the application for material help cast a doubt on his ability to provide for the family, but eventually he said his wife could apply 'just for this once'. The caseworker had noted that Mrs. D. had asked only for the children and not herself. She provided the children with two sets of clothes and also took some clothes for Mrs. D. In this way her gift not only helped at a time of financial difficulty, but also communicated to Mrs. D. that she valued both children and mother and that it was possible for them to be given things by the same person.

(2) The V. family had been known to the family casework agency for three years and during this time there had been three changes of worker. The V's were always asking for material help usually in the form of clothes for every member of the family. Requests began as hints and then developed into what amounted to demands.

On one occasion Mrs. V. asked if the worker had an old suit that he did not want, adding that the children were also short of clothes. The worker wondered how this would help. Mr. V. said that was a silly question. He spoke at some length about the former worker who had never made a fuss. 'It wasn't as if they were new clothes; they were only second-hand and he knew the agency was full to bursting with clothes and here was his family with hardly a thing to their name.' The worker said that Mr. V. obviously felt that he was being unhelpful, but he wanted to try to see if there was not some other way that might be more beneficial in the long run. Mr. V. said that the worker should not worry so much. He knew that the worker would find them something if only he tried. The worker said that the V's could see he was trying to help them reach a point at which they could get new clothes. 'That'll be the day' said Mrs. V.

Some months later when the worker was leaving the agency he had a long discussion with Mr. V. about the agency. In the course of the interview Mr. V. made the following remarks: 'We've been a nuisance about asking for clothes and things, haven't we? We've been a trouble to you.' The worker agreed that he had not always known the best way to help with their frequent requests for material aid. Mr. V. said that it was their job to make the demands and the worker's to control them.

This case raises a number of important issues in the handling and understanding of requests for material aid. The absence of an agency policy in regard to the function of giving such help created a situation in which the family was encouraged to regard the clothes as the personal gift of the worker. Consequently, they adopted strategies of coercion, persuasion and coaxing. They reiterated the fact that their request was only for second-hand clothing, and this acts as a reminder that we should view the giving of material help within the context of communication. Does the gift of second-hand clothing, for example, suggest to the recipients that they are 'second-hand' people? Certainly, in the V. case the parents seem to be basing their request on a fantasy picture of the agency, full to bursting with 'good things', and of themselves as essentially 'empty', unable to create 'new or good things' for themselves. The final comment of Mr. V. could be seen as an indication of his emotional immaturity,[10] since he appears to be drawing a picture of himself and his family as a group of greedy, demanding children who cannot control themselves and who need the guiding hand of others. He suggested that the worker should have set some limits to their greedy demands. His behaviour bore some resemblance to that of a two-year-old. Yet of greater significance is the fact that he knew he wanted to be treated as a young child and a two-year-old, of course, does not. Consequently, the response of the worker should not be one of simply complementing Mr. V.'s role expectation, but rather of questioning the role he offered, of asking why Mr. V. wanted to be treated as if he were a child by that particular worker on a number of particular occasions.

RELATIONSHIPS WITH THE OUTSIDE WORLD

In helping the family in its relationships with the world outside its boundaries, the family caseworker recognizes the importance of these relationships and uses his position as an 'outsider' within the family. This position helps him to mediate between the family and outside agencies in a way that encourages the family members most concerned with playing instrumental as contrasted with expressive roles. The caseworker will help the family both with its feelings about outside agencies and also with its actual transactions with them, but in both instances the aim is to enhance rather than depress their own capacities.

(1) In the V. case, the family caseworker helped Mrs. V. to make contact with the hospital by making an appointment for her and calling to collect her to go there. When she visited it was obvious that Mrs. V. was not going. She made various excuses, but the worker who had had this kind of experience with Mrs. V. before, refused to accept them. She admitted her annoyance and said it was due to the fact that she was concerned about the seriousness of Mrs. V's ill-health. The worker suggested that all the reasons for Mrs. V's refusal could have been met in one way or another and she wondered if there was a reason they had not yet discussed. Eventually, Mr. V. said that Mrs. V. should tell the worker and Mrs. V. said she was frightened because she had nits in her hair. The worker said she was sorry not to have thought of this. She offered to get the family the

necessary equipment, but they insisted they could manage. New tentative arrangements were made about a hospital appointment.

Later, the worker telephoned the hospital. She spoke with the ward sister who was angry about Mrs. V's non-appearance. A new appointment was made.

On the day of the appointment the worker called and accompanied Mrs. V. to hospital. She was detained and the worker spent some time settling her in and helping her with the formalities of admission. She discussed with Mrs. V. how she would cope with her feelings in hospital and talked over some of Mrs. V's problems with sister, after she had obtained her client's permission to do so.

(2) Mr. V. was feeling extremely aggressive towards his eldest son, George (14). He burst into the house while the worker was there and began hitting George about the face. He accused him of truanting from school and stealing and he said he was going to the headmaster to drag George's name in the mud and then he would go to the police and tell them. The worker suggested that he accompanied Mr. V. to the school. They all went to the school and George admitted truanting and stealing; he had given the money to his mother. It was discovered that he had not in fact had many absences that term and Mr. V. eventually became more calm. He asked the worker if he would like a word on his own with the headmaster, but the worker did not think this would be necessary. Mr. V. seemed puzzled by this and once they were outside the school, he questioned the worker. He said that the former worker would have talked with the head on his own. The worker said that he did not feel he should say anything that Mr. V. did not hear. He suggested that Mr. V. had managed the interview well; he had found out what he wanted to know and he had not lost his temper. Mr. V. listened to this with some interest and said he had decided not to go on to the police station.

It is not always possible, of course, to avoid the anger clients sometimes feel towards the casework agency as one of the depriving 'them'.

A few weeks after the above episode, for example, Mr. V. called at the casework agency and demanded why no one had been in court when George had been charged. He thought that the service given by the agency to his family had deteriorated considerably since the days when Miss Q. used to be their worker. He drew a detailed picture of those halcyon days and became more and more angry. The worker wondered where all this was getting them, adding in a quiet but firm tone that really Mr. V. was angry because he had not been to court himself. This halted Mr. V's angry torrent.

In this situation it is important for the caseworker to avoid the proferred roles of becoming angry and retaliating or of placating the anger. Instead the worker should attempt to initiate a new role, that of withstanding in order to understand. Why was Mr. V. feeling so angry? In some ways, it seems, he is expressing the frustrated fury of the infant who has lost the all-powerful, all-giving Mother. At the same time his aggressive, demanding behaviour represents his conception of the adult masculine role. It is also possible to see his aggression as a defence against the realization of his own considerable unmet needs.

MULTIPLE INTERVIEWING

The family caseworker who visits the family in their own home often finds herself conducting multiple interviews rather than the more traditional one-to-one interview of the office or clinic. In family casework this kind of interviewing is frequently the method of choice. In the first place it encourages the integrative forces within the family, by symbolically and literally 'keeping things and people together'. Mr. E., for instance, had been an invalid for a number of years and to match his uncertain view of his own masculinity he had married a rather unfeminine woman, whom he encouraged to remain unclean and unadorned by make-up. (When she began to take a pride in her appearance he became anxious, saying, rather fearfully, that he did not recognize her.) On one occasion the worker called and discussed Mrs. E.'s gynaecological problems.

> Mr. E. became restless and said that he wished there was another room in which they could talk about 'these female things'. He seemed relieved, however, when he was included much more obviously in the conversation. In this way he was helped not to feel excluded from 'these female things' which frightened him, but which he would have to begin to face if he was to become more certain of his own sexual identity.

The multiple interview also shows the participants how they react upon one another and is perhaps particularly useful for those clients who act out their relationship problems. In the multiple interview, whether this is at the client's home or at the agency, the caseworker is able to see how the family wants to present itself to the outside world represented by his presence. At the same time he should appreciate the difference that his presence makes to the interaction within the group. In the Z. family, for instance, the following extract from an interview illustrates the effect that a caseworker's intervention might have on family relationships:

26. 4. 61. (In the previous interview Mr. and Mrs. Z. had been seen and Mrs. Z. had complained about not getting out of the house, and about her depression. The worker had offered to baby-sit one evening whilst Mr. and Mrs. Z. went out.)

The worker said that she could baby-sit on Monday night. Mrs. Z. rather too quickly said that the Darts Match for that night had been cancelled. The worker talked a little of Mrs. Z's depression and Mr. Z. agreed that his wife had been feeling low recently. Worker wondered if he had considered taking her to the cinema. He said he was bored with T.V. and with the cinema. The worker offered to baby-sit on another night. Tony (15), the eldest son, then volunteered to take his mother out, saying that if she waited for his father to take her out she'd wait for ever. Mr. Z. appeared restive, but said nothing. (It later transpired that Tony did take his mother to the cinema and that Mrs. Z. refused to go out with her husband.)

The important feature of this extract is not so much the pressing of an issue in terms foreign to the norms of the family (encouraging joint husband and wife recreation), but the effect of the caseworker's intervention in exposing Mrs. Z. to a plight from which she had to be rescued by her son. In pressing Mr. Z. the worker encouraged an oedipal definition of the situation and did nothing to help the family to face and begin to remedy some of the difficulties involved.

Naturally, it is not always possible or advisable to use multiple interviewing. At times it may be important to give special, individual attention to a particular member of a family. Quite often children (particularly adolescents) could profit from separate help from the caseworker and some aspects of the parent–child relationship might be reserved for discussion with parents who need considerable support before they can begin to examine the parental roles. Where the destructive impulses in the family are directed towards wrecking or persistently confusing channels of communication, it would seem advisable to avoid multiple interviewing as a regular method.

At present social workers have not given very much attention to interviewing the family as a multiple unit. Scherz[20] in America has suggested four special techniques for this approach—intervention in terms of the family's interaction; empathetic neutrality on the part of the worker; ensuring that the family group knows the worker will not allow one member to destroy another; and using non-verbal as well as verbal behaviour as a basis for interpretation. These, however, seem not to be techniques. Rather they concern the clarification of the worker's identity and function and his 'openness' to every kind of communication and these features are fundamental to casework in any kind of interviewing.

NOTES

[1] See e.g. Donnison, D. and Stewart, M., *The Child and The Social Services*, Fabian Research Series, No. 196, 1958.

[2] Hill, R., in his revision of Waller's, *The Family*, Dryden Press, 1951, p. 460.

[3] Hill, R., *Families Under Stress*, Harper, 1949, p. 10.

[4] Waller, W., *The Family*, Dryden Press, 1951, p. 33.

[5] Sumner, W. G., *Folkways*, Ginn, 1906, pp. 345–6.

[6] Bosanquet, H., *The Family*, Macmillan, 1902, p. 242.

[7] Winch, R. F., *The Modern Family*, Holt, 1952, pp. 408–9.

[8] Spiegel, J., 'The Resolution of Role Conflict Within the Family', in Bell, N. and Vogel, E. (eds.), *A Modern Introduction to the Family*, Routledge & Kegan Paul, 1961.

[9] The twofold analysis of existing role-playing and of the internalized images of the individual family members can be seen in the fruitful work of Elles in this country. See: Elles, G., 'Treatment of a Family Problem Linked with Psychopathic Illness', *Case Conference*, Sept., Oct., Nov. 1962; 'The Closed Circuit: the Study of a Delinquent Family', *British Journal of Criminology*, Vol. 2, No. 1, July 1961.

[10] Reiner, B. and Kaufman, I., *Character Disorders in Parents of Delinquents*, Family Service Association of America, 1959. For a recent discussion of families like the D.'s see Philp, A. F., *Family Failure*, Faber, 1963, Chapter 16.

[11] Rees, J. R. and Robinson, D. F., 'Modern Psychiatry and Social Work', *Almoner's Year Book*, 1930.

[12] Hale, M. B. and Hale, S. M., 'Visiting', Chapter V in *Social Therapy*, London 1943.

[13] Bogue, K., 'Three Homes', *Social Work*, Oct. 1943.

[14] Tod, R. J., 'Why Visit?', *Social Work*, April 1950.

[15] Paterson, J. and Cyr, F., 'The Use of the Home Visit in Present-Day Social Work', *Social Casework*, April 1960.

[16] Howarth, E. E. *et al.*, *The Canford Families*, The Sociological Review Monograph No. 6, 1962, p. 166.

[17] Both Paterson and Cyr, op. cit., and Howarth, op. cit., have called attention to the ways in which the home visit reproduces or can be made to reproduce some of the positive features of the clinic interview.

[18] Williams, R., *Culture and Society*, Chatto and Windus, 1958, p. 213.

[19] For comments on this concept see my *Casework in the Child Care Service*, Butterworths, 1962, pp. 137–8.

[20] Scherz, F., 'Multiple-Client Interviewing: Treatment Implications', *Social Casework*, Vol. XLIII, No. 5, May 1962.

Chapter Nine

PSYCHIATRIC SOCIAL WORK

INTRODUCTION

PSYCHIATRIC social work is the youngest of the casework specializations, with the exception of child care. It has become the most established of the branches of casework and its prestige has grown to considerable proportions within and outside social work. The history of the profession,[1] however, shows much uncertainty about the nature of psychiatric social work—a form of psychotherapy, a particular level of casework (psychotherapeutic casework), or social work carried out in conjunction with psychiatry? The latter conception obviously describes psychiatric social work in mental hospitals and child guidance clinics where psychiatrists have the main authority for treatment. It seems less appropriate to the field of community care where there is no teamwork in the usual sense and very limited psychiatric consultation on cases. Some psychiatric social workers in this field see their service as the nucleus of a general family casework service department in a local authority, viewing their problems of special interest as those of mental ill-health widely defined rather than those of psychiatric illness. They base their service on the client's everyday life at work and at home rather than on his role as a past or possible future hospital patient. It is arguable that this conception of a form of casework should be seen as family casework in a statutory agency rather than as psychiatric social work. Community care in general, however, is included in the present chapter as one of the three main fields of psychiatric social work, though it is important to note that it is still creating its own identity and that the form this eventually takes will have many implications in a consideration of the functions of community care agencies.

What can be said in general about the three fields of psychiatric social work, the child guidance clinic, the mental hospital, and community care? The psychiatric social worker has been trained to work in institutions and organizations carrying out a series of *treatments* or rehabilitation usually under psychiatric auspices of those defined (by themselves, by their relatives, by social agencies) as maladjusted or mentally ill; the availability of these treatments is authorized generally by the community. These institutions (hospitals, clinics etc.) have general and special characteristics and it is part of the function of the psychiatric social worker to understand them.[2] Similarly, it is her obligation to keep her knowledge of treatment up to date because it might involve a change in the world she, the patients and their families inhabit. The clientele of the psychiatric social worker will differ in some respects according to his or her field, but they will themselves tend to occupy a particular deviant role ('problem child', mentally ill person) and to exhibit failure in one or more significant 'normal' role-relationships (e.g. those considered appropriate to a child of a certain age and sex etc.) or they will be intimately concerned with such a deviant.

The psychiatric social worker's problems of special concern lie in the world of madness, its manifestations and treatment, and our social attitudes towards it. This, of course, makes considerable demands upon her. She works to a considerable extent in consultation with or under the direction of psychiatrists and this has often in the history of her profession posed problems of rivalry and envy. At times psychiatric knowledge (particularly of the psychoanalytic schools) has appeared as a body of wisdom to be incorporated wholesale rather than selectively adapted. It is, however, contact with madness that constitutes the psychiatric social worker's main challenge, just as in the work of the probation officer it is contact with deviance requiring legal remedy or treatment. Our present attitude towards madness clearly represents a revolutionary change from the days when the mentally ill were punished or shut away and neglected as a shameful disgrace. Yet the extent and depth of change over the last few years must not be exaggerated. We say, for instance, that we are now becoming more used to treating mental disease as an illness, just like a physical illness. This is perhaps a rather loose way of questioning why mental illness should be stigmatized if physical illness is not. It can also, of course, represent a denial of the simple fact that mental illness is not entirely and exactly like physical illness. The term itself is sometimes used to hide our fears of certain kinds of behaviour more evident perhaps in the more stark, old-fashioned notion of 'madness'.

We are certainly more informed about madness and its treatment, but progress in the extension of humane understanding is limited by the fact that many of our ideas of madness have their source in unconscious fantasy. Some of the implications of this approach have been usefully discussed by Williams[3] from the viewpoint of the patient, the members of his family and the social worker. The epileptic patient, for example, may feel a deep stigma because her illness 'is a symbol of all the sadistic phantasies and destructive impulses inside her, and the sign to others of her imperfection and incompleteness . . .'. Families with a mentally sick member may find their unconscious wishes reactivated in a way that threatens their control by the behaviour of the mad person. Social workers have to acknowledge the irreversibility of organic damage and chronic dependency and 'The sufferer who fails to improve is in danger of meeting primitive human behaviour disguised as treatment'.[4]

Faced with the depth and complexity of the world of madness social workers may sometimes feel that their skill and knowledge can make little or no therapeutic contribution. In some particularly taxing cases they may suggest that only the psychiatrist can help their clients. In this context the possible goals of casework and the minimum conditions for its efficacy assume more than usual importance. Caseworkers cannot, of course, expect to cure mental illness, but they can help a person to sustain and consolidate the healthy aspects of his personality for more satisfying performance in one or more of his significant roles. Even for psychotics mental illness does not usually have a complete and uniform effect on the whole personality; it often affects social functioning in an essentially 'patchy' manner. (I remember once visiting a woman diagnosed as a paranoid schizophrenic. She complained at length of the electrical charges coming from the flat above and from the neighbour at the end of her garden. Her daughter (aged 18) came into the room to ask if her mother wanted her to do some shopping. The mother at once 'switched off' her delusional system and gave her daughter what appeared to be a realistic list of requirements.) Caseworkers must be able to establish a system of communication as a minimum condition for successful work and it may seem that this is often impossible in the case of deluded people. It is, however, a mistake to consider their unrealistic and bizarre conversation as so much nonsense. Mental illness does not constitute a total breakdown in communication, but does introduce a considerable degree of distortion into the system. This underlines the importance of the caseworker's purposive attention not simply to what the client is saying, but to what he is trying to tell the worker by direct or indirect means.

MENTAL HOSPITAL WORK

Social work in the mental hospital has many similarities with the medico-social work we have already discussed in chapter five. Its special characteristics spring from the task of the mental hospital, the treatment of mental illness. The following case illustrates the kind of work this may entail for the caseworker.

Vera L.

When Miss L. (aged 30) was referred to the psychiatric social worker in July 1961 by the hospital psychiatrist, Dr. X, she had been known to the mental hospital as an in-patient or an out-patient for about eight years. She had been admitted to hospital on three occasions following suicide attempts. Her diagnosis at the time of referral was hysteria?, schizophrenia? She was referred because her move to another area made the continuation of out-patient therapy from Dr. X impossible. Little was known about her childhood. Her mother was alive, but had advanced paranoid schizophrenia and the grandmother was apparently the most stable figure in Vera's childhood. In the work undertaken by the hospital psychiatric social worker attention was focused less on the past and more on the problems Vera was facing in the present. What follows is an account of some of this work in which the social worker tried to help Vera to value herself and her job (she was a teacher), and to maintain her independent functioning as a person, in spite of her feelings about herself. The main means of help chosen by the psychiatric social worker were support and interpretation of the meaning of some of the transactions of their developing relationship. Vera was seen over a year, usually once, but sometimes twice, a week. The worker would often arrange to meet Vera after school and interviews would then be conducted

in her car. Sometimes Vera would say very little and on occasions
when she came to the hospital she would spend much of the
allotted time in an adjoining room.

23. 7. 61. The psychiatric social worker arranged to meet Miss L. at
a railway station on her way home from school and the first interview
took place in her car. An attempt had been made to arrange an
interview at the hospital, but Miss L. had said she had just started at
a new school and did not want to take time off.

Miss L. greeted the worker by saying in a hostile, challenging
manner, 'Give me one reason for living'. She did not know how she
had managed to get through the day at school. Her colleagues were
kind, but she did not want kindness nor even contact with people.
The worker wondered if this was what she felt about her also. Miss
L. said she did not know. She said she could not give of herself as
she used, that she wanted to help people, but it was as if she had to
make herself suffer. The worker wondered if she could explain. She
said that she wanted to find God. She used to teach in a Sunday
School, but she felt the devil was behind her. She went on to ask how
it was that worker could help people, and the worker said that
perhaps she was wondering if the worker could help her. Her reply
was an aggressive affirmative: 'You've got to make me feel better'.
Worker suggested that Miss L. wanted someone who could change
things in a flash. This apparently quietened her because she said she
knew this was not possible but she did want to get better. She feels
that at the moment she can only live for her father, since she is sorry
for him because of her mother's nagging. Yet she hates him and
cannot bear him to show her any affection. This was followed by a
long pause. Then a crowd of people came out of the railway station
and Miss L. wondered if they looked like wild animals to the worker.
Miss L. thought they did: like wild animals about to attack her. The
worker asked if she looked like a wild animal, too, and Miss L.
replied that she did not sound like one. She felt safe only in hospital.

She returned to the subject of 'giving' and said she used to be able
to give of herself until about two years ago. Worker wondered what
happened then and Miss L. replied she had quarrelled with her
boyfriend. It had, she supposed, been all her fault; she criticised
everything. Suddenly she said she should go. The worker made no
comment except to confirm the arrangement that they should meet
next week.

30. 7. 61. Miss L. arrived 55 minutes late for her hour's appointment
in the out-patient department. Worker explained that she had another
appointment in five minutes. Miss L. could not say why she was

late, but said she might be going to her sister this week in Birmingham and might stay permanently. She was not sure of this, because being with people worried her. She seemed relieved when the worker said she would keep her appointment open for the next week.

6. 8. 61. Miss L. did not come. Letter from worker and a further meeting was arranged.

18. 9. 61. Worker met Miss L. from work. She seemed restless and fidgety throughout the hour. She complained that she felt empty, that she could not give anything in her work. She asked about Dr. X. and said she loved him. The worker suggested that she felt badly because she was seeing her instead of Dr. X. Miss L. denied this and went on to say that she was wasting worker's time because she could not say all the things she wanted to say. Worker suggested that Miss L. perhaps felt that worker would suggest it was not worth their while meeting. She glowered at the worker and said nothing. Worker said that possibly Miss L. felt that when she became fond of people, sooner or later, they disappeared from her life. Miss L. was silent for about ten minutes and then got up to go. Worker reaffirmed the next appointment and as she went Miss L. asked in an aggressive way 'I wonder how you knew', presumably in connection with worker's last comment about her feelings.

19. 9. 61. Letter from Miss L., saying that everything she said was degrading and hopeless and she hated the fact that the worker had to listen. She wished she could say something good that would make sense. She knew that all the people at the hospital thought dying was wrong, but that was all she wanted to do. She said that the worker had hurt her yesterday, and she had to run away, because she hated the worker so. If the worker came again Miss L. could not promise to be any different, but she did appreciate the worker's interest.

23. 9. 61. Worker met Miss L. at the station as arranged by letter. (This addressed Miss L. by her Christian name). Vera was unable to say what had upset her last week. She felt guilty because she could not talk. The worker wondered why she felt guilty. There was a very long pause and the worker suggested that it was perhaps because Vera felt she was wasting the worker's time, and that perhaps she wanted to please the worker by talking. There was another long pause and Vera said it was a bit of both: she always lets down the people she is fond of. The worker wondered if this also applied to her. Vera coloured and then said she did not know. Worker wondered if Vera felt Dr. X. had let her down. Vera said she hated men (except Dr. X.) because they let you down and she was afraid of them. She could not expand on this fear. Worker discussed her going on holiday next week and arranged the next appointment in two

weeks. The worker linked the fact of her approaching holiday with Vera's feelings of rejection. Vera denied this, but turned very pink.
8. 10. 61. Worker had had to change time of appointment and was on the 'phone when Vera arrived. When she came into the worker's room after a delay of approximately five minutes she was very angry. She sat down and all she said was that the worker seemed like a stranger again. Worker commented on Vera's great distress and asked if this was linked with the fact that Vera had not seen her for two weeks or with her anger at being kept waiting. Vera sat in silence for about ten minutes and then said she should go. She did not reply to the worker's question about this for about five minutes and then said she felt she was going to explode and she did not want to do that here. By the time she had said this she was out of the door.
9. 10. 61. Worker wrote saying she would be pleased to meet her next week.

11. 10. 61. Vera wrote apologising for her rudeness and saying that there was no goodness in her. She had hated worker for being so much in charge of the situation. She felt at times that she hated all the world: the worker would not know this feeling but Vera was glad she bore with it.

15. 10. 61. Interview at hospital out-patient department. Vera apologised for rudeness and then asked if Dr. X. told the worker that she *had* to see her. Worker commented that Vera found it difficult to believe that anyone would want to see her, to which Vera replied that she hated people, so how could they want to see her. Vera said she felt worse at the hospital because everyone was so busy helping people and she could not even help herself. She asked again if worker was sure she was not wasting her time. Worker wondered if perhaps she had felt like this with other people. Vera said that she had always been in her mother's way; her mother had never wanted her and Vera hated her. She recalled that when she first went to school, mother had been very jealous of the fact that she held the teacher's hand. Worker linked Vera's mixed feelings for her mother with her relationship to the worker and Vera nodded.

25. 10. 61. Vera flung open the door of worker's car and threw herself into the seat, almost literally spitting at the worker, 'Why do I have to live?' Worker commented on her angry and upset feelings. Vera made no reply, but ceased playing with the door handle. When they reached a convenient place at which to stop and talk, Vera said she could not go on for long like this. She asked if the worker thought God would damn her if she committed suicide. The worker said she could not answer that for her, but it seemed a pity to waste her potentialities in this way. Vera said that she had none. Worker

said that it was not easy to face problems in oneself, but if one could then one often had more to give. Vera said that she hated everybody; she did not want to, but she could not help it. Worker commented that some part of her did hate people, but another part did not. Vera said that she had phoned Dr. X. last week and the worker commented on her positive feeling for him. Vera said he was very helpful and understanding and the worker said that perhaps Vera felt the worker did not understand. Vera replied by saying in a very controlled way that she hated the worker. Worker said that there was a part of Vera that did feel like this, but that Vera also had more positive feelings for her, and it was really these that made for difficulty for her. Vera became sarcastic at this point and said that the worker must be very happy, knowing and watching everything and not caring at all. The worker was sorry Vera felt like this because she was concerned for her, but perhaps Vera had had similar feelings in the past. Vera said that worker was just like her mother and she hated her and she hated the worker. She expressed her hatred with venom and then broke down in quiet sobbing, saying she could not love anybody. Worker said she was sure Vera could, but that mixed feelings could be very painful and sometimes it was easier to feel angry than to take the risk of being hurt too much by people one was fond of. They drove back in silence to the spot where Vera usually left the worker. The worker repeated the arrangements for next week and Vera thanked her quietly and calmly.

Other interviews followed and the problem on each occasion seemed to be Vera's great sense of failure and her fierce ambivalent feelings. At the end of October she had a short period in hospital. Arrangements were made for her to continue seeing the worker after her discharge, but the first of these new appointments was broken by the worker because of illness. Vera was very upset by this and wrote (6.11.61) accusing the worker of making excuses because she did not wish to see her, and calling her a Judas. The worker replied by simply restating the fact of her illness and making an arrangement to meet. Vera was admitted to hospital later in December, and the next recorded interview took place after her discharge.

7. 1. 62. Vera had written to ask for the appointment. She said that she wanted to talk, but it was just the same. Worker wondered if she meant her feeling that she could not talk. She nodded and the worker talked about other ways of communicating. She suggested that Vera and she were communicating even though Vera sometimes just came

and sat. There was a long pause and then Vera said that she was all bad; how could anybody like her. Worker suggested that she felt the worker could not like her and Vera replied that, of course, she could not, as Vera hated her. She did not reply when the worker asked her why, and when the worker wondered if she did something that upset Vera, she simply said 'no'. Worker wondered if she reminded Vera of someone else. After a long pause Vera mentioned her Sunday School teacher: she said that she loved her, but she disappeared like all the people she had loved. The worker wondered what love meant for Vera, and Vera described it as the sort of love a child gets from a mother, from someone who made you feel safe and who looked after you when you were afraid. Vera denied any sexual aspect to love. The worker suggested that Vera's feelings towards her were a mixture of feelings she had towards the Sunday School teacher and towards her mother.

The themes of Vera's badness, her fear of desertion by the worker, and her feeling that she has always loved the wrong people (i.e. women and not men) were continued in the next interviews.

17. 3. 62. Vera asked the worker how *could* she help her; she could not go on struggling, never getting any better. The worker suggested that, in fact, Vera was now much more able to talk about her feelings. Vera said that this was so, but when the worker knew how weak Vera was she would. . . . There was a long silence and the worker wondered what Vera thought she would do. At last, Vera said the worker would put her in a pram like a baby. Worker asked what Vera meant. There was another long pause and then Vera talked of her teacher at school whose help Vera had wanted: she had always wanted to hold her hand. When she was at school the children used to have to stop before crossing the road, but Vera always ran on: she wanted to go back and hold teacher's hand, but always ran on. One day the teacher had a pram and put Vera in it. Vera almost exploded whilst describing this episode and added that the teacher had been so kind and good like the worker. Worker suggested that Vera thought that the worker would do something like that to make her feel small and unwanted. Vera suggested that the worker would do this. Worker reassured her that she would not and thought that perhaps the teacher had not really understood what Vera had been trying to tell her. Vera said she hated her and ran home to her grandmother who went to the Headmistress and told her that the teacher had been right. Worker thought that Vera must have felt it was she who was bad. Vera agreed and asked worker how she knew

and how could Vera trust her. Worker said she could see it was very difficult for her, and reassured her that she could understand how Vera felt. She said that although Vera's feelings towards her were often mixed with those towards others, including the teacher, worker was a different person.

Vera refused a lift in worker's car and said as she left that she would kill worker if she let her down.

22. 3. 62. Interview at hospital. Vera went at once into the adjoining room and sat with her back to worker. There was a very long silence. The worker suggested that Vera was feeling as she did about the teacher; she ran away from her, though she wanted her help. There was another silence, but Vera came and sat facing the worker. She said she could not go on living as she was; she had no reason to go on living; nobody wanted her. Worker wondered why Vera felt like this. Dr. X., and the worker and nurse B. were all interested in her. Vera said that nurse B. had not written to her and that she had let her down. Worker said that this was how Vera felt when the people she was fond of seemed to let her down. Worker said she was sure there was a reason why nurse B. had not written, but it was easier to think badly of nurse B. than to feel let down. Vera began to cry quietly and said that she liked nurse B. because she left her alone. Worker commented that Vera felt that she did not and that perhaps Vera felt let down because worker had had to change the day of her appointment. This made Vera feel perhaps that other things were more important than she was. Vera wondered if she could trust worker and commented that her feelings were so strong. Worker said that perhaps Vera felt frightened of the seemingly great demands that she made on people, demands which could not be satisfied. Silence followed and then Vera asked how worker knew these things. Worker talked of how frightening and overwhelming feelings can be, especially when we cannot allow ourselves to share them with other people.

Worker again offered a lift in a car, but Vera declined. Worker said it was not a pram and that she would not laugh at her and make her feel small. Vera almost accepted and then declined in a calm manner.

31. 3. 62. Worker met Vera at the station and they drove to the hospital. Vera demanded if worker had written to nurse B. Worker said she had not. Vera said she had had a letter from her, but had destroyed it because she was sure it had been written at the worker's request. Vera said that God would punish her for failing and that the only thing to do was to die. Worker commented that Vera was punishing herself: God could understand her feelings and her at-

tempts to deal with them. Worker spoke of Christ's Agony in the Garden. During the interview Vera became increasingly drowsy. She denied that she had taken any sleeping tablets. After the interview Vera admitted in the car on the way back to the station that she had taken six tablets in case the worker had told her that she had asked nurse B. to write.

Later worker consulted psychiatrist who felt that it was reasonable to assume that Vera had not taken more tablets than she admitted.

These interviews illustrate episodes in the life of a very disturbed and unhappy woman. During most of the period covered, however, she continued to teach and it was probably partly due to the help she received from the mental hospital that she was able to isolate her work from her illness so successfully. What were her problems and what was the nature of the help she received?

It is perhaps over-optimistic to refer to Vera as a person with 'problems', since this kind of language might be taken to imply the existence of 'solutions'. 'How can I go on living?' has the form of a problem, but it is really of a different order from the question 'How can I get enough to live on until next week?'. None the less, it is helpful to try to analyse Vera's basic question into its component parts. Her difficulty is clearly one of object relations and within this context she is asking certain crucial questions. How can she trust the world outside herself? It is full of 'wild beasts', and when she does begin to love someone he or, usually, she 'vanishes'. What is it about her feelings that makes people leave her and why does she seem to find it easier to hate than to love? These questions lead to a second group of doubts which Vera raises implicitly or explicitly in connection with her own identity and value. Why is it that she falls in love with women, though relationships with women are more threatening for her? She feels 'bad' and incapable of giving, and doubts her ability to play any role to her own satisfaction or that of any particular role partner. These questions are basically important for Vera and through words or behaviour she asks them all in her transactions with the caseworker.

The caseworker centres her 'treatment' from the beginning on the relationship between herself and Vera, since within it can be seen a microcosm of the client's larger world. No work was undertaken with the parents with whom she lived, because Vera would not allow it and because it was judged that the main chance of effecting an improvement in the situation lay in giving help to Vera. The worker consulted with Dr. X from time to time and the support of his judgment was clearly valuable, as the last recorded interview illustrates. The worker was able at times to indicate to Vera that she was one of a group of staff (including Dr. X and nurse B.) who were all concerned for her, and on one occasion Vera wrote to the doctor about her desire to become a psychiatric social worker.

In the initial stages of the contact the worker helped Vera by some very practical illustrations of her interest. She maintained throughout a very flexible approach to the arrangement of interviews, and, by changing their *venue* and offering her client a lift, from time to time, she demonstrated her concern and her 'human' reality. In helping Vera to move towards receiving help from a caseworker she discussed her feelings at not seeing Dr. X, assisted her in forming some realistic expectations, and recognized that she did have strong positive feelings for the psychiatrist. In conveying this recognition she reassured her client that she could have 'good' feelings for another and that she need not fear the worker's jealousy.

Throughout the case the worker maintained a consistent attitude to Vera, though this was subjected to considerable testing by the client. The reality of Vera's hatred and of her love towards the worker was acknowledged. It was important that Vera could experience the fact that her feelings towards another person could be endured, and that the worker was not destroyed or seduced by them. At the same time, the worker paid continual attention to the implicit and explicit roles the client was asking her to play. In responding to Vera's changing role expectations the worker was at times reassuring and at other times she interpreted the meaning of Vera's expectation. Thus, in the interview of 31.3.62 the worker's comments on Vera's statement that God would punish her for failing were partly interpretative (you want to punish yourself) and partly a complementary response of reassurance (the reference to Christ's Agony).

Can any criteria be discerned in the interview material to suggest when the worker considered she should reassure and when offer an interpretation? It seems that reassurance and support were offered (*a*) when Vera seemed quite overwhelmed by the strength of her inner feelings, but could not accept intrusion (of a questioning or contradictory kind) from outside i.e. when she was nearly crossing the psychotic borderline; (2) when her feelings of guilt or hopelessness seemed 'real', in the sense that her inner problems had created a situation in reality to which she then responded fairly normally. Interpretations of what Vera was fearing or wishing for in her relationship with the worker were offered (1) when Vera's fantasy interfered to a marked degree with her relationship with the worker, thus preventing her from seeing and benefiting from the latter's *real* helpfulness; (2) when acute anxiety, anger or fear, was being expressed within the interview itself.

WORK IN THE CHILD GUIDANCE CLINIC

The attitudes of therapists towards their patients' families have varied strikingly over the years. Sometimes they have been seen as simple providers of the information required by the therapist. Sometimes they have been used as his allies or agents. On other occasions relatives have been seen as the main cause of the patient's illness or the therapist's bafflement. Freud at one point in his career reflected that 'As regards the treatment of relatives I must confess myself utterly at a loss, and I have in general little faith in any individual treatment of them'.[5] The beginning of the child guidance movement reflected a more optimistic view. The maladjusted child and his parents were to come to a clinic where the combined skills and knowledge of three disciplines would be used to help them. The child would be tested by the psychologist and given a psychiatric examination, while his parents (usually his mother) would be interviewed by the psychiatric social worker who would take a social history. The findings of the three inquiries would be combined to form the clinic's assessment of the case. Treatment, if given, would take the form of regular interviews between psychiatrist and child, and between parent (usually mother) and psychiatric social worker.

This was the model of child guidance work, but it was never generally applied. Clinics approximated, more or less, to its dimensions. Since the early days of child guidance, moreover, there have been several significant developments. As the team of workers became more secure with each other and more experienced in the work of the clinic, increasing role flexibility became noticeable. Some psychiatric social workers interviewed the child, for instance, while his mother was seen by the psychiatrist or psycho-therapist.[6] Psychiatrists and psychiatric social workers took initial interviews jointly with parents and children.[7] On the other hand, it has been suggested that teamwork as a co-operative endeavour has broken down once the stage of diagnosis has been reached.[8] Valiant efforts have been made to correct the early over-emphasis on the mother[9] and they have had spasmodic success. For the young child, however, the mother has pre-eminence and psychi-atric social workers have at times offered a service for the mother and young child together.[10] It will not be possible to illustrate each of these important developments, but the rest of this section will be devoted to an illustration of psychiatric social work on an 'intake' case in a child guidance clinic.

Robert N. (3)

Mrs. N. appeared at the child guidance clinic one day with Robert. She said she knew no one could see her, but her husband had suggested she came. The secretary said that the work was usually based on an appointments system, but she would see what could be done if Mrs. N. would not mind waiting. The psychiatric social worker (who was male) could give Mrs. N. 30 minutes as another appointment had been cancelled.

Mrs. N. said that Mr. N. had suggested her coming; he read lots of psychology books and would be in his element here. The psychi-atric social worker suggested that Mrs. N. must be wondering what sort of place the clinic was. Mrs. N. agreed that this was so. During this part of the interview Robert had clung to mother who was holding him off rather awkwardly and telling him, from time to time, not to crumple her dress.

The worker gave Mrs. N. a brief outline of the way the clinic worked, and suggested that Mrs. N. could best see how it worked if they discussed why she had come. Mrs. N. said that she knew what the social worker would say, that she should give up working. The worker wondered what problem that was intended to solve. Mrs. N. said that she had really come about Robert's tempers. She wanted some advice that was all. She looked crossly down at Robert who had started to play with some toys the social worker had put on the floor near his mother's chair. The social worker commented that Robert must also have been thinking about the place he had come to, and that he was there to help them both. He asked Mrs. N. to describe the tempers. Robert hurried to his mother's side. 'Well', said his mother, 'his father thinks I exaggerate, but they're awful. He just lies on the floor and screams and screams. I don't know what the neighbours think'. Mrs. N. said that if he was deprived of anything he reacted in this 'savage' way. His father usually took his side. The worker commented that it sounded as if Mrs. N. expected the clinic to be on the side of Robert against her. Mrs. N. seemed to relax at this point and though she made no comment Robert returned to playing with the toys.

Mrs. N. said she had a part-time job. She knew what the worker would think—she was a barmaid. The worker said that Mrs. N. seemed to have come determined that he should think badly of her. Mrs. N. became flustered and said all she wanted was advice. The worker said he would be pleased to help Mrs. N. to work the problem out. Their time was up for that date, but . . . Mrs. N. interrupted that she was sorry to have taken up the worker's time like this. The worker said that possibly she was feeling she was no further forward with her problem. Mrs. N. said she was not sure. She accepted the offer of an appointment in two weeks and at the door of the office mentioned that Robert was soiling during the day.

In this first interview the psychiatric social worker has not attempted the systematic collection of a social history. Instead he has concentrated on the actuality of the present as Mrs. N. presents her reasons for coming and her ambivalence about the clinic. He attempted to show her that, in spite of her guilt and fear, the clinic was not the 'strange' place of her husband's books, but a place where she could receive understanding and help. In order to increase and convey his understanding the worker responded differentially to Mrs. N.'s role expectations. Some of these he accepted (he gave information about the clinic), some he enlarged or developed (he suggested that she would satisfy her expectation of being informed if they jointly discussed her reasons for coming). Other expectations he made explicit and corrected implicitly (he said it seemed that Mrs. N. was determined she would be blamed, whereas his whole attitude was non-condemnatory). The worker could also use his observation of the mother's behaviour towards her child to add to his picture of their relationship. Mrs. N. held Robert awkwardly and seemed concerned about his possible intrusion into her world; she took no initiative in comforting or directing him in the clinic.

Second Interview

Mrs. N. arrived at the clinic on time for her appointment. She said she was still very worried about Robert. It was difficult to talk with him in the same room. The worker said that Mrs. N. seemed to feel restricted by Robert. Mrs. N. agreed, but thought the social worker would blame her for this. The worker suggested that Mrs. N. was very concerned about blame; perhaps she sometimes blamed herself. Mrs. N. burst into tears and sobbed for some minutes. The social worker commented that she must have been blaming herself for a long time. Robert, who had been playing in a corner of the room, came and put his arms round his mother. Mrs. N. lifted him onto her lap. When she was quieter the social worker drew attention to her two-way feeling towards Robert. Mrs. N. agreed, but expressed concern about her crying. The social worker said that Mrs. N. was perhaps worried about what he would think of her. Mrs. N. said she had not let go of her control like this before. The worker mentioned that control seemed to be an important theme and drew attention to her reference at the end of the last interview to Robert's messing. Robert snuggled to his mother who held him more closely. The social worker asked how long the messing had been going on. Mrs. N. said that there had been no sign of it until her mother had come on a long visit to their home. She was always picking Robert up and demanding how Mrs. N. could possibly let him cry. Then Mrs. N. looked down at Robert and suggested that sometimes he cried for the sake of it. Mrs. N. said that when her mother used to rebuke her for leaving him she would become afraid of the hatred in her mother's eyes. The worker suggested that Mrs. N. was also worried about the hatred she felt within herself. She agreed and said she always had been angry. The worker wondered what used to make her angry. Mrs. N. went on to talk of her fear of her brother; he was her mother's favourite and was never blamed for anything. She talked of his dare-devil exploits but she was never allowed to join in. (By this time Robert was again playing with the toys on the floor.) There was a long silence and Mrs. N. suddenly asked what all of this had to do with her problem. The social worker suggested that Mrs. N. was perhaps concerned that things were getting out of control. He retraced the course of the interview to show Mrs. N. how they had reached the present point. He said that mothers were naturally closely involved with their children and sometimes felt criticised if their feelings were discussed. Mrs. N. said that the worker could say that again. It was all very well for the experts, but who had to bring children along to the clinic, who had to clear up all the mess the men made of the world. The worker remarked on Mrs. N's feelings about men. Perhaps Mrs. N. felt that men and boys had to be controlled because they would confuse everything and mess things up. This, he said, was what she seemed to feel about the worker also. Mrs. N. made no reply and then said that the worker's remark had been rather like a blow. The worker commented that Mrs. N. had felt he was being aggressive, but he wondered if he really was. Mrs. N. agreed that this was not so.

The time was up and the worker asked Mrs. N. what she would like to do in regard to further clinic appointments. He felt that they had been making progress. Mrs. N. agreed and said that she would like to see the social worker a few more times before deciding whether or not she wanted Robert to be put on the waiting list to see the psychiatrist.

In the second interview Mrs. N. appeared to be more trustful of the clinic and less afraid to show her feelings about Robert. It seems that she can allow him to come close to her when she needs comfort and the social worker might well have drawn her attention to this. Instead he helped her to see that her negative feelings towards Robert were a reflection of earlier intense feelings for her brother. Mrs. N. was also encouraged to express her feelings about aggression and control, and she gained some reassurance from the social worker's ability to trace the pattern of the interview with her. Towards the end of the interview Mrs. N. was encouraged to learn something about her general attitude to men by reflecting on the questions she seemed to be posing about her developing relationship with the worker. Finally, the social worker drew Mrs. N.'s attention to the immediate problem—what did she wish to do in relation to the services offered by the clinic.

Fifth and final Interview

Mrs. N. came with Robert and they seemed to be much more relaxed in each other's company. She reported some improvement in his tempers and that he had ceased to soil himself. She expressed very considerable gratitude to the social worker. He had been wonderful. The social worker commented that first men had had to be controlled and now, it seemed, they had to be praised. He said that Mrs. N. should recognise the part she had played in the improvement by coming in the first instance, which had not been easy for her, and by working hard on her problems. Mrs. N. remarked that she now thought she had many problems. The social worker acknowledged that this was true of everyone. He asked what she now felt about keeping Robert's name on the waiting list for psychological and psychiatric examination. Mrs. N. said that she had consulted Mr. N. and they had agreed that they would not proceed. They would, however, both like to feel free to contact the clinic if necessary in the future. Mrs. N. said, rather defiantly, that she would not give up her job, but that she was going to give Robert more time. She was talking to his father much more about Robert and was feeling much less guilty. The social worker acknowledged Mrs. N's feelings about the improved situation, and said that the clinic would be pleased to see her and her family if she wanted to renew contact in the future.

In an abbreviated account of short-term work such as this it is difficult to avoid creating an impression of 'magic' for the 'un-initiated' or of 'superficiality' for the purist. Yet, there has clearly been improvement in the situation between Mrs. N. and her son—an improvement seen in the description of the mother at work on her problems and also in the judgment of the participant observer, the social worker. It is likely that Mrs. N. has other and more serious problems (perhaps a basic insecurity about her identity as a woman), but she was able to use a limited amount of help to question and to redefine, to an extent, her situation. She began to see her role-taking and role-making with her son in the context of previous role relationships and this change in perception helped her to develop potentialities for different behaviour towards her-self and her son. The worker helped Mrs. N. to enter the 'organiz-ational' role expected by the clinic (first as an informant, then as a co-operator) and encouraged her to see in their transactions a miniature of Mrs. N's problems in relation to her son.

COMMUNITY CARE

The first extensive arrangement for social work help to the men-tally ill in the community is to be found in the Regional After-care Scheme inaugurated in the war by the National Association for Mental Health. The ideas contained in, or developed from, this experiment in community care have received renewed emphasis as a result of the new policy for mental health. If this policy is to be effective and the community is to care for many of its mentally ill members outside the mental hospital, the quality of social work help for such patients and their families is crucial.

What are the main characteristics of the agencies offering such help? They are local authority departments operating under the general direction of medical officers of health, and endeavouring to carry out a general policy of community care. This is, of course, a concept in the process of social definition and the community care agencies are, as we have observed, still at the stage of creating their functions. Some, apparently, would see these in terms of the mental hospital for which they provide a pre-care or after-care service. Others wish to expand their work on the basis of a general service for the mental health problems of the community. Yet, whatever definition is finally accepted, the community care agency is concerned with both the mentally ill person and with his family. This is a difficult focus to maintain and some caseworkers, as Irvine has pointed out, have tended to emphasize the 'patient's' problem or that of the relatives in so far as it affects the 'patient'.[11] Yet families need help in dealing with mental illness, whether they are called to nurse a sick member or to face the repercussions of his illness on the 'healthy' others. Parsons[12] has stated some general reasons why the family may react unhelpfully to a physically sick member and these would seem to apply to a mentally ill member also. He has suggested that each member of the family has to defend himself against latent dependency needs. Consequently, a family will over-react to its ill member, either by being more supportive than necessary (thus, bolstering their own defences by projecting their need to be taken care of on to the sick person), or by being more severe than necessary.

The setting of community care is not clinical (like the child guidance clinic or mental hospital) and the workers are continually involved in the business of their clients' daily lives and with the general community social services. Their work requires knowledge of the medical and social services, recognition of the attitudes to mental illness among different sections of the community, and a knowledge of the family context of mental illness. This is likely to prove an especially fruitful area of exploration for the community care worker, though the knowledge we possess at the moment is rudimentary.

Yet it is now clear that the family participates in many complex ways in the mental illness of its members. Brown and Carstairs[13] have found, for example, that discharged chronic schizophrenics were more successful in lodgings or with siblings than with their family of origin. Goldberg has recently given sensitive examples of the kinds of entanglement possible between families and their mentally ill members, and Searles has graphically discussed the different motives behind 'The Effort to Drive the Other Person

H*

Crazy'.[14] Wynne and his associates[15] have suggested an interesting viewpoint on factors in the family that are productive of schizophrenia. Their study was based on the assumptions—made also in this book—that man is inherently concerned with object-relations and with the search for identity. Three main forms of relatedness are possible—mutuality, non-mutuality and pseudo-mutuality. In a family whose basic form of relatedness (or style of role playing) is one of pseudo-mutuality there is 'a predominant absorption in fitting together, at the expense of the differentiation of the identities of the persons in the relation'. Any transient non-reciprocation in a role relationship is experienced as a threat to the whole relationship rather than a possible questioning of a particular transaction. There is, thus, a tendency to maintain the role structure of the family despite important changes in family members (e.g. the children growing up). The family acts as if it constituted a truly self-sufficient social system within a completely encircling boundary. Role behaviour comes to be largely disassociated from subjective experience: the pattern of roles within the family is internalized by each member, but is not integrated into the functioning of an actively perceiving ego. We are only beginning to acquire knowledge of the functioning of families with a mentally ill member, but the kind of approach towards understanding suggested by Wynne and his associates, together with pragmatic findings on the outcome of mental health policies and descriptions of actual work with such families, constitute a particularly fruitful beginning for the community care worker.

Two Case Illustrations

The two following case extracts show two different approaches to casework. In the first, the worker made a vigorous and persistent effort to put the client in touch with the necessary and appropriate social services, though the final interview shows that this was not achieved to the detriment of the client's developing perception of his situation. In the second case, one interview illustrates a more family-centred approach, in which the psychiatric social worker participated in the family group as an 'intimate outsider'.

(1) *Jack Taylor*

Jack first came to the notice of the Mental Health Services in June 1955. His widowed mother had been sent along to the office by the

Youth Employment Officer after she had called seeking help for him. She explained that he was 17 years old, had not worked for eighteen months and had refused to go out of the house for several months. She had seen the family doctor about him, but Jack had refused to keep an out-patient appointment at the General Hospital and the doctor had then said that he was unable to help further. An appointment was made for the senior psychiatric social worker, Mr. Hinton, to call and see Jack with his mother.

Jack was seen the following Saturday morning when his mother was home from work. He lived with her and his younger brother in a post-war municipal flat which was poorly furnished and rather drab. Mr. Hinton was shown into a bedroom where Jack was sitting nervously on the edge of the bed, his eyes fixed to the floor. He was thin and pale, his blonde hair curling over his shoulders. He complained of various aches and pains and wondered whether he had a weak heart or kidney trouble. He admitted that he had lost confidence in himself and said he was afraid to go out because he could not face people. He spoke fairly freely during this first interview and appeared grateful for the interest taken in him. He had thought of himself as a complete failure, but readily accepted that he might in fact be ill and agreed to see a psychiatrist.

Mrs. Taylor was seen again in order to obtain a history. He had been born in 1937 and was a sound, healthy baby. He attended an elementary school until the age of 15, and was about average. He made one or two close friends but was never very active. He got on well with his brother and parents. Mr. Taylor had suffered from ill health. As a child he was said to have had a weak heart and later in life had a good deal of trouble with a duodenal ulcer and with a kidney complaint. He had died in July 1953. Jack left school soon after the death of his father and worked as an electrician's mate. He was made redundant after five months but found another job where he worked for two months. He then had influenza and from that point lost confidence in himself, refusing to leave the house or even answer the front door. Mrs. Taylor had kept him supplied with cigarettes and sweets from her own small earnings, but after six months felt obliged to seek help for him.

Mr. Hinton called to take Jack in his car to keep the appointment with the Consultant Psychiatrist. The Consultant felt this might be the beginning of an insidious schizophrenic process or a chronic anxiety state and recommended admission to hospital. Jack was reluctant to enter hospital as it meant facing people again, but he was persuaded that it was in his own best interests and a week later was taken to a mental hospital and admitted as a Voluntary Patient.

Once in hospital Jack changed remarkably and on the first visiting day his mother found him playing football with the other patients. He became more lively and alert and really regained altogether his self-confidence. He wrote a cheery letter to Mr. Hinton thanking him for all his help and saying how well he now felt. His attitude towards his mother changed completely and instead of being utterly dependent on her he seemed to resent her at visiting times. He did not like her visiting him, was rude to her and even avoided her altogether sometimes. For her part Mrs. Taylor appeared relieved and if his attitude towards her upset her she never showed it.

After six weeks in hospital he was given parole to find employment. He attended the Youth Employment Office where he was fixed up with a job as a warehouse assistant with a firm of electrical engineers. It was felt at the hospital that his rapid progress was entirely due to the change of environment and it was hoped that once in employment again he would quickly establish himself in the outside world.

A week after Jack left hospital Mrs. Taylor came to the office and left a message asking Mr. Hinton to call urgently. When he called she showed him into the tiny scullery which was to be the scene of many interviews to come. The curtains were drawn and the oven full on with the door open. The heat was stifling, but Mrs. Taylor had a black overcoat on and appeared not to notice. She explained that Jack had worked for a week and then taken a day off because he was not feeling well. Since then he had gradually slipped back again to where he was before. She showed the worker into the bedroom where Jack was sitting, with his chin cupped in his hands, a posture he kept throughout the half-hour interview. He did not look up at all, but stared vacantly at the linoleum. It was not difficult this time getting him to talk although he was thoroughly dejected. He said he did not like his job in the warehouse and still felt unable to face people. He did not want to return to hospital but felt he might manage another job. The worker felt it best not to encourage him in his desire to run away from difficulties and suggested that he should return to his job the following day and perhaps ask for a transfer. Jack was not sure about this, but eventually agreed if the worker came with him to explain this to the manager.

The following day Mr. Hinton and Jack went to the firm where the manager, who already knew a little about Jack's background through the Youth Employment Office, agreed to accept him back.

Four evenings later Mr. Hinton called to see Jack and mother showed him into the living room, saying Jack was shaving and would not be long. She said he did not start back at work as arranged and she was worried about him. After nearly 20 minutes he had not come in despite several calls from Mrs. Taylor, so the worker put his head round the scullery door and Jack came out, eyes downcast and thoroughly miserable. He said he had got ready to go to work but at the last moment could not face leaving the house. He could not be brought to make any decision as to the next move, but the worker said he would call three days later and take him along to the Youth Employment Office.

When Mr. Hinton called again it took a good deal of persuading to get him to agree to visit the Youth Employment Office. Eventually he was coaxed out of the house, but he felt very embarrassed walking along the road and thought the neighbours might be laughing at him. Once on the bus he was quite chatty—mainly about his interest in radio. The Youth Employment Office had nothing to offer him and over a cup of tea with Mr. Hinton he agreed to return to the job he had just left—if they would have him back.

After warning Jack that he would have to attend regularly, the manager took him on once more. Four days later Mr. Hinton received a telephone call from Jack at about 5.0 p.m. He said he was 'fed up'. It was raining and he had no coat to go home in.

The pattern of attempts at helping the client to make and keep contact with the outside world followed by the client's withdrawal continued for some months. Mr. Hinton, the psychiatric social worker, supported the client throughout this period, holding him to his obligations but also giving concrete help in helping him to meet them. The work entered its second phase in May 1957 with a prolonged period of testing out.

May 1957

The worker called at his home and saw Jack in a particularly despondent mood. He persuaded him to return to the lodgings which had been found for him previously. He again settled quite well and Mr. Hinton was optimistic of the outcome. He worked as a nurseryman from August to November, and was then made redundant, so packed his bags and went to his mother. A month later he found himself a job with a Corporation Parks Department. He telephoned Mr. Hinton and asked for help with overalls and when he found that the worker could not supply him with some right away, he became resentful and said he would now manage on his own and there was no need for the worker to help again.

Mr. Hinton called to see Mrs. Taylor to learn how Jack was progressing, a week later. While she was showing him into the living room Mr. Hinton caught a glimpse of Jack's pale and frightened face as he darted across the room and up the stairs. Mrs. Taylor said she was extremely pleased he had called because Jack had been sitting at home refusing to go out. He had managed very well at his job for six months but then, on Whitsun Monday, had been detailed to stop children running on the flower beds. This had upset him. He did not feel bold enough to order anyone about and half way through the day had come home in a very distressed state. He had not been out since but had got progressively more depressed and now stayed in bed half the day, and spent the rest of his time in the living room staring into space. Mrs. Taylor went upstairs to ask Jack to come down, but he refused, so the worker said—rather than force the pace—he would write and fix an appointment for later in the week.

When he called again, Mrs. Taylor was in the back yard hanging out the clothes. She opened the door for him and once again Jack bolted up the stairs. Mrs. Taylor called to him but he refused to come down. Mr. Hinton went to the bottom of the stairs and called up but it was a long time before Jack would answer. Then he was extremely hostile, saying that it was his own business what he did, that Mr. Hinton had no right to hound him like a criminal. The worker stressed that he was acting for Mrs. Taylor who could no longer afford to have him sitting about the house drawing no money. Jack still refused to come down and told the worker that when he wanted some help with overalls at his last job he had let him down, so he wanted nothing further to do with him. Mr. Hinton said he would call again the following week at the same time so that they could talk again.

As he approached the house the following week Mr. Hinton was confronted by Mrs. Taylor who was very distressed. She said she had gone out to do some shopping two hours previously, and when she returned Jack had locked her out and refused to let her in. He had said he would not see the worker again and had locked her out to prevent her letting him into the house. The worker went with her to the door, but Jack would not open it. Mr. Hinton explained to Mrs. Taylor that he would be on holiday for the next two weeks but would call after that time. He suggested she should get in touch with the office in the meantime if Jack became really unmanageable.

While Mr. Hinton was away, Mrs. Taylor called at the office and saw the worker in charge of the department. Jack was no worse but she wanted to make sure that something was done for him. When he returned Mr. Hinton discussed matters with the senior worker. He wondered whether he should visit the house with a Duly Authorised Officer, force his way into the bedroom and remove Jack on a three day order under the Lunacy Act, but it was finally agreed he should try once more to see Jack and perhaps get him to agree to enter hospital again. Mr. Hinton then composed a carefully worded letter in which he reminded Jack that on previous occasions when he had been very ill he had received treatment and improved, that it was unlikely that he would get better without help and that his mother must have some income to keep him. Finally, the letter pointed out that unless Jack was prepared to see Mr. Hinton and at least discuss his difficulties in a reasonable way, his mother would have no alternative at some future date, but to ask for his compulsory removal to hospital.

Jack evidently gave serious thought to this letter, for at the next appointment Mrs. Taylor opened the door to reveal Jack seated at the table, with head in hands. The room was unbelievably stuffy and the curtains drawn as usual. It took about 15 minutes of patient coaxing to get a word out of him, but he slowly responded to Mr. Hinton's remarks. He said he felt he was a coward, he was no good and never would be any good. No one wanted him, he could not face people, certainly could not attend the Labour Exchange or get a job. It was no use seeing a doctor—they could not help him, and the hospital was no good. He would rather stay as he was, perhaps he would die soon anyway and that would solve everything. He felt so strange and awful sometimes that he was sure he would not live long.

The interview ended quite inconclusively with no apparent progress being made. A week later Mr. Hinton called again and the week after that once more. Jack's attitude was the same. It took 10 or 15 minutes to get any kind of reply from him and then in his slow, halting, flat voice he countered every suggestion or proposal with a despondent negative. On the fourth interview, after the same sort of start, he was a little more open to suggestion and finally agreed that before anything else could be done he must smarten his appearance by getting a haircut. He had not left the house for 15 weeks and his hair had once again nearly reached his shoulders. He would not consider going to a hairdresser because he was afraid of being laughed at, but agreed to come with Mr. Hinton to the hospital where a nurse who was used to such things would cut it for him. As they passed from the darkened room into daylight, Mr. Hinton suddenly became aware of how pale and thin Jack had become. His eyes were sunken into his head and during the car journey to the hospital and back he would not make any conversation.

There followed several weekly interviews each starting with a prolonged silence from Jack which was extremely difficult to break down. Eventually he agreed to see the hospital doctor again and Mr.

Hinton accompanied him to the hospital. The doctor invited him to become an in-patient, but Jack would not hear of it so was given some tablets and asked to come up again the following week. Jack now seemed a little more optimistic but when he found, a few days later, the tablets were not having a magical effect on him he sank into despondency and refused to see the doctor again.

Eventually, Jack entered hospital again and this time showed considerable improvement and in 1958 the worker recorded the following final interdiew:

Jack had changed considerably. He was friendly and cheerful, his head was held high and he was dressed quite smartly. He said that he no longer felt moody and depressed as he did in the past, and although he had no job at the moment he was optimistic about finding one soon. The conversation naturally turned to the past and Jack said he had shied away from Mr. Hinton because he wanted to be independent and find his own way in the world. He had been grateful for all Mr. Hinton's help, but he reminded him of his past failures and he could never feel really well while he was calling.

Mr. Hinton asked him if he knew why he had experienced such an unhappy time and he said he thought it might have been due to his mother. She was a timid, anxious woman who depended on his father a good deal and when father died she had turned to him, her eldest son. He said 'She used to treat me as though I was her husband' and he recalled how, when she visited him in hospital, she used to worry him about the outstanding debts and about his younger brother's behaviour. He said he had always been a little afraid of life, but his mother had expected him to be too grown-up and he just could not take it. He thought she realised what she was doing but could not help it, so appeased her feelings of guilt by buying him cigarettes when he was home. He also thought she quite enjoyed having him home anyway and to some extent resented it when he got a job.

This case illustrates long-term, patient work with a severely disturbed client. The focus was held largely on the patient's role as a worker, and continuous efforts were made to encourage him to resume this role and forsake that of a deviant. The main part of the work was done with Jack, and it is arguable that more could have been done to deepen the caseworker's understanding of the crucial mother–child relationship. There seems to be some evidence in the record that the worker does not always maintain a consistent view of who his client really is. For instance, at times the pressure on Jack to work is represented as action by the worker on Mrs. Taylor's behalf. A more consistent focus on the mother–son relationship might have avoided the impression of the worker taking sides. However, the worker represented for Jack a continuing adult-figure who offered a warm and understanding relationship that also made explicit demands upon him. At times the worker took strong action (as, for instance, in the letter he wrote) and this seems to have been appreciated by the client, although he expressed considerable ambivalence about it.

(2) *A Family Interview*

The F case was referred to the community care worker by the G.P. who attended Peter (18). (The other members of the family, Mr. F (50), Mrs. F (49), Jill (20) each had a different G.P.) Peter had left grammar school at 15, though the doctor thought he was quite intelligent. He had been at home since then and had never attempted to get a job.

The worker made an appointment to see Peter and called at his home. Mrs. F. was present at the first interview. She insisted on giving the worker a full history of Peter's development, stressing his good behaviour. She hardly knew she was having a baby when he was delivered and 'as he began, so he has continued'; he never had to be told to behave well, it came naturally. Her daughter, on the other hand, had been difficult at birth and had been a talented, wayward child. Mother softened a little as she commented that she had been like this, but 'marriage changes you'. The worker asked about Mr. F. and Mrs. F. said he was an accountant in a bank, but they did not see much of him at home. She hinted that she had a hard life. The worker tried to make contact with Peter, but he just moved over to sit beside his mother and made no response. The worker said he would like to see all the family together to talk about the problem.

When he called a week later by appointment, the whole family was present, but the T.V. set was on and everyone seemed intent on watching the programme. The worker waited a little and then suggested that perhaps the T.V. set could be turned off. Mrs. F. looked apprehensively at her husband. The worker said he was sorry to interrupt their programme, but he was sure they did want to talk about Peter. He thought that everyone had probably been concerned, and he hoped they could discuss it together. Mrs. F. kept looking at Mr. F., who eventually said, in a hesitant manner, 'We've been managing very well up 'til now and we feel that your interference will stir up a lot of trouble to no good'. The worker said it must seem that he was coming into their home and laying the law down. Mrs. F. interrupted and said Mr. F. would never allow that, and Jill moved towards Peter and sat with him on the sofa. The worker said that the family had agreed to his visit and they were in fact all present at the time of his call. He thought that this meant they did want to talk, however painful it might be. Jill said that it was about time they talked, all the bottling up they had had to do! Mrs. F. said that Jill was upsetting the peace; they had tried to keep things nice for Peter. Peter laughed, and began to recite the Apostles' Creed. The worker said that it sounded as if keeping the peace had been very difficult and he suggested that perhaps only God could go on keeping things nice. Peter became more excited and the family froze into silence. Jill moved away from Peter and mother moved to the sofa to comfort him. After a pause, she said that he had been studying a lot recently and must have been overworking. Peter got up and walked away from his mother who looked dejected. The worker commented that it was hard when her comforting was not experienced by Peter as helpful. Mr. F. wondered where all this was getting them. Surely there were some things better left unsaid. 'Words can be so cruel'. Jill sighed and said they would all slip back if they were not careful. The worker thought that they were trying to say something important, but it was difficult and painful. Peter suddenly exclaimed, 'There's never been any fight in me'. Mrs. F. said fighting was dreadful and the worker wondered why she felt this. Mrs. F. said that one never knew where it would stop. Mr. F. burst out angrily, 'Talk, talk, it's all we ever do. You get up talking, you talk all day and you go to bed talking, and no one can think'. Mrs. F. turned on Mr. F. and said that thinking never got him anywhere. When she thought of what she had been before her marriage. They shouted at one another for a few minutes and then Mr. F. rounded on Peter, saying it was all his fault. Everyone was quiet again. The worker said that they were probably wondering about what they had said and done to each other, but that it was important to see what in fact each had been trying to say. Mr. F. felt shut in and resentful of Peter, and Peter must feel he is blamed for something which he is unsure about. Mrs. F. has wanted to keep things peaceful, but they had lost their tempers tonight and they could see that the harm they feared had not materialised. Jill had wanted to talk, but was perhaps urging the family to move at too fast a pace. It was agreed after discussion that some progress had been made and that the worker would call in a week's time.

In this interview the worker began by firmly calling the family's attention to the purpose of their meeting and holding them to it, whilst he recognized some of the feelings they might have about this approach. His main role in the interview is that of the involved observer. He noted the changes of seating position during the interview as an indication of shifting allegiances and of roles offered and accepted or rejected. For instance, he tried to help both Mrs. F. and Peter to understand Peter's rejection of his mother's proffered comfort. The worker also tried to help the family members to communicate about previously unacknowledged feelings and expectations, partly by encouraging them by showing the positive aspects of their meeting and partly by suggesting what each was trying to accomplish. This interview represents only the beginning of work with the family. Yet by showing them that they and he could not only survive the exposure of feeling, but also begin to make the situation more coherent as a result of their learning through a joint experience, he had placed the casework on a firm basis.

NOTES

[1] See the author's account of the history of psychiatric social work, *Psychiatric Social Work in Great Britain (1939–1962)*, Routledge & Kegan Paul, 1964.

[2] The social organization of the mental hospital clearly affects the welfare and recovery of the patients. See, for instance, the following studies: Caudill, W., *et al.*, 'Social Structure and Interaction Processes on a Psychiatric Ward', *American Journal of Orthopsychiatry*, Vol. 22, 1952; Stanton, A. H. and Schwartz, M. S., *The Mental Hospital*, Tavistock Publications, 1955; Weinberg, S. K., *Society and Personality Disorders*, Prentice-Hall, 1952.

[3] Williams, M., 'Mental Illness and the Community', *British Journal of Psychiatric Social Work*, Vol. IV, No. 3, 1958.

[4] Main, L. T., 'The Ailment', *British Journal of Medical Psychology*, Sept. 1957, quoted in Williams, M., op. cit.

[5] Freud, S. (1912), 'Recommendations to Physicians Practising Psycho-Analysis', Standard Edition of Complete Works, Strachey, J. (ed.), Vol. XII, Hogarth Press, p. 120.

[6] For an interesting example of this reversal of traditional roles see Lloyd-Davies, B., 'Psychotherapy and Social Casework', in Goldberg, E. M. (ed.), *et al.*, *Boundaries of Casework*, Association of Psychiatric Social Workers, 1956.

[7] This is suggested as a helpful general procedure until the child is eleven by Martin, F. and Knight, J., 'Joint Interviews as Part of Intake Procedure in a Child Psychiatric Clinic', *Journal of Child Psychology and Psychiatry*, 1962, 17–26.

[8] Harrington, M., 'The Integration of Child Therapy and Casework', *Journal of Child Psychology and Psychiatry*, Vol. I, No. 2, 1960.

[9] See e.g. Hunnybun, N., 'A Short Communication on the Place of the Father in Child Guidance', *British Journal of Psychiatric Social Work*, No. 2, 1948.

[10] See e.g. Hunnybun, N., 'David and his Mother', *British Journal of Psychiatric Social Work*, Vol. VI, No. 3, 1962.

[11] Irvine, E. E., 'Psychosis in Parents: Mental Illness as a Problem for the Family', *British Journal of Psychiatric Social Work*, Vol. VI, No. 1, 1961.

[12] Parsons, T. and Fox, R., 'Illness, Therapy, and the Modern Urban American Family', in Bell, N. and Vogel, E. (eds.), *A Modern Introduction to the Family*, Routledge & Kegan Paul, 1960.

[13] Brown, G., Carstairs, G. and Topping, G., 'Post-Hospital Adjustment of Chronic Mental Patients', *Lancet*, 958, Vol. II, p. 685.

[14] Searles, H., 'The Effort to Drive the Other Person Crazy', *British Journal of Medical Psychology*, Vol. XXXII, Pt. 2, 1959.

[15] Wynne, L., Ryckoff, I., Day, J. and Hirsch, S., 'Pseudo-Mutuality in the Family Relations of Schizophrenics', in Bell and Vogel, op. cit.

CONCLUSIONS

THIS study has been concerned with a review of the knowledge, principles and skills used by social caseworkers in almoning, child care, probation, family social work and psychiatric social work. We have not considered all the settings in which caseworkers practice; there has been no reference, for instance, to the important field of moral welfare or to casework in penal institutions. We have not exhaustively considered all the problems in the five main settings that have been discussed. Yet, the main features of social casework have been outlined and studied in this book, and a number of significant conclusions can be drawn.

Firstly, social caseworkers, irrespective of the setting in which they work, are involved in intricate and baffling psychological, social and moral problems. This will not, of course, surprise caseworkers, even if they have not studied the complex of problems as fully as they might. It is, however, a conclusion of some importance in view of recent criticisms of social work training. These have suggested that caseworkers, because of professional ambitions to be considered a kind of therapist, convert the molehills of practical problems into psychological mountains and spend the rest of their professional lives in a series of tunnelling operations. They thereby ignore the valuable function they could perform as the poor man's secretary. Yet, it is clear that most of the problems illustrated in this book would never have been taken by any prudent man (however rich) to his secretary—in the hope, that is, of reaching a solution. It has been one of the aims of this book to question the separation of the 'practical' from the 'psychological', whether this is advocated by critics in terms of their definition of illegitimate and legitimate social work functions or by caseworkers in terms of 'symptoms' and 'basic problems'. It has been my argument that the 'practical' is always joined to the 'psychological' and that there should be no divorce between them in regard to the appraisal of a problem or its treatment. This does not, however, confirm the caseworker as an expert in human relationships without focus or function, a kind of free-lance, unobtrusive, therapist.

Secondly, caseworkers should respond to the challenge of the complexity of the human and theoretical problems they encounter. This response can take a number of different forms. Caseworkers in any setting can use opportunities to develop a new focus for their work—offering a casework service directly to children, seeking to help with difficulties in the marital relationship etc. They can explore much more fully the nature of the institutions in which casework is practised, so that in particular cases and also in general terms they come to appreciate the impact of the institutions on their personnel and on those coming for help. Caseworkers should also endeavour to find new ways of working in view of the serious shortage of trained staff, which is likely to be a permanent feature of the social services. The place of a consultative service for untrained and inexperienced staff and of short-contact casework are two problems which merit serious attention.

It is important, however, that each particular line of inquiry, each new development is considered in terms of the more general theorizing about social casework. This is still in its infancy, but an attempt has been made in this book to outline the main components of a theory of casework. Emphasis has been given to the knowledge caseworkers use, to the principles of value and the instrumental principles they apply, to the skills and attitudes they develop as they try to help agencies to attain their objectives of helping people with different kinds of social problem. Each component presents its own difficulties. We have seen, for instance, the complex intermingling of value and instrumental principles, and the 'knowledge' used by caseworkers has been shown to consist of varying psychological and sociological content and of theories and concepts at different stages of development. Nevertheless, any theory of casework in the future must encompass and connect the components described above.

As we have seen in this book, high claims are sometimes made for social work knowledge and skill. The attractions of a contemporary synthesis of principles and practice are obvious. Premature formulations or overbearing claims may well escape genuine criticism in the present climate of opinion, which is conducive to the growth of social work, but will ultimately bring the profession into general disrepute. Any framework (such as the one presented in this study) must be regarded as tentative. There are, as has been indicated, many exciting new developments in theory and in practice, but very few rest on any solid basis of tested validity, and we are still ignorant about the relationship between knowledge and the effective practice of casework in each setting. Caseworkers accept different kinds of psychological and sociological theory and some, of course, have no explicit theoretical frame of reference at all. What differences, if any, does this make to their practice? This is a fundamental issue requiring sustained thought and empirical research. We are beginning to study the actual operations of the social services, but we know very little about the results of social work, or about ways in which a casework service is regarded by actual and potential clients. This latter gap in our knowledge is particularly important for caseworkers, since their occupation is more of a discourse than the application of techniques, a moral as much as a scientific discipline.

Thirdly, this book has given a central place to the functions of the social agency and their essential contribution to the specific character of casework. The implications of this have been discussed particularly in chapter one, and the theme has been illustrated throughout the book. Two additional comments are appropriate. The first concerns the social caseworker's general attitudes towards society. In discussion of the functions of a social agency importance has been attached to the wider functions of the agency within society. Thus, it has been suggested that the social services 'represent' in some way the organization of the altruistic and compassionate impulses within society. Society in this context is seen as a personified mother-figure creating services to 'reclaim' the deviant and to help the maladjusted and underprivileged. This can be a useful point of view, as the present study suggests. However, exclusive attention to the 'positive' and unitary aspects of society can be particularly misleading for social workers. Social workers should also look to the elements of conflict in modern society. A rounded approach to society includes reference to society as an arena of conflict as well as a consensus of values. Social workers characteristically find themselves 'standing for' the elements of solidarity in a society, but it is important for them to appreciate that the social services are often the meeting-point of two or more groups whose interests may be, partially at any rate, in conflict.

The emphasis on function in this book raises questions about the place and nature of specialization in social work training and the organization of the social services. The present style of training favours a 'generic' approach, which stresses the elements common to the practice of casework irrespective of the setting in which it is practised. Clearly, general features of casework practice can be discerned. There are certain requirements for practice in any field. The caseworker should have certain general attitudes towards people and their problems. These have been broadly described in the present work, and seem to consist in an 'openness' towards people, an acceptance of the worker's and the client's personality, a willingness to acknowledge that the present may be understandable only in the light of knowledge not yet available. The caseworker should also possess certain skills (e.g. in communication) which are applicable in any setting or with any group, be they clients or colleagues. These skills will be used in accordance with the general values and the technical skills of casework. Yet, casework is never 'generically' practised; the knowledge, attitudes and skills of the caseworker are always applied within a particular setting. Casework is not a kind of therapy *sui generis* that can be either practised or described without essential reference to the social agency or institution, whose objectives it helps to achieve.

The agency or institution exercises a decisive influence on the worker, on what he or she does for the client, and on the problems presented. There are, for example, different degrees of visibility of success and failure in the different services. In child care serious failure is widely publicized, partly because of the history of the service and because of the meaning of the service to the wider public. In probation the failure of an order is more public than the failure of casework in a family agency. The organizational roles of worker and client are different in each setting. The person in a particular kind of trouble does not come for help as a social worker's client, he comes, or is sent to, a particular agency, because it has been established to achieve certain objectives which seem appropriate in his particular case. It is, of course, possible to abstract from the problems presented to social agencies certain 'generic' features. One can discern, for example, the problem of separation in child care, in social work for the old and for the mentally ill, and it is clearly helpful to consider the common psychological problems and processes. Yet the problem is always presented in the field in concrete terms—a particular old person (who is not a child or mentally ill) has doubts and fears about entering an old people's home. The whole social situation in which problems of separation arise is different for each group and the problems are presented to workers in different organizational structures.

The issues of 'generic' and specialist *training* have not been carefully discussed in this country. We need to keep a balance in our training programmes between the abstraction of common elements and the implications of the fact that practice is always concrete, specialized and functional. The emphasis of this book can perhaps be most clearly summarized in the words of the sociologist Durkheim:

'We can then say that, in higher societies, our duty is not to spread our activity over a large surface, but to concentrate and specialize it. We must contract our horizon, choose a definite task and immerse ourselves in it completely, instead of trying to make ourselves a sort of creative masterpiece, quite complete, which contains its worth in itself and not in the services that it renders.'*

* *The Division of Labour in Society*, Macmillan, 1933, p. 401.

INDEX OF PROPER NAMES

INDEX OF SUBJECTS

Index